A Simple Life

*Roland Walls & the Community
of the Transfiguration*

John Miller

SAINT ANDREW PRESS
Edinburgh

First published in 2014 by
SAINT ANDREW PRESS
121 George Street
Edinburgh EH2 4YN

Copyright © John Miller, 2014

ISBN 978-0-86153-713-6

British Library Cataloguing in Publication Data

A catalogue record for this book is available from the British Library.

It is the publisher's policy to only use papers that are natural and recyclable and that have been manufactured from timber grown in renewable, properly managed forests. All of the manufacturing processes of the papers are expected to conform to the environmental regulations of the country of origin.

Typeset by Regent Typesetting

Printed and bound in the United Kingdom by
CPI Group (UK) Ltd, Croydon

Contents

Preface

The Community of the Transfiguration has benefited throughout its life from the discerning eye of a Warden, who looks after the well-being of the Community's spiritual life. The Community's most recent Warden was Church of Scotland deaconess Kay Ramsay, who died in June 2013.

One day in 2010, Kay was among a small company of people who were sitting at lunch in 'the Tin Tabernacle' in Roslin, at 23 Manse Road. It was 6 August, the date on which the Church celebrates the Feast of the Transfiguration. A few minutes earlier, Brother Roland, Brother John and Sister Patty, together with this small group of friends, had celebrated the Eucharist in the little wooden Chapel in the silent Enclosure at the back of the house. Kay put into words people's unspoken recognition that the Community was approaching the end of its life.

'We must have a record of all of this,' she said. 'Who can do it for us? Who will write it?' Then, pointing at me, she said, 'John'. There was no room for argument. I had been invited to write the Community's history.

I knew the Community from its very beginning in 1965. Roland was teaching theology at New College when I was one of his students from 1964 to 1967. I enjoyed Roland's classes, and I loved his humour and incessant theological reflection on life and work. Later, when I was employed as a minister in a busy housing-estate parish, my wife Mary and I took the unconventional step of moving out of the congregation's manse – a Victorian villa in a nearby town – into a small council house up a communal stair. The Community liked what we were doing, and sensed a shared spirit. In 1971, Roland wrote to us, 'We see your plans and ours as closely linked ... May the Lord keep us together in his kingdom.'

While I knew there was a permanent friendship between us and the Community, the pressures of my own life meant that there was only intermittent communication. Yet the bond was expressed in many ways. Many years ago, on a visit to our family home in a Glasgow housing scheme, Roland expressed his approval of it by saying, 'Yes. I could quite happily die here.' It was an unusual compliment, never offered to us by anyone else before or since. But we received it as Roland's affirmation of our effort.

There came, however, a particularly stressful era of my parish life. For more than a year, I used to go to Roslin every two months. I would spend three nights – two complete days – in the quiet of a hut. The Community welcomed and sustained an exhausted visitor; I revived. Furthermore, through the Community's engagement with Holocaust literature, I encountered the work of Elie Wiesel and other Jewish writers. These writers articulated many of the issues which perplexed me in the parish setting, and they gave new resources for my thinking.

In addition to these specific benefits, I found that, whenever I reconnected with the Community, even after intervals of some years, I received reassurance from the stability and constancy of their pattern of life.

Thus it was as a long-standing friend that I was glad to accept the invitation to write the history of the Community. As a friend, I have written it as a chronicle rather than as an analysis. I have tried to describe the main themes and emphases of the Community through the decades. When a small Community contains a figure as significant as Roland Walls, it is necessary to ensure that such a book does not become simply a biography of that one person. But equally, it is important that the influence and attainments of that individual are given the attention they deserve. Roland Walls, with his learning and his extraordinary ability to communicate about matters of faith, is himself worthy of a major study. But this book is not it. This is an attempt to write the story of the Community as a whole.

Nor does the book attempt a detailed critical analysis of the policies and values of the Community as they are set out in the Rule (Appendix 1). Where possible, I have tried to describe the way the Rule is embodied in the Community's life. Although I myself might have observations and even reservations about some features of the Rule, I have not written about these at any length. Instead, I have tried to give sufficient information to enable readers to make their own evaluation.

The Community began in 1965. It was a time when people were exploring the possibilities of communal living. Many young people, sometimes influenced by the drug culture, tried living in 'communes'. The Community at Roslin engaged with one such commune for many months. In Scotland, the Findhorn Community was established beside the Moray Firth in 1962. In 1974, the Lothlorien Therapeutic Community began in Dumfriesshire. There are many other examples. There would be value in a study comparing the pattern and effectiveness of different forms of community. But again, this book is not it.

In the second half of the twentieth century, the churches in Europe and in North America were trying by every means to respond to an era of change, hoping to demonstrate the continuing relevance of Christianity and the Church in the new cultural climate. Worker priests and industrial chaplains sought to counteract the alienation of industrial workers from the Church. The Charismatic Movement infused some church worship with excitement, with modern music and with an element of drama. Evangelical campaigns generated huge public meetings with the opportunity for individual religious commitment. And, as mentioned above, it was a time when numerous religious communities emerged to test styles of communal Christian living – a movement akin almost to a new monasticism.

Church movements arose, and often fell; and many sought or received considerable publicity, and even acclamation in their day, for the 'solutions' they proposed. The Community of the Transfiguration, living their simple life, never made mighty claims or sought the headlines. However, I consider that, as a body that sought to live out its understanding of the Gospel, the Community of the Transfiguration is worthy of close attention on three important grounds at least. First, in total contrast to the consumerism of the times, the Community have been committed to a life of simplicity. Almost all their furnishings and clothing were second-hand. Their diet was basic in the extreme. They spent little on heating. Second, in contrast to the exclusivity of most people's domestic setting, the Community have kept an open door, ready to welcome anyone who came – with a meal, a listening ear and a bed constantly on offer. Friend, stranger, professor from the university, tramp from the highways – all have been welcome at their table, and accepted just as they are. And third – while one of the Community was in low-paid work as a worker priest, another taught at university, and others were employed in youth work and pastoral care – the central activity of the Community as a whole was contemplative prayer. These three features of the Community in Roslin have marked them out as exceptional. So, although the Community have shunned publicity and published nothing about themselves, and although they have intentionally avoided any public stance on issues of Church or state, their fame and influence have spread widely throughout Britain and beyond. People wanted to know more about them.

These were the reasons why I accepted the invitation to write the history of the Community of the Transfiguration, as a friend. So began the process that has led to this book. Having been granted this 'official' status, I was able to introduce myself to a host of other friends of the Community. In the light of my role as historian, they in turn were willing to speak freely of their connection with the Community. Sometimes, individuals would reveal confidential issues on which the Community had given them indispensable help. Whenever I interviewed someone, with their agreement I took full notes. I would then write out the notes in detail and send them to the interviewee. An interviewee could amend, expand or delete the notes and then agree the final form in which I would present their contribution in the book.

I have done my utmost to ensure that dates and facts in the book are correct. Placing a high value on their contacts with the Community, people have extremely vivid memories of events and encounters in Roslin. Yet no two people remember things in exactly the same way. Occasionally, therefore, readers may find something in the book that they regard as inaccurate. And they may be right. I can only assure readers that I have tried to present matters as accurately as possible.

Such accuracy as there is owes an immense amount to John Halsey, who, with characteristic patience and humility, consulted his memory and scrutinised and corrected successive manuscripts. Patty Burgess was similarly generous with her time and her memory. Her gift for life was never better illustrated than when, one Friday, at the age of 95, she made her way delicately up the uneven stone path to Eucharist in the Chapel. She suddenly stopped, unable to breathe. A chair was fetched. She sat down. Paramedics were summoned. 'I can't find a pulse,' said a companion anxiously as we waited for help to arrive. 'That's because I'm deid [dead],' explained Patty calmly. Which, happily, she was not.

It is perilous to write a book about an enterprise, a way of life, which has shunned publicity and has remained hidden and confidential. I became increasingly uneasy about the risk that a book would pose to the Community's privacy. I wanted to share my anxiety with Kay Ramsay. She had already seen the manuscript of the book and approved it. But, by the time my anxiety had crystallised, she had suffered a stroke and was lying in a semi-coma in hospital, seemingly unable to respond. Nevertheless, at her bedside I asked her two questions.

'Kay. This is John Miller. Should I be worried about the book making public the life of someone as private as John Halsey?'

Kay slowly opened her eyes and said, 'Yes.'

'Kay. Should I delay publishing the book until after John's death?'

Kay slowly opened her eyes again and said, 'No.'

So, with Kay Ramsay's approval, here it is.

*John, Patty and Roland with
Father Gero McLoughlin SJ visiting the Community*

The Chapel

Roland and Patty with visitors

Roland with Jean Vanier, founder of L'Arche, in the Chapel

Acknowledgements

Each reader of this book will recognise my debt to the many people who have been willing to entrust their recollections to me. John Halsey and Patty Burgess of the Community of the Transfiguration have been exceptionally generous.

I thank Rosemary Lee and Jonathan Jamal, who have both spent many years in religious communities. Jonathan was 14 years in Roslin; Rosemary was for over 20 years one of the Sisters of the Love of God. Both of them have now left their communities and are lay-people. They have both given me invaluable insight into the character of the religious life.

From the large numbers of other people whose names or profiles are found in the text and the footnotes, I have received invaluable assistance as I traced the life of the Community through the years. To Ron Ferguson, whose book of conversations with Roland Walls, *Mole Under the Fence*, captured many facts and much of the atmosphere of the Community, I am indebted for freedom to use whatever I found there. To Roland Walls' godson William Henderson in Australia for memories of Roland's Cambridge friendships; to Roland's 'spiritual son' Franciscan Brother Johannes Kuepper of Cologne; to the Abbot and the Cistercian monks of Sancta Maria Abbey, Nunraw; to Jean Vanier of L'Arche; to Father Jock Dalrymple, parish priest of St John and St Mary Magdalene in Edinburgh; to personnel engaged with L'Arche in Scotland and England; and to friends of the Community in many countries I express my gratitude for revealing to me the distinctive spirit of the Community.

I have benefitted greatly from the assuring influence of commissioning editor Ann Crawford of Saint Andrew Press. I thank copy editor Ivor Normand and proof-reader Jill Wallis for detailed improvements to the accuracy of the text. I record my gratitude to Susan Sirc for translating the German text of Brother Johannes' correspondence.

Finally my thanks to my wife Mary for her exceptional editorial skills, her inexhaustible patience and her devastating humour, and for finding the perfect title for the book.

I

A Place in History

In his very old age, Father Roland Walls was walking up through
the garden of the Community's house, steadied by the arm of a
friend. He paused for a rest. His eye caught sight of a tiny blue
flower growing beside the path. 'Look at that!' he said in a tone of
awe. 'Isn't it beautiful? Just sitting there. Not drawing attention
to itself. Just being itself.'

Roland's words about the flower might be applied as fittingly
to the Community which he had founded in Roslin many years
before. Not drawing attention to itself. Just sitting there, just
being itself. Beautiful.

At the foot of the Pentland Hills to the south of Edinburgh lies
the small, seemingly obscure country village of Roslin. In contrast
to its immediate appearance, it has a substantial history. The early
spelling of its name persists in the hereditary title of the Earl of
Rosslyn and in the name of the historic Rosslyn Chapel. But, for
more than two centuries, the village's name has been spelled as
'Roslin'.

In 1303, it was the site of a Scottish victory over the English
army in the initial battle of the First War of Scottish Independence. In medieval times, William Sinclair, the 1st Earl of Caithness,
founded Rosslyn Chapel with its carved-stone 'Apprentice Pillar'.
Standing at the edge of the village, on a hillside overlooking the
River Esk, the Chapel has an association with the Holy Grail,
the cup supposedly used by Christ at his Last Supper in Jerusalem. Legend has it that the Knights Templar brought the cup
from Palestine to Scotland and concealed it in Rosslyn Chapel's
foundations. In 2003, the Chapel became the focus of world-wide
interest through Dan Brown's best-selling novel, *The Da Vinci*

Code. The book incorporates the legend that the Holy Grail is concealed within the Chapel. However, the author postulates that the Holy Grail was not a chalice but the very person of Mary Magdalene. He writes that Mary was secretly married to Christ and bore him children, and thus carried within her the bloodline of Christ himself. Mary's bones, posits the book, now lie within the Chapel. The helicopter-borne arrival of the film actor Tom Hanks to shoot some scenes for the film of the book attracted several thousand people to the fields beside the Chapel. In subsequent days, the Roslin farmer, on whose ground the helicopter landed, enterprisingly offered for sale 'Da Vinci Horse Manure' at 50 pence a small bag.

Set in the midst of farming land, with good grazing for sheep and cattle, Roslin village was the birthplace in 1839 of John Lawson Johnston. A butcher by trade, Johnston invented a beef-based drink called 'Bovril', a thick, salty meat extract sold in a distinctive bulbous jar. In 1870, he supplied this liquid nourishment to the army of Napoleon III in their campaign against the Prussians. By the 1890s, Bovril was synonymous in Britain with good health and physical strength, and so successful was the business that Johnston's son was later ennobled as Lord Luke of Pavenham.

The industrial revolution brought the village a new role. Coal was found far beneath the surrounding green fields. Farm workers became miners, and a rail link from the Roslin pit carried coal from the village to steel foundries and power stations in the central belt of Scotland and beyond.

In 1807, a gunpowder factory was built at Roslin beside the River North Esk. For the next 150 years, the factory supplied gunpowder for the mining and quarrying industries. It also manufactured munitions for the Napoleonic, Crimean and Boer Wars, and for the First and Second World Wars. 'Lord Haw Haw', the broadcaster of Nazi propaganda, in a radio transmission warned that the Luftwaffe, the German Air Force, knew of the 'Fox in the Glen' (the continuing manufacture there of munitions) and would destroy it. Many of the buildings were recessed into the steep banks of this wooded glen to prevent any chain reaction in the event of an explosion in one of the sheds. Latterly the site was run by ICI Nobel, and when it closed in 1954 it was one of only two such factories in the United Kingdom.

In the late twentieth century, the village's name came to prominence through the work of the Roslin Institute, a department of the University of Edinburgh devoted to animal husbandry, located on farmland at the village. In 1996, researchers at the Institute created Dolly the Sheep, the first mammal to be cloned from an adult cell. Dolly, and the implications of her arrival, and the details of her short life, sparked world-wide scientific interest and attention. The origin of the sheep's name had been a well-kept secret. Apparently the cell from which she was cloned came from the mammary gland of an adult ewe. The cloned animal was named in tribute to the famously well-endowed country-and-western singing star Dolly Parton.

But this book will suggest that, among all the associations and adornments for which Roslin may be acclaimed, none is more significant than the small religious community founded in 1965 which adopted the name 'The Community of the Transfiguration' and which thereafter resided at 23 Manse Road. Its members were bound by the threefold vows of poverty, chastity and obedience. The focus of their life was prayer and contemplation, together with employment in unskilled work, and hospitality. When a much-loved member of the Community, Father Roland Walls, died in 2011, his three-column obituary in The Times spoke of him as 'the founder of the hugely influential Community of the Transfiguration'.[1]

The Community at its outset had only three members; at no time was their number greater than five. They lived in great simplicity and for their first 30 years had no telephone. Hospitality was at the heart of their way of life; and homeless men, travellers of the road with difficult lives and difficult personalities, were welcomed at table and given a bed. Roland himself was an outstanding academic scholar and teacher, and professors would call by, hoping to be guests at their meal-table; yet the Community published only very occasional, tiny, fragmentary writings. They shunned publicity and had no interest in celebrity. Though for decades recognised by the Vatican as an Ecumenical Community, after their first year they received no financial support from any Church denomination. The mantle of quiet anonymity which thus veiled the Community ensured that no-one encountering them ever felt in the least intimidated by their eminence.

Beloved of friends on five continents, viewed as a companion by numerous communities of prayer and contemplation across the world, their kitchen table in Roslin a centre of hospitality and unquenchable laughter for enquirers and lost souls, this Community of the Transfiguration has been likened to the Little Gidding of T. S. Eliot's poem:

You are not here to verify,
Instruct yourself, or inform curiosity
Or carry report. You are here to kneel
where prayer has been valid.[2]

In its initial form, the new religious community, being composed only of men, took as its name 'The Fraternity of the Transfiguration'. But, after a short number of years, the arrival of a new member, a woman named Patty Burgess, required a change. It became 'The Community'. 'Yes,' said John Halsey, a founding member, 'Patty came, and changed the points!'

They quickly established the shape of their common life. By the time Patty arrived, two of the members were working, one underground as a miner, the other as a teacher. Another early member, who left after five years, was a local-authority youth-worker. The Community was determined to share the working life and working conditions of ordinary men and women.

Their main house was a former community library, donated to the village by a benefactor 60 years earlier for the benefit of Roslin's coalminers and their families. It was a simple wooden-framed building with an outer cladding of corrugated iron. The various rooms had high ceilings, and, although there were coal fires in most parts of the house, it was a draughty dwelling-place. The toilet was outside the house, in an adjacent unheated shed.

They were at heart a contemplative Community, seeking through silence and prayer to witness to their dependence on the life of

Christ and on his sufferings and death and resurrection. Accordingly, a six-foot-high wooden screen divided the house and the front garden from the back garden. The back garden became an area of silence called the 'Enclosure'. There, a variety of shrubs and flowers flourished among the free-growing meadow grass. Located in this Enclosure, each member of the Community had a separate small wooden hut, a garden shed. For each, this was their cell, in which they could read, pray and sleep. In addition, a double wooden hut – two adjacent huts placed end to end – served as the Community's chapel.

In the chapel, the Community's members gathered four times a day for prayer; those who were in employment attended as their working hours allowed. In this way, the Community alighted quietly in the landscape of the Scottish Churches.

Not everyone, of course, identified the character of the Community in exactly the same way. 'I must be honest,' confessed an able and distinguished Scottish Church leader, George Wilkie, whom the Community of the Transfiguration at one time approached for advice, 'I can never quite understand what the Community is about.'

The Community set its compass firmly towards an engagement with the poor and with those who were employed in unskilled industrial jobs. This orientated them towards a new field of activity which the Churches were exploring.

The British Churches recognised that their traditional parish focus had resulted in them having virtually no contact with working men who spent their lives in industry. During the Second World War, the chaplains to the armed forces had played an important role. Although non-combatants, chaplains were present at the centre of the action, often in the front line, often under fire. The troops came to value the chaplains as a resource to assist believers and non-believers as they faced the fears and horrors of war. Observing this, the Churches, including the Church of Scotland, developed a new approach to industry, promoting the presence of industrial chaplains in factories and other work-places.

George Wilkie was one of the first of such Church of Scotland chaplains, serving as industrial chaplain to the Lower Clyde. His responsibilities included building good relationships with management and unions in the shipyards of the Lower Clyde, and with the workforce and management of the huge factory which the American company IBM established in Greenock. Politically, George was known to be left-wing. Indeed, it was rumoured that his Church employers at one time warned him that this tendency was putting at risk his impartiality, his ability to relate to both management and workforce. Evidently, when he was away at a conference, he arranged for his van to be part of a street cavalcade on behalf of the Labour Party in the run-up to an election. Plastered with Labour posters and topped with loudspeakers, the van was recognised campaigning particularly loudly outside the offices of Lithgows' shipyards. 'That's the end of Wilkie's access to my yards,' said Sir James Lithgow. This restriction was of limited importance, for plenty of other yards were still open to him, and even Sir James in due course welcomed George's successor Cameron Wallace as an industrial chaplain.

By the mid-1960s, the mission arm of the Church of Scotland had clearly come to terms with George's approach, for they appointed him Industrial Organiser. He was at the centre of an ecumenical drive to enable the Scottish Churches to engage with industry. George led a team of industrial chaplains who came from several different Church denominations. They were placed in strategic industries such as coal, steel, engineering, shipbuilding and information technology. George ensured that the new ideas and thinking being generated by this team of chaplains were fed into the thinking of the Churches, the unions and industrial managers.

At the very time that preparations were being made for the Fraternity at Roslin, a group of members of the Scottish Episcopal Church were keen to initiate the engagement of their Church with industry. They were ready to fund a part-time industrial chaplaincy. Thus John Halsey, with his experience of Sheffield Industrial Mission, was enabled to join George Wilkie's team of industrial chaplains, supported by the Scottish Episcopal Church. George wanted to develop work with British Rail and the National Coal Board, and arranged for John to be a part-time chaplain at the British Rail depot at Haymarket in Edinburgh, and at the NCB pits at Bilston Glen and Roslin. After a year, with his time so divided between the different work-places, and the chaplain's role so detached from the conditions of the working men, John found this arrangement unsatisfying. Accordingly, it was agreed that he should develop the relationship established with the Roslin pit by leaving chaplaincy work and taking full-time work at Roslin as a miner underground. He was to find this personally more satisfying as well as more in line with the general vision of the Fraternity.

In the early years of the Fraternity's formation, one of their foremost influences was a religious fraternity called the Little Brothers of Jesus. This is a Roman Catholic community, established in the 1930s, inspired by the life and witness of Charles de Foucauld. Foucauld, born in 1858 into the French aristocracy, had a brief but colourful career as a cavalry officer in the French Army in North Africa. He became an acclaimed explorer of French Morocco, and then after a dramatic conversion to faith he became a monk in the strand of the Cistercian Order known as the Trappists. Seeking to follow Jesus in solidarity with the poorest of the poor, he was released from the Cistercians, and he made his way back to North Africa. There, among the remote Touareg tribes of southern Algeria, he lived as a hermit at Tamanrasset in the Sahara. Devoting his life to the Touaregs, he compiled the first dictionary of their language. Making no attempt to attract converts, his mission was simply to live in such a way as to make Christ real to the tribal people of the area: 'To shout the Gospel with [his] life,' as he wrote, 'living in such a way that people would say, "If such is the servant, what must the Master be like?"' He had hoped to found a religious community to share his work and his vision, but so strict was his asceticism that during his lifetime he could find no companion to share his life.

In 1916, his home and his tiny chapel were ransacked and he was murdered by passing marauders. Later, his meticulous writings were discovered. In the 1920s, several brotherhoods were created, inspired by his life. In the 1930s, the Little Brothers of Jesus, and the Little Sisters, emerged as a radically new form of religious life. They lived in small communities, often of three or four people. They embodied Charles de Foucauld's vision by their solidarity with the poor in their working lives, in prayer and in commitment to following Jesus.

Contact with the Little Brothers and with the spirituality of Charles de Foucauld provided the impulse for John Halsey's move from the 'chaplaincy approach' to seeking employment as a labourer underground.

Many years later reflecting on John's working life, George Wilkie remained puzzled by the Community's character. 'For myself,' he said, 'I have always wanted something which gave more tangible results.'[3]

George Wilkie was not the only person to be perplexed by questions about the identity of the Community of the Transfiguration. Another was Andrew Parker, who studied theology at New College, Edinburgh, where Roland Walls taught from 1965 to 1974.

'So, your strategy, Roland?' Andrew enquired earnestly. 'What is your strategy?' By then it was 1973. The Community of the Transfiguration had been in existence for eight years. Around the coal fire in the main room of the Community's house in Manse Road sat a small group of young Church of Scotland ministers. All, like Andrew Parker, were former students at New College.

Andrew was one of Roland's ablest scholars. He had arrived at New College in 1964 as an orthodox young Christian on course for the ministry of the Church of Scotland. He attended Roland's course of lectures on Dogmatic Theology, and was intrigued. While Roland's entire presence radiated a sense of confident faith, he addressed great theological issues with the lightest touch. He spoke with sympathetic understanding about the historic interweaving of error and discovery in the development of Christian teaching. At home with the Greek and Latin Fathers of the Church, the theologians of the early Christian centuries, Roland brought to life the development of Christian doctrine and the growth of the Church. His readiness to open debate on matters of dogma – the fixed points in Christian theology – characterised him in the conservative Scottish theological scene as a radical, although a more sceptical student remarked that Roland seemed to pull up only one single root at a time. His classes were alive with laughter, and such was Roland's gift for extemporaneous expression that few students found it possible to take notes of the lectures. Instead, they entered into the flowing river of Roland's thoughts to see where the current would take them.

In class and over meals, however, Andrew would raise searching questions with Roland, sometimes about the detail of a particular lecture, but also about the whole enterprise of theology. If the Bible was written by human hand, how can we claim it is divinely inspired? What makes the Hebrew stories more important than the same stories which are carried in the texts of other Middle Eastern religions? If the Bible is just another literary tradition, how can it be a guide to life? Perhaps the urgency of Andrew's search arose from a hunger for certainty about the foundations on which he hoped to build his life.

Roland confessed later that it required all his knowledge and intellectual power to do justice to Andrew's questioning. 'It was as if I was walking along a cliff-edge,' said Roland, 'delicately balancing the points on this side of the argument and that. And along would come Andrew with a question and push me over the edge.' Andrew expressed his despair at the Church's ineffective response to the vision of life promoted in the Bible, demanding that Roland justify anyone's continued loyalty to so lame an institution. Andrew was searching for a way of engaging with the major issues of society from the standpoint of Christian faith. Roland understood Andrew's questions, although he himself had different certainties from those which Andrew sought. But Andrew found in Roland a sympathetic ear and a perspective which enabled him to retain an interest in continuing his course of study. The importance that Roland gave to the life of the poor chimed with Andrew's understanding of the Biblical imperative, although the paths by which they each pursued it were to diverge dramatically.

On leaving New College in 1967, Andrew Parker was ordained as a minister but immediately felt stifled by the atmosphere of the Church of Scotland. Sunday sermons and parish visiting seemed a pale response to the Biblical description of Christians turning the world upside down. So, Andrew travelled to France to work with the McAll Mission, which had been founded by a Scot among some of the poor of Paris. By then known as *La Mission Populaire*, the '*Miss. Pop.*' provided Andrew with a theology and a structure through which to engage with the political life of the world. His time in France in 1968 coincided with a period of major social unrest across Europe – and Paris was in ferment following a summer of riots and street demonstrations by workers and students. Andrew's role in the *Miss. Pop.* brought him into close touch with the poor and the unemployed, working among Portuguese immigrants and Arabs from North Africa. With companions from the *Miss. Pop.*, he held radical Bible-study meetings, engaging with students from the Sorbonne University, Paris Quatre, in the debate about what kind of society should emerge from the struggle.

He was appointed to lead the *Mission Populaire*'s Foyer in Nemours. He worked there with students, many of them Maoists, whose dynamic espousal of continuous revolution complemented Andrew's growing sense of a political dimension to the Christian Gospel. As a community activist, he quickly incurred the wrath of the local mayor, who happened also to be the Vice-President of the French Senate. Soon, by order of the Minister of the Interior, Andrew was expelled from France, speciously accused of incitement to arson. One morning, in the early hours, a force of armed police surrounded the Foyer in Nemours – but Andrew was away teaching in Paris. Later, he gave himself up and under police escort was conveyed to the airport and despatched to England.

On his enforced return to Britain in 1973, he moved north to Scotland to stay with friends who lived in one of Glasgow's large housing estates – a 'housing scheme'. He trained as a motor mechanic and then became a porter in a huge Glasgow psychiatric hospital. His study of the Bible drove him to become a fellow-activist with local people immersed in community issues in the housing scheme. He was seeking the fuse that would detonate the revolution that would give the community control over its own life. Roland's was still a voice he trusted, but Andrew was baffled by the pattern of the Community's daily life and by the

Community's apparent reluctance to become involved in radical political action. On the occasion of his question to Roland about the Community's strategy, Andrew was visiting Roslin, still searching for answers.

The Community was composed at that time of four members. There were three ordained Anglicans from England – Roland, John and Neil Russell, the exiled Bishop of Zanzibar. At that time, the Anglican communion still ordained only men. The fourth member was Patty Burgess, a widow whose four children were now adult, and who herself had grown up in the Scottish Episcopal Church. The Community were following their simple way of life, giving hospitality to visitors without disrupting their own regular pattern of turning to prayer four times a day.

But Andrew, carrying within him a sense of urgency about making an impact on the world's injustices, interrogated Roland about the Community's purpose. What was it all for? How did the Community's life interact with the world's intolerable problems? Was it not merely commenting harmlessly on the global scene? Did Roland not see that the Bible demanded of us that we make a real difference?

'Roland,' he asked, 'what is your strategy?'

In some consternation, Roland responded, 'Oh, Good Lord! Andrew! Our strategy? I don't know if we really have a strategy. Do we?'

The ensuing discussion made it clear that, whatever might be the meaning and purpose of the Community of the Transfiguration, it would not embrace Andrew's vision for the revolutionary, real-time changing of the world. On the strength of his Christian faith, Andrew was committed to joining the struggle of the oppressed; in the process of achieving justice, he was prepared for conflict, though he would not espouse violence. On the other hand, while the Community of the Transfiguration was anxious to identify itself with ordinary working people, it was concerned to do so from the standpoint of the Community's shared life. Andrew's understanding of the Bible required political activism, which led him to a critique that sharpened through the years of the Community's commitment to contemplation.

His debate with the Community would continue for many years. He would engage closely with that aspect of the Community's life which shared the life of ordinary working people. But he could not grasp the Community's sense of its own overall identity.

Andrew Parker was disappointed in his hope that the Community might work with him to bring about major, revolutionary political change. Equally, George Wilkie was unable to understand how this Christian Fraternity, which recognised the significance of the industrial world and the importance of making substantial contact with the working man, could settle for what he himself regarded as such a quietist role in relation to it all.

John Halsey's godfather had a different opinion.

John had taken a path other than the one which life seemed to have marked out for him. The son of a distinguished Royal Naval officer who before the Second World War had been an outstanding sportsman, John seemed destined to follow in the family tradition, to look after the family estate and undertake a significant public service. It was enough of a surprise to his father when John announced to him that he was going to theological college to train as an Anglican priest. Saying farewell to John as he left for the college, his father mused, 'You'll probably come back a bishop.'

Little can he have imagined that within a few years John would become a worker-priest, working underground as a labourer in the Scottish coalfield and at the same time, as a monk, devoting his life to a communal discipline of prayer and contemplation. John and his father were not adept at communicating with each other, and John had no idea how his father viewed this very different life on which he had embarked.

The answer to this question was revealed to John in a conversation with his godfather, Kenneth Sellar – 'Monkey' Sellar, as he was known in his wartime years as a Royal Naval commander.

'In about 1976,' said John, 'Monkey had been visiting his daughter who lived in Alexandria outside Glasgow, and he fell and broke his hip. So I went over from Roslin to visit him. He wanted me to know that my father was sympathetic to what I was doing – Monkey and my father were close friends. They were both naval officers and both exponents of the Naval Grace before meals: "Is the Padré there? No? Thank God."

'Monkey wanted to assure me that my father appreciated what I was doing, and that he did too. He wanted me to know that he regarded what I was doing as significant, that he recognised that my life was "the real thing".

'"I've tried your sort of Christianity once," he said. "But never again." He came out with a story. Towards the end of the war, Monkey was in command of a mixed bunch of ships, a motley group of naval vessels. They were in the English Channel and were given an assignment. It was before the D-Day Invasion. Their job had two aims. Firstly they were to bottle up the Germans in a particular Normandy port, and secondly they were to keep the gun emplacement on the nearby cliff busy.

'They were told it was to be brief, but the exercise dragged on for weeks. The men became bored and impatient from simply sitting in the Channel. In order to restore flagging morale, Monkey decided to call a Sunday Parade "in No 1's" – the formal naval uniform for ceremonial occasions. He himself would give an address, culling texts from the book of the Prophet Isaiah, summoning the men to faith.

'To bring the men together, it was necessary to bring them all on board the two largest vessels, which were strapped to each other. This made them sitting ducks for the gun on the cliff. Monkey was in mid-flight in his pep-talk when the first shot came. It exploded just short of them. Then the second shot came, landing just beyond them. Classic sighting shots. The gun has found its range; now it can land its third shot exactly on target. Should he abandon the exercise and scatter the ships? No! This would be a total denial of what he was saying.

'The third shot never came.

'"But I never tried that again. But isn't that what you are doing all the time?"'

John was astonished as much by his godfather's revealing a side of himself he had never glimpsed, as by Monkey associating the enterprise at Roslin with his own sally into 'real Christianity'. Yet the admiration with which both father and godfather viewed John's pioneering path need not have surprised him. For they were men of adventure. In the course of his naval career, Commander Sellar was awarded the DSO and Bar, and the DSM, decorations for a courage surely not unconnected with his sort of Christianity. John's father, also, had once spoken diffidently to John of an undertaking he had embarked upon just after the First World War. As a young midshipman aged 20, he had taken leave of absence from the Royal Navy in order to experience a way of seafaring life which was about to come to an end. He joined the crew of the last sailing clipper, in order to sail before the mast on its final voyage from London to Adelaide.

So there it is, the Community of the Transfiguration. A disappointment to some. Baffling to others. To others again, 'The real thing'. What were its origins? What has been its purpose, what its significance and what its effects?

2

Roland Walls and the Sheffield Twelve

In a garden a hundred flowers bloom, each one the product of an age-long process of accident and experiment, of elemental forces and hopeful intervention. That each now appears with its unique form and colour is a consequence of a long series of steps and progressions. Similarly, the emergence of the Community of the Transfiguration was the result of long-standing processes, concealed influences and roots that had become invisible. What historical precursors and personal histories made it possible for this small religious Community to come into existence and to present its distinctive face to Scotland and to the world?

Of pivotal significance in the origin and history of the Community was the life of Roland Charles Walls. Roland was born on Thursday 7 June 1917, at 2 Hope Cottages, Bembridge, Isle of Wight. It was the day of the Feast of *Corpus Christi* – the famous Latin words meaning 'the body of Christ'. On that festival Thursday, the Christian Church traditionally celebrates the infinity of the Divine becoming present in the finite human life – in the body of Christ. In the sacrament of Holy Communion, this mystery is presented to Christians when they receive the communion bread or wafer, consecrated and now held to be 'the body of Christ'.

The date and the Feast met again when Roland was 11. Then his birthday and the Feast Day did not coincide again for a third time until he was 90. Yet the Feast of Corpus Christi held great significance for Roland from his childhood. When he was just 3, the family moved to Ryde, and in 1929 he was confirmed in the Church of England at the age of 12. Around this time, he visited the Benedictines' Quarr Abbey, not far from Ryde. The abbot and the monks befriended him and gave him the run of their library, providing him with access to an important new resource.

Roland recalled how, when he was at Sandown Grammar School, he had gone, at the age of 11, to his headmaster's study to ask if he could have the day off school on the Feast of Corpus Christi.

'Why on earth should you get the day off school?'

'Because I want to go to church that day to celebrate it.'

'But the idea of infinity in the finite is absurd! Surely you don't think that Christ can be present in that little wafer?' said the headmaster. 'Do you seriously think that a person like me could become small enough to go through the keyhole of that door?'

'But you are not God,' replied the child Roland.

So the headmaster gave Roland the day off school, and he went to church to celebrate the Feast of Corpus Christi. At that stage of his life, Roland already had a sense of the immensity of God and could clearly comprehend major theological and philosophical concepts in some ways akin to the frontiers of theoretical physics. And, when Corpus Christi Day coincided with Roland's 90th birthday in 2007, the Community celebrated the mystery which Roland had contemplated throughout the intervening years.

Roland grew up in an observant but not conspicuously devout Anglican family. His father, also Roland, was frequently unemployed during the 1920s. As a regular soldier, he served in the First World War, and, when his baby son Roland was born, he had just been posted to India. He did not return to the Isle of Wight until his term of service in the Army was completed. By that time, Roland was four years of age. Mr Walls spent five years unemployed, and then worked as a kitchen porter in a hotel. Roland's mother Mrs Albertina Walls, Tina, had two more sons younger than Roland, and a daughter who died at the age of nine months. Tina worked in domestic service. Roland saw her as having a proud and unquestioning Christian belief without being dependent on impeccable church-going. Roland always looked back to his childhood in the Isle of Wight with gratitude for happy years on an island rich in history and beauty. In his old age, he would smile with recollection as he sang from a hymn of Isaac Watts, one of England's best-loved hymn-writers. Watts, from the window of his rectory near Southampton, could look out over the stretch of water known as the Solent to the Isle of Wight in the distance, pondering the mysteries of creation and redemption.

> There is a land of pure delight
> Where saints immortal reign.
>
> Sweet fields beyond the swelling flood
> Stand dress'd in living green;
> So to the Jews old Canaan stood,
> While Jordan rolled between.

In his years at Sandown Grammar School, Roland carried the nickname 'Bem', given to him earlier at his school in Ryde when he went there from Bembridge. He was expected to leave school when he reached the age of 14.

The school, however, recognised his able mind and persuaded the family to keep him in school. Roland had a yearning to be a priest. But the family was without means, and so that thought could never be encouraged. Most candidates for the Anglican priesthood in those days were from the families of the well-to-do. But to Roland's parish came a young curate who recognised Roland's longing for the priesthood and saw his gifts. This new curate also knew of a recently founded theological college, Kelham Hall in Nottinghamshire, which was specifically tailored to cater for boys without means who sought to become priests. Before long, then aged 17, Roland set out from the Isle of Wight to undertake a course of study at Kelham.

Kelham was the home of the Society of the Sacred Mission, founded in 1893 by the Revd Herbert Kelly to train men for service in the Church of England, usually with ordination as their goal. The Society had strong connections with Korea and Japan, and had actually started as 'the Korean Brotherhood'. Kelham was unique in that it provided general education and theology, with personal and communal prayer at the centre, totally free of charge and completely independent of the Universities of Oxford and Cambridge. It was thus liberated from the 'Establishment' entanglements of the Church of England. Consequently, those whose ministries were formed at Kelham were marked out from other Church of England clergy, who for the most part looked down on them as being of inferior status. At Kelham, Roland encountered a pattern of daily life where study, for which he was intellectually equipped to a high degree, was closely woven together with prayer, to which he was temperamentally attuned. The disciplines of Kelham found in Roland a most fertile field. Kelham's influence shaped his thinking and affirmed his gifts, and marked all the subsequent years of his life.

Roland recalled the first lecture on theology he received at Kelham, delivered by the college's founding principal, Father Herbert Kelly. Father Kelly was tall and gaunt, and his monk's habit was shabby, and his tunic had seen better days. He was hard of hearing and used an ear-trumpet. Entering the classroom on that first day, Father Kelly greeted the students and invited them all to rise from their desks and follow him out of the building. He led them across the yard to a low building which housed the college's collection of pigs. Gathering the students around him, Father Kelly paused at the entrance of a sty containing a large sow resting in her straw. 'Do you see that sow?' he asked them all. The young men looked at the sow. 'Now, either God has everything to do with that sow,' said Father Kelly, 'or He's about nothing at all.' That was the lecture, the beginning of it and the end of it. They were dismissed.

Subsequent classes covered other fields of knowledge more regularly associated with developing the minds of young priests in training, but that first lecture made its impact on Roland. Perhaps his sensitivity was already attuned to seeing God in everything. Certainly, in future years the walls of the Community's kitchen in Roslin – the common dining area and the place of welcome for visitors – would be adorned with pictures of animals and birds, little marks of beauty and wonder. Many visitors remember, on the wall next to the dining table, a photograph of a tiny bird peering up the snout of an enormous elephant seal.

Father Herbert Kelly fitted no ordinary categories. He was a former soldier who had become a Christian missionary in Korea. Influenced by F. D. Maurice, a nineteenth-entury Christian Socialist, Kelly founded both the Society of the Sacred Mission and Kelham Theological College. He was an Anglo-Catholic who had a significant role in the Edinburgh Missionary Conference of 1910. This conference marked the start of the Ecumenical Movement, which in turn led to the founding of the Student Christian Movement and in time to the forming of the World Council of Churches. Kelly's life-long commitment to Church unity meant that ecumenism was an underlying theme in Kelham's training for ordinands.

On one occasion, in 1937, Kelly invited to the college the most famous contemporary Roman Catholic advocate of ecumenism, Abbé Paul Couturier of Lyons. In his day, Couturier was often a lone Roman Catholic voice in honouring the Christian credentials of Reformed Churches at a time when, for the Vatican, 'ecumenism' meant the Reformed Churches returning to Rome. His visit to Kelham was a sign of his passion for unity in the Church and of his respect for fellow Christians in the Anglican communion. When Couturier came to Kelham, Father Kelly appointed the student Roland Walls as his guide to the college. At the end of the visit, Roland accompanied Abbé Couturier to the railway station. Roland asked Couturier to give him a blessing. 'I will give you a blessing on this condition: will you promise to do all in your power, in your ministry, to work for the unity of all God's people?' Roland considered his life forever marked by his own promise and by Couturier's blessing.

Roland lived and studied at Kelham from 1934 to 1940. He quickly showed an aptitude for study; and, as the years progressed, his gifts of understanding and insight may already have encouraged the Kelham staff to see him as a potential teacher and colleague. In 1940, he went to a parish in Leeds and was ordained as a deacon and then a priest. In 1943, he moved to the Sheffield parish of St Cecilia's, Parson Cross, which was run by a team of priests from Kelham. This move from Leeds was in part to repay the debt he felt to Kelham for his training. After two years at

Parson Cross, Roland decided to join the Novitiate of the Society of the Sacred Mission (SSM), taking his first steps towards becoming a monk.

By then, Roland was 28 and had never given a thought to going to university, far less to the prospect of an academic career. The leadership at Kelham, however, saw that he had already demonstrated an expertise in Biblical studies, fired by his passionate commitment to Jesus and to the Church. His entry into the Novitiate gave them the opportunity to send him to Cambridge University to study for a degree in theology. The underlying intention of this was undoubtedly to enable Kelham in future to demonstrate that it had teaching staff of high attainment. Accordingly, in 1945, Roland matriculated as an undergraduate in Corpus Christi College, the very name of the college having great appeal to him. A brilliant degree, awarded with a rare distinction *magna cum laude*, 'with great praise', saw him proposed and accepted as a member of the prestigious International Society for New Testament Studies. In that same year, 1948, he was elected a Fellow of his college. The college accepted and respected his Novitiate with the Society of the Sacred Mission, and Roland fulfilled his teaching responsibilities at Kelham. But by 1950 he was aware that there was a clerical and authoritarian aspect to Kelham which did not altogether suit him. A distinct trace of insubordination in Roland was making him suspect that perhaps he was not in the end an ideal aspirant to full membership of the SSM. At any rate, Roland terminated his Novitiate, left Kelham and accepted the post of chaplain to the Bishop of Ely for a year until a resident post at Corpus Christi College became available.

The Bishop of Ely, Edward Wynn, was himself a member of a religious order called the Oratory of the Good Shepherd. The members of this order did not live in community; they were dispersed, but they maintained their common spiritual disciplines. So, while Roland had withdrawn from the community of Kelham, he remained in close contact with similar community disciplines.

In 1952, Roland was appointed chaplain and Dean of Chapel at Corpus Christi College. He quickly gained a high reputation for teaching and for inspiring students and all kinds of people, and was being recognised as a rising personality in the Anglican Church. He established life-long friendships with the families of academic colleagues and was cherished by children as an anarchic influence, on their side rather than on that of their parents. One child of those times remembers Roland leaving him under a laburnum tree, with its poisonous pods, while Roland read a book. Friends had high hopes, at one time, that they might see him marry: they knew of a most eligible lady, a Mrs Chivers, widow of the head of a family who made marmalade and fine jams. Perhaps, though, Roland already recognised that he was not on course for marriage or family life. He was fulfilled as part of the Church and of the academic community and of the family life of his friends.

Then all of a sudden he disappeared to Sheffield, effectively annihilating any prospect of an academic future. This was inexplicable to many close friends, at least four of whom later became bishops, others advancing to high-profile academic and Church appointments.

The call came when Bishop Leslie Hunter of Sheffield arranged to attend a meeting of Cambridge chaplains, pastors and teachers of theology who periodically gathered to reflect on the relationship between the academic world and the Church of England in the parishes. 'Why is it', asked the bishop, 'that when I am provided with the "best" ordinands, the ablest ones with the best training and preparation that the Church of England can provide, comparatively few stay long in parish life in the industrial urban area of Sheffield? Why do so many move away, to rural or suburban parishes, or into specialist ministries and chaplaincies, or leave the ministry completely? Has their training been out of gear with the job?'

After letting the group reflect on this, Bishop Hunter then said he wanted one of those present to commit himself to a pilot project in his diocese to address the issue. 'I'm not leaving this room', he said, 'until someone makes this commitment.' Of this meeting, only Roland's account has survived. The men listened to the bishop's challenge and fell silent. Here were people with big responsibilities, scholarly ambitions, academic careers, families. Roland recalled that the silence lengthened. He gradually became aware that, one by one, the others had turned their eyes to look at him.

So it came to pass that Roland went to Sheffield as a canon of the cathedral.

With the bishop's support, Roland designed a one-year course for young men preparing for ordination to the ministry, 'ordinands'. The course was to run for three consecutive years, with six students in each year. Modelled on the pattern of the disciples of Jesus in the Gospels, the candidates were to be known as the Sheffield Twelve (each year's group referring to themselves disparagingly as 'the mucky half-dozen'). After a fortnight's orientation, the candidates were to spend their first six months working in industry. They would live in digs with families in working-class areas, and take unskilled employment in Sheffield's steel-related industries. For the second six months, they would all live together with Roland in the canon's large house at 393 Fulwood Road. There, living on the pooled savings from their earlier months of employment, they would spend their time in study and discussion, in prayer and in widening their understanding of parish life by visiting hospitals and old people's homes and other institutions of society.

Roland selected three books for the students to read as preparation for their year in Sheffield:

- *Seeds of the Desert* by René Voillaume is the life story of the hermit Charles de Foucauld who, as we have noted, lived in solitude in the mountains of the Sahara desert and was eventually murdered by thieves. The book also recounts the emergence of the Little Brothers and Little Sisters of Jesus.
- *Life Together* is the account by Dietrich Bonhoeffer of his underground theological seminary in Finkenwalde during the Nazi years.
- *The Twelve Together* by Ralph Morton, then Deputy Leader of the Iona Community, is a study of how Jesus developed a community life with his disciples.

All the students were encouraged to read these books and to deepen their understanding of their own discipleship before they arrived in Sheffield. The brief, one-page course outline given to each of the first year's candidates on arrival presents the aim and purpose of the Sheffield Twelve: 'By prayer, work and study, to put ourselves to school in Gospel discipleship, and to learn the compassion of Jesus, for the Evangelism of the world and the Glory of GOD'. The course outline also contains a simple Rule, its essence distilled from the monastic tradition. This Rule shaped the experience of many of the candidates, and presented itself again in the life of the Community of the Transfiguration.[1]

Roland issued an invitation to young men already in training for the ministry and the priesthood to join him in Sheffield. Five accepted the challenge. Then George MacLeod, the Leader of the Iona Community, heard that Roland was about to start this new form of training for ordinands, and hoped that he might have room for a candidate from Scotland. Accordingly, he wrote to Roland with this suggestion. Roland's reply was as follows:

> My dear George,
> Your letter comes as a gift – the gift of the possibility of a sixth man. I've got 5 Anglicans, and was looking about for a 6th. If he can be Church of Scotland so much – so very much – the better. I will certainly try to fit him in.[2]

And fit him in he did. In October 1958, the first half-dozen young men, the first of the Sheffield Twelve, travelled to Sheffield to begin the adventure of their lives.

Apart from the one from Scotland, they were products of the English public-school system – from Harrow, Eton, Lancing, Haileybury and St John's, Leatherhead.[3] For them, the sudden introduction to industrial life, to hazardous working conditions and to cramped domestic accommodation came as an excitement. One of them recalled with remembered exhilaration, 'The factory that employed me specialised in wire-drawing and heat treatment – very hot and nasty heat-treatment of steel wire in large vats filled with sodium nitrate at a temperature of about 1,400 degrees Centigrade. The challenge was to keep all ten fingers intact and avoid a rather bad burn. At the time, however, it seemed that with my £15 per 60-hour week I was well paid.'[4]

Another recalled, 'the stark contrast between Cambridge and the six months in the steelworks, and the satisfaction of being accepted in such a different world. Something of the attitude to life of my workmates has stayed with me.'[5]

Six students trained with Roland in the first year, six in the second and five in the third; a total of 17. Most of them did indeed proceed to ordination; several advanced to senior posts in the Church of England, and one became a bishop. Others went into academic life or into social work, and one became a globally distinguished psychoanalyst. Eight of the 17 shared a 50-years-on reunion with Roland in 2008. Their conversation and their written recollections[6] demonstrate the lasting effect of their year in Sheffield, with its opportunity for them to interact with Roland.

Several recalled that Roland sent them out to their six months of industrial work with something to assist their prayers when they were on the shop-floor: a simple nail. The nail spoke of three mysteries: the nail of Jesus in the carpenter's shop at his daily work; the nail of crucifixion, sharing the world's suffering; and the nail holding together the simple cross on the altar of the upper-room chapel in the house at 393 Fulwood Road – their connection with the here and now.

The focus on prayer was combined with a programme of serious study. In their months together in Fulwood Road, the students engaged in daily Bible study together and were encouraged to read theological works by Paul Tillich and Karl Barth. During their year, the Sheffield Twelve had regular contact with the Little Brothers of Jesus, the originally French religious fraternity whose origins lay in the inspirational life of Charles de Foucauld. The Little Brothers had a house in Leeds, where a small number of men lived in community under a simple discipline and worked in unskilled industrial jobs. At some time during their year of training, each year group was in contact with the Ecumenical Community at Taizé, and the concluding event of the year was a week spent on the island of Iona with the resident members of the Iona Community.

Each member of the Sheffield Twelve was thus invited to immerse his life for a year in the experiences Roland had prepared for them all: industrial work, personal and communal prayer, rigorous intellectual discipline and lightness of heart.

The concluding event of their year as members of the Sheffield Twelve was on the day they left Iona, which was timed to be on 6 August – the Feast of the Transfiguration. During their Sheffield year, the Transfiguration was a frequent focus. With their ecumenical perspective, they honoured the Orthodox Church's celebration of the Transfiguration as one of the four great Christian feasts along with Christmas, Easter and Pentecost. They also recognised the significance of that date, 6 August, as the date of the dropping of the atomic bomb on Hiroshima in 1945. In the words with which Robert Oppenheimer, 'father' of the atomic bomb, greeted the sight of the first atomic explosion, 'brighter than a thousand suns',[7] they saw an antithesis to the brightness of Christ's Transfiguration on the Judaean mountainside, when 'his face shone like the sun and his clothes became as white as the light'.[8] That date therefore attained a great significance for them, as commemorating both the transfiguring and the disfiguring of humanity.

So, at 5am on the morning of their final day on Iona, they held a celebration of holy communion, the Eucharist, in the tiny chapel of St Oran. Then, having celebrated the Feast of the Transfiguration in this way, they took the early-morning ferry towards the rest of their life.

Asked to recall significant moments of their Sheffield year, the former students, by the time of asking all in their 70s, needed no second invitation.

'Roland set me an essay on Paul Tillich's *Systematic Theology*,' wrote one. 'Eventually I was forced to ask him about the meaning of the recurrent word, "ontological". "Substitute it with the word 'bloody'," said Roland, "and all will become clear."'[9]

'While we were in community we all had our jobs,' wrote another. 'Mine was to do the laundry for the eight of us living together: Roland, Miss Black (Roland's housekeeper) and the six of us. The washing machine used to make quite a noise so I used to sing while I worked, sometimes a bass solo from the Brahms *Requiem*. Another thing I remember especially about our time with Roland was how much fun we had with him. He used to regale us with his stories.'[10]

Another wrote, 'Miss Black the housekeeper came from the Isle of Lismore in the Inner Hebrides, and was a lady of eccentric ways and indomitable scepticism about the Christian faith. Early in 1961, when Yuri Gagarin became the first man in space and reported no sign of God up there: "I told you so!" said Miss Black with a triumphant smile.'[11]

'One Sunday Miss Black went to the Presbyterian Church in Sheffield,' contributed another.

'"I'll not be back there," she said to us.

'"Oh? Why not?"

'"They're much too friendly."'[12]

One by one, many of the former Sheffield Twelve contributed.

'The months in 393 Fulwood Road were the basis of my theological and spiritual training; the two following years at Westcott House were only a comment on this fundamental experience. For me it was unique – the heady mixture of our prayers in the attic, the almost intense devotion to the person of Christ, but also the bubbling joy and humour, the sense of the absurd!'[13]

'Undergirding our corporate life was the daily worship, morning and evening, in the small chapel at the top of the house.'[14]

'The task I was allotted in the house, much to my initial disgust, was to care for the top-floor chapel – I was not at all into sanctuary slippers and sacristies. But I came to love that chapel dearly, lavishing a lot of time on cleaning, polishing and dusting, and doing my best to fill it with flowers from the fairly wild garden at 393. Roland knew best, of course.'[15]

'I learned to appreciate the liturgy, the Daily Office in the little chapel. The way Roland addressed these things showed me that something could be simultaneously the most important thing in the world, yet not be taken too seriously. There were always jokes with Roland. I remember him telling us of a parish he'd visited where there was a misprint in the prayer book. Instead of "Compline"[16] it had the word, "Bompline"!'[17]

'Roland made a bedroom for himself in the garage, putting a mattress on to a ping-pong table. Beside this he had put the remains of the Easter candle which he used as a bedside light while he read his way through the novels of D. H. Lawrence, which was part of his reading while we were there.'[18]

Several of the Sheffield Twelve recalled an incident which illustrated Roland's love of animals, and their love for him. A Sheffield cathedral family lived near the house at 393 Fulwood Road, and they regularly welcomed Roland for a meal. They had a dog called Buster who liked Roland immensely. One day, the family were preparing dinner for themselves, roast chicken. The cooked chicken was on the counter just before being served to the family. Buster jumped on to the counter and made off with the chicken. He raced up the street with the chicken in his jaws, pushed into Roland's house, and buried the chicken in Roland's bed. A present for his friend.

Bishop Leslie Hunter, at whose behest Roland went to Sheffield, has been described as 'both a thinker and a doer'.[19] He pioneered many national initiatives within the Church and was seen as 'one of the most forward-looking bishops of his generation, regarded by many as a prophet'.[20] He had a gift for appointing people to undertake significant work. In 1950, alarmed at the wide gulf between the Church of England and the people of industrialised cities, Hunter appointed the Revd Ted Wickham as industrial chaplain to the diocese, and forcefully directed him to engage with the steel industry. With the example of wartime forces' chaplains in mind, many European Churches were seeking to connect with the industrial world through introducing the presence of ordained ministers into factories and other work-places. Wickham was an admirer of the German theologian Horst Symanowski of Mainz, who guided young Lutheran ministers into working with apprentices in the steel-making factories of the Ruhr.

Wickham sought to build and sustain an engagement with the working population by visiting steelworks and other heavy industries. His style was participatory. He and his chaplains made regular factory visits, engaging people in informal conversation and holding formal break-time discussions about issues of importance to them. Wickham was also the author of a seminal book on Industrial Mission.[21] His intense concentration on the interaction of the Church and industry led him to develop a distinct theology and to design viable methods for establishing links between them. His work constituted a template which was followed by mission teams in other parts of the country and abroad.

However, it is not clear how Bishop Hunter envisaged the relationship between the work which Wickham had pioneered and the task he had invited Roland Walls to undertake. Indeed, the bishop did not consult Wickham about the new project. The first Wickham heard of it was when Roland arrived in Sheffield. And he was none too pleased.

A member of the earliest year group of the Twelve recalls, 'Roland's plan needed the co-operation of Ted Wickham and his Sheffield Industrial Mission. But Ted regarded Roland as effete and eccentric, and resented what he saw as Roland setting up a counter-movement to his own, in an Anglo-Catholic Cambridge kind of way. Wickham interviewed us all, in preparation for helping us to find industrial jobs. He said to me, "What you want to do is come and join the Sheffield Industrial Mission, and forget that other stuff."'[22] By the second year, however, Wickham had recognised that Roland was offering a pattern of training that could be complementary to his own. His industrial chaplains readily offered assistance to Roland's students in finding six-month industrial posts, and he and Roland became very firm friends.

Whatever course their lives subsequently followed, it is evident that all the men who lived for a year among the Sheffield Twelve regarded the experience as having influenced them permanently.

Bruce Anderson's widow was in no doubt about how her husband viewed that year. 'What Bruce learnt in Sheffield became a life-long resource for his ministry ... and he had an enduring affection and respect for Roland, with his radical commitment to discipleship, his quirky sense of humour, and his total disregard for the wealth and status that this world hankers after.'[23]

A range of others looked back on the year as a milestone in their lives. Ted Longman remarked, 'As I look back, I think Roland has been a role model for me. Not that I have tried to imitate him, but he has been a check on what I might have done, a healthy balance to other influences and inclinations. His simplicity of lifestyle has been a constant reminder that we can easily get distracted by attachments.'[24]

'That Year was more about "being" rather than "doing",' said Kenneth Hughes, 'and what was gained from it came more from osmosis than from any cut-and-dried package of instruction. Roland of course was the guiding light whose personality affected us as much as the many insights that first made us laugh, then reflect and later still re-visit frequently in a variety of circumstances.'[25]

John Oliver reflected, 'How lucky we were to have had that year, to have lived together under Roland's leadership, our faith nurtured by his, teased and challenged and inspired alternately. He was the best teacher I ever had.'[26]

Kenneth Boyd, another Church of Scotland candidate, mused: 'I've been thinking about that Year on and off. Thinking, "What was it about?" and thinking, "How valuable it was." I suppose I got so much from it that it takes the rest of my life to work it all out. It is a kind of standard, a level of excellence, for ever afterwards.'[27]

From our vantage point of 50 years later, we can sense the significance, for these men, of spending a year as one of the Sheffield Twelve. In September 1961, three months after the third and final year-group of the Sheffield Twelve had dispersed at the end of their course, Roland delivered a report on the experiment to the Church of England committee which supervised the training of ordinands (the Church Advisory Council on Training for Ministry, known as CACTM). Roland was a member of this committee, which met in Church House at the side of Westminster Abbey. Explaining that, in Sheffield, Ted Wickham had pioneered a Church engagement with industry, Roland then enthusiastically outlined the programme he and the ordinands had followed in the Sheffield Twelve. Among the 40 committee members present were seven bishops (another six sent apologies) and six theological-college principals. After general discussion, it was agreed that a working party should be set up to investigate the various schemes for incorporating an industrial thread into the training of ordinands, and to make recommendations as to how they might best be used in the future. The working party would be set up at the next meeting.[28]

At that next meeting, in January 1962, the committee learned that 'it was now clear that the Board for Social Responsibility was going into the matter of the Church in Industry, and that any enquiry about ordinands in industrial schemes would best be undertaken as part of a larger enquiry. It was agreed that CACTM should not appoint a separate committee at this stage.'[29] Roland remained a member of CACTM until May 1965, but in minutes of meetings from those succeeding years no remnant of the Sheffield experiment is to be found. Nor, in the subsequent minutes of the Board of Social Responsibility, is there any trace of the experience of Roland and the Sheffield Twelve.

As a consequence of these apparently innocuous decisions, no committee or working party evaluated the report; no hint was given as to whether the three years of work had resulted in anything worthy of comment, good or bad. Seen by many as a prophet, Bishop Hunter had hoped to transform the training of priests and ministers for work in industrial areas. In Roland, he had discerned the creative potential to make it happen. 'I believe this may prove to be a very valuable variant on the normal course for ordinands.'[30] So, how could the report and the project itself now disappear into oblivion?

The years 1958 to 1961 were of critical significance for CACTM itself. Its original responsibility had been to select and train men for ordination, and to secure and distribute grants for their education. Now major new issues were forcing themselves on to the Church of England's agenda, and in February 1959 the Church Assembly voted to add several new areas of responsibility to CACTM's remit.[31] With a fall of more than a third in the number of candidates for ordination, a review of the theological colleges was to be undertaken to determine whether they were all now needed. A new graduate theological college had been proposed. In addition, a major question was arising about the possible ordination of women to the priesthood. And finally, there was a perceived need to train lay people for unpaid leadership in the Church, a movement which would lead to Non-Stipendiary

Ministry. With these major responsibilities now occupying their attention, perhaps CACTM simply had no capacity to incorporate the results of the Sheffield Twelve experiment into their agenda.

Another hint is found, however, in the account which one of the Sheffield Twelve gives of how he came to join the second group of ordinands. 'I had done my first year at Westcott House. I was taken aside by the then Principal Ken Carey, who told me in his avuncular way that some of the chaps who had been with Roland Walls in Sheffield had rather gone off the rails theologically, and it would be a good idea if someone who had done a good bit of theology went on this occasion.'[32] Perhaps, therefore, influential voices were already threatening the outcome of Bishop Leslie Hunter's bold idea.

If the pattern of training offered to the Sheffield Twelve was to continue, it would require an advocate. Roland himself was no strategist, nor was he a church politician. It would have to be someone else. But there was no-one. Ted Wickham had left Sheffield in 1959 when he was appointed Bishop of Middleton. His successor as chaplain of the Industrial Mission, Michael Jackson, proved to have little sympathy with Wickham's programme of training industrial chaplains, far less with Roland's programme of more direct industrial engagement. Discussion within the Sheffield Cathedral Chapter had already begun to weigh the high cost of the Sheffield Twelve project in terms of staff time, speculating about reassigning the post of Residential Canon currently filled by Roland. Bishop Leslie Hunter was himself approaching retirement. He would be succeeded in 1962 by Bishop John Taylor, who did not share Hunter's concern for engagement with the industrial scene. The climate for the Sheffield Twelve was turning cold.

At what seemed the call of God, Roland had abandoned an academic career in order to develop a new form of training for the ministry. Now his best efforts, and the achievements of the young men who had entrusted themselves to him, were counted as nothing. The silent oblivion into which the Church swallowed these richly creative years seemed to beckon Roland also.

Disconsolate, he left England for France, taking up residence in the fledgling Protestant religious community at Taizé.

3

The Inexplicable Journey to Edinburgh

A key source of information about Roland Walls is *Mole Under the Fence*, a book of transcribed conversations between Roland and Ron Ferguson and Mark Chater.[1] The book wonderfully conveys the quality of Roland's engagement with theology and the world, but being a single book of less than 200 pages it is unable to present the entire range or depth of Roland's experience. For instance, when Roland offers his reflection on the end of the project with the Sheffield Twelve, the *Mole Under the Fence* records him as saying, 'By 1962 it was clear that the Church of England, whatever else was happening, wasn't particularly interested in [the Sheffield Twelve]. I would be going on doing that as a rather peripheral little experiment that wasn't really getting into the heart of training for the priesthood. And in my last year there I was made very uncomfortable by the fact that I might be left there doing this odd thing on my own, with my bishop's approval, but not with much effect on the general thinking of the church.'[2]

Roland goes on to say, 'My bishop said to me, "Go off to Taizé. Go and spend three or four months in Taizé to find out if that's what you ought to do."'

But another book, *Britain's First Worker Priests* by John Mantle, gives a more dramatic account of the end of the Sheffield Twelve:[3] 'After three years' work at [Bishop Leslie] Hunter's invitation, Walls prepared a report for CACTM arguing for a radical shift in theological education. Its committee, however, engrossed in discussion on the establishment of a new ecumenical Queen's College in Birmingham, only received this, and in a loss which has never been calculated, it was never heard of again. Walls, disappointed and alarmed, abandoned Sheffield in 1962.'

John Halsey, too, remembers Roland's sense of personal and professional rejection at the complete ignoring of the report and of the work embodied in the project of the Sheffield Twelve. It seems possible, therefore, that in leaving for France Roland was at that point turning his back on England and shaking her dust from his feet.

In attributing to Bishop Leslie Hunter the impulse for going to Taizé, Roland is exhibiting one of his marked characteristics. When attempts are made to assess his motivation, or his reason for making a particular decision, Roland proves elusive. His own wishes, his own personal preferences, his weighing of specific factors and arguments, all tend to remain invisible. The final outcome is often expressed as the decision of 'the bishop', or later as the view variously of 'the abbot', or 'the cardinal', or 'the Community'. So, while Bishop Hunter may well have articulated approval of Roland's visit to Taizé, it is also true that Taizé was already familiar to Roland from earlier contact.

While he was still working in Cambridge but preparing for the Sheffield Twelve, Roland spent a summer travelling in Europe, visiting and observing places where new flames of church life were arising. He visited Pontigny, where priests were trained for *Mission de France* – part of the movement to present the Christian message to the working people of France. That same summer, he went to Annemasse, on the border of France and Switzerland, and visited a working fraternity of the Little Brothers of Jesus. The pattern of their life and thought impressed Roland profoundly and established a benchmark in his thinking about the life of a Christian believer. He was moved by their determination to remain in their current location for life; by the simplicity and yet the severe demands of their prayer programme; and by their hospitality – on Roland's first visit, the brother in charge gave up his bed and slept in the corridor so that Roland had somewhere to sleep.

During that summer, Roland also visited, not for the first time, the ecumenical community in Taizé. Taizé was founded in 1940 by Roger Schutz, a young Protestant Christian from Switzerland. Searching for an authentic way of living a life according to the

Gospels in the turbulent years of the twentieth century, Brother Roger eventually settled in France, in Taizé, a small desolate village just north of Cluny, historically a key centre of Benedictine monasticism. In September 1940, Roger bought a small house there that would eventually become the home of the Taizé community. It was only a few miles south of the line which divided the war-torn country, and from its beginning the little Community gave welcome and shelter to refugees fleeing from danger and persecution. On his early visits, Roland responded positively to the atmosphere which he found there. Through the entire life of the community ran a commitment to peace and justice, expressed in regular times of prayer and in an explicit encouragement to kindness in relationships, to simplicity in style of life, to ecumenism, and to reconciliation between individuals and nations.

Two incidents from the years of the Sheffield Twelve reveal that within Roland an inclination had been developing towards life in a religious community. First, Ted Longman, one of the second-year group of the Sheffield Twelve, was talking with Roland on Iona during the final week of their year of study.

'I've enjoyed my year with you in Sheffield, Roland. But of course what you're doing isn't really to do directly with training for Ordination.'

'Oh? Do you not think so? What is it, then?'

'It's really something to do with "community" – about how to be a religious community.'[4]

This observation startled Roland, and he remembered it.

Later that same year, 1960, at Christmas, Roland was spending a week on retreat in the Monastery of Our Lady of the Cross at Glasshampton near Worcester. Many years before, Father William Sirr had lived there for 20 years as a hermit, devoted to contemplative prayer but profoundly hoping that he might found a religious community there. Not one other enquirer, however, came to join him. When he died in 1937, he was buried in the little cloister garden. Not until ten years after his death did a company of Anglican Franciscans take up residence again. On a moonlit winter night in 1960, Roland looked across the cloister to William's grave and was aware of making a commitment to God. 'I don't know what it was about, but only that I would be prepared to leave anything that I was doing, and anything I had, in order to follow up in some completely undefined way what Father William had been about.'⁵

In his discussions with Bishop Leslie Hunter before he left for Taizé, it was evident that Roland might one day be part of a religious community. Leaving Sheffield for France, he paid a brief visit in London to Lambeth Palace, to his friend Michael Ramsay who was by that time Archbishop of Canterbury.

Roland then made his way to Taizé. Those features of the Taizé Community's life which had originally appealed to him soon fulfilled his hopes. Within months, he was considering committing himself to membership of the Community. But two factors now entered the equation. A visitor came to stay at the Community of Taizé, a bishop of the Orthodox Church. Roland used to relate how he accompanied this bishop on a walk. The bishop gave his opinion that if Roland wished to introduce new patterns of religious life to Britain he could not hope to do so from Taizé. He would need to return to Britain, and the new religious life would have to be home-grown. The Taizé community had already tried to establish a sister community in Sheffield, but it had not taken root. And, as for Scotland, Brother Roger avowed that, 'as far as a religious community is concerned, Scotland is the stoniest ground in Europe'.

Around the same time, however, a deputation arrived at Taizé from England to meet with the leader of the Taizé Community, Brother Roger. The group included the leaders of the Church of England's religious orders – the Superiors (the senior figures) of the Anglican Benedictines and Franciscans, and the Community of the Resurrection from Mirfield. They had come not to see Roland but to enquire of Brother Roger whether his order, the Monks of Taizé, had Episcopal authority. They asked Brother Roger by what authority he, a Protestant pastor of Reformed, Calvinist origins, received the vows of the men who joined the Community. Could he demonstrate that his authority was in direct line from St Peter? Less than content with his response, the leaders of the religious orders returned to England and contacted the Archbishop of Canterbury, Michael Ramsay. They informed him that if Roland, a priest of prestige in the Church of England, was to become a professed member of the Community of Taizé, it would create a break in the communion they all belonged to. They would regard the Archbishop of Canterbury as conniving in this betrayal, and a significant number of members of their orders would become Roman Catholics.

Ramsay wrote to Roland about this, saying, 'I think you should know.' Confronted by this contradiction, preparing to join a Community dedicated to ecumenical unity but thereby causing disunity within his own Church, Roland reconsidered his future. He explained his dilemma to the Brothers at Taizé, and expressed his regret at having to make this new decision. Roland swiftly returned to Britain. He went back to Sheffield, where he was still a canon, and to the canon's house at Fulwood Road.

Within a short space of time, Roland received two unsought invitations: one to a Fellowship at Merton College, Oxford, the other to become leader of a famous charitable institution, the Royal Foundation of St Katherine in Stepney in the East End of London. Unsure whether to accept either of these invitations, Roland then received an unexpected phone call from his close friend, the former principal of Westcott House, Kenneth Carey, now Bishop of Edinburgh. Carey invited him to come north.

Roland went to Edinburgh to visit his friend, who offered him the post of priest-in-charge of Rosslyn Chapel, six miles outside Edinburgh. Roland visited the chapel. There it stood, a small, medieval architectural jewel set in a farm field with a little museum standing alongside it. To Roland, it made no sense. Carey said to him, 'Come to Edinburgh and see what happens.'[6] Roland's answer was required within ten days. He returned to England by train to decide.

The story of how he made up his mind has been told and retold many times with a variety of details, both by Roland himself and also by people upon whom the story had a powerful impact.

'I went on that lovely train from Waverley through Carlisle,' said Roland. 'When I got to Leeds City station I remember I was praying to the Lord, and I was getting mad at him, and I was saying, "Now Lord, I don't know what you're doing" – because I was 45! Was I? Yes. Ridiculous! So I said, "Lord, you've got me where you want me, because I will do what you say as long as you make it perfectly clear to me what it is. I really don't mind what I do of all these things but I will do anything as long as you make it clear: so jolly well get on with it." That was the kind of prayer I was saying, when, all of a sudden, coming out of Leeds the other way, was a big coal train, all of twenty trucks, and on the back, on the guard's van, it had a big notice – I've not seen one before or since. It was a paper notice, big red letters, and it said, RETURN EMPTY TO SCOTLAND. The word "Empty" was underlined.

'"Right, Lord."

'This event, on my return from seeing this highly unpromising little Chapel, is the only reason we're at Roslin. I mean, that is utterly irrational.'[7]

Roland was inducted as priest-in-charge of Rosslyn Chapel, and in November 1962 he moved into the parsonage with his house-keeper, the irreversibly irreligious Miss Black. Word soon spread among the church-going Episcopalians that a fresh voice was to be heard in Rosslyn Chapel. Before long, Roland had attracted a variety of new faces, some coming from a considerable distance. One of the new arrivals recalled, 'He started a thing he called W.U.S.H. This was a set of groups: groups centred on Worship and Unity and Service and Healing. So these groups started off. And I went to the one on Service.'[8] These groups injected new energy into the congregation's life.

Roland, however, still had hopes of a surprise. He hoped that some other priests looking for surprises might come and join him. In the following two years, a number of people enquired, but none came to stay. In 1964, finding himself thus becalmed, Roland experienced a form of panic. Without telling his Edinburgh bishop, Kenneth Carey, he wrote to Donald Coggan, the Archbishop of York, to see if there might be some opportunity in York with more potential. The archbishop invited him to visit, and talked and listened to him. Then he took him round some potential parishes and other posts. But, on the way back to Edinburgh, Roland heard the voice of God saying to him, 'Roland, you Rat. You said you'd wait in Roslin for something to happen.' So he wrote to Dr Coggan with his sincere apology, and called a halt to further search.[9]

Later that same year, Bishop Leslie Hunter again entered Roland's life with an initiative which would lead to changes. By now retired, and aware that his successor as Bishop of Sheffield had very different priorities, Hunter called a meeting of people who had worked with him in the industrial programme of the Sheffield Diocese. Living by then in Beaconsfield, he invited them to a 24-hour informal gathering. Eighteen of them joined in discussion of how the Church was to engage with society in the coming decade. Before lunch on the second day, just prior to their departure, Roland said he would like to speak. 'You'll need to be quick, then,' said Bishop Hunter, 'because my wife Grace has made the lunch, and it's ready.' Roland quite hesitantly spoke of his hope of starting a new type of religious community, on the Celtic model. John Halsey was at the meeting in Beaconsfield, as were two others from the Sheffield Twelve, John Ware and Hugh Maddox. Another young priest from Sheffield was with them, Robert Haslam. He had not been one of the Twelve, but he knew them because he also worked in the Diocese. These four drove back from Beaconsfield to Sheffield together, and John Halsey and Robert spoke excitedly about Roland's plan. The ground was prepared for planting the new community.

John Halsey was perhaps a surprising candidate to be among the founding members of a new religious community. He belonged to a prominent Hertfordshire family. The family home, Gaddesden Place, was built in the late eighteenth century, though Halseys had lived in Great Gaddesden since at least the fifteenth century. John's father Sir Thomas Halsey was the 3rd Baronet. John's mother was a niece of the third and last White Rajah of Sarawak, Sir Charles Vyner Brooke, whose great-uncle James Brooke, the first White Rajah, was the inspiration for Joseph Conrad's novel *Lord Jim*. In another literary connection, Oscar Wilde dedicated one of his fairy-tales for children, *The Young King*, to 'Margaret, Lady Brooke, Ranee of Sarawak', John's grandmother. From his childhood, John was aware of his family's traditions, and grew up anticipating, albeit perhaps uneasily, that he would fulfil the family's expectations and bear responsibility for the family estate. Two of his great-uncles were Anglican clergymen, and one of them had been rector of the Church of St John the Baptist at Great Gaddesden. As a child, John often accompanied his great-uncle on visits to small churches in the area and regularly attended worship in the church on a Sunday.

One Sunday when he was about 10 years of age, he was listening to the Gospel reading: it was the story of Jesus and the rich young man who wanted eternal life. Jesus told him to give his wealth to the poor and to come and follow Jesus. The young man 'went away sorrowful, for he had great possessions'.[10] Although he was only 10 years of age, the story resonated with John.

After his schooldays at Eton College and two years of National Service as an officer in the Army, in the 60th Rifles, the King's Royal Rifle Corps, he went up to Cambridge to study geology. While his chosen subject would be germane to the work of caring for the family estates, John knew that it might also open doors to a different life. In 1955, the second year of John's degree course, Billy Graham visited Cambridge with his mission team. John, through his college chapel, attended some of Billy Graham's rallies and found himself profoundly stirred by the experience. Hitherto, the Church had been an important part of the social fabric of John's life, with church-going an unquestioned personal duty. But, through the words of Billy Graham and the atmosphere of the crowded rally, John received a powerful call to evangelical conversion. He sensed the power of the call of Jesus to his disciples that they should leave everything and follow him. John became part of the Magdalene College Christian Union.

On graduation, John joined an oil firm who assigned him to their team of scientists who were prospecting for oil in Canada. He had been in Canada less than a year when the curate of the local church in Calgary asked him to help with a mission which was to be led by the Revd Tom Allan from the Church of Scotland. Rather reluctantly, John agreed. Working with the mission team, however, reignited the feelings and interests which had been awakened when John had listened to Billy Graham in 1955. Although unsure where it would lead, he felt he had to change course and prepare for the ordained ministry.

Accordingly, he made contact with the Revd Simon Barrington

Ward, his college chaplain at Magdalene. Barrington Ward arranged for John, on his return from Canada, to see Canon Kenneth Carey, principal of the theological college Westcott House. The interview took place a few days before the start of term, and coincided with the withdrawal of one of the students from the ordinands' course. Carey thus had a vacancy to fill, and he offered the place to John. Since Carey's offer required an immediate response, John next day accepted the place at Westcott House.

Aware of his own very limited experience of life and ministry at a grass-roots level, John had been exploring a possible 12-month venture into the mission-field or industry before entering formal training for ministry. The day after he accepted the place at Westcott House, he received an offer of a teaching post in a school in Penhalonga in what was then Southern Rhodesia. But the choice was already made.

John encountered a signpost to where this might lead early in his Westcott House days. Over his first Christmas holiday, John visited a new experimental community. Near Bridport in Dorset, the Revd Percy Smith had established a religious community at Pilsdon Manor in 1958. An Anglican foundation, it developed a communal life based on prayer, on manual work on the small 15-acre farm, and on recreation, and it offered a refuge for people whose life was in crisis. John spent several days on a working party there, and was attracted by its conscious resonances of the historic community of Nicolas Ferrar at Little Gidding.[11] He liked its commitment to offering care and hospitality to wayfarers and to people facing personal crisis.

At the same time, however, he heard about Roland and the Sheffield Twelve, the project which had just begun. When Roland came to Westcott House a few weeks later to recruit for the second year of his course, John was among those who applied.

Thus the second year of John's training was spent with Roland and the Sheffield Twelve. For the first few months, he lived in digs in Stocksbridge near Sheffield, working in Samuel Fox's steelworks (later United Steel). He attended the local parish church, St Matthias, and became friendly with the vicar, Randolph Wise.

Wise asked him to consider working with him in the ministry team when he was ordained.

However, on a Christmas retreat in his final year at Westcott House, just six months before his ordination, he recognised that he had no sense that he was made to be a parish priest. He confided in the retreat leader, who affirmed that it might be sensible to withdraw from the path to ordination. Ken Carey subsequently persuaded John that experience in parish ministry was always useful and could also lead elsewhere.

So, after completing his final year back at Westcott House, John returned to Stocksbridge, now as a curate. 'I was ordained deacon in 1961, and priest in 1962,' said John. 'After a year in the parish church, I was put in charge of St John's, Deepcar, a daughter church within the parish.'

As planned, John spent four years in the housing estate of Deepcar as an ordained curate, and year by year he became familiar with the duties of a parish priest. As his final year neared its end, John received various offers of posts within Sheffield Diocese, but none seemed right.

As John approached the end of his four years as a priest in Deepcar, he spoke with Percy Smith. Percy was pondering the possibility of opening an associated small community in an urban setting, perhaps in Birmingham. Percy clearly would have welcomed an offer from John to share in this project; but, while John was attracted by the life and the work of the community, he did not feel it was for him. (Later, John and the Roslin Community were to remain in touch with Pilsdon through the following decades, and John sustained a close friendship with Percy and his wife.)

The solution came from an unforeseen quarter, at the gathering convened in Beaconsfield by Bishop Leslie Hunter, to which John had unexpectedly been invited. When Roland at that meeting outlined his hope of a new type of community, John felt enthusiastic at the opportunity of starting something fresh and worthwhile. For him it reawakened echoes of the call of Jesus to the 12 disciples who left all to follow him – a call which first resonated in him during Billy Graham's mission to Cambridge in 1955.

Others, however, saw it differently. John's spiritual counsellor, an eminent priest who soon afterwards became a bishop, issued a warning: 'If you join this venture of Roland's, you must know that it will be the end of your career in the Church.' The counsellor had correctly judged that Roland's programme had a thread of anarchy which would ill accord with the main fabric of Church thinking. But he had utterly misjudged John's motivations. To John, high office in the Church was irrelevant. As far as John understood it, his calling was to discover what it meant for him to follow Jesus.

Some of John's wider family were dismayed. It had been surprise enough when he had chosen to train for the ministry rather than prepare to take charge of the family estate. But the family could still envisage him serving locally one day as vicar of Great Gaddesden. Now, however, they saw him as not only abandoning the tradition of Christian duty and public service which successive heirs to the family's estates had fulfilled faithfully through the centuries, but also he seemed to be deserting the Christian ministry as they understood it, to live in Scotland with two others in a ramshackle old house, perhaps soon to be working down a coalmine. What was going on? But John, arranging for the family responsibilities to be passed into other hands, set his compass towards the new Fraternity.

Who else might join?

On the journey back to Sheffield from Bishop Hunter's meeting in Beaconsfield, John and Robert Haslam had reflected on Roland's contribution and what it might mean. At this time, Robert was curate-in-charge of Rawmarsh in Sheffield. He was ready to take a new step. 'As a boy, I went to Rugby School,' he said, 'and although I was a Presbyterian I went through the sausage machine by which the school turned out Christian lads, and I was confirmed. So in that way I became a sort of Anglican.'[12]

After doing his National Service in the Army, Robert went to Cambridge, to Corpus Christi College where Roland was chaplain. He had no notion for ordination at all when he went. But around that time, when he was about 20, he thought very seriously about becoming a Roman Catholic. His Presbyterian father persuaded him to visit the Franciscan monastery at Cerne Abbas in Dorset. This was Robert's first contact with a religious community. It was an Anglican foundation, at what is called the 'High Anglican' or 'Anglo-Catholic' end of the theological spectrum: it was formal and dignified, with a deep respect for the sacramental powers of the priest. For Robert it was a formative encounter, and the poise and the gravity of the ceremonial rites appealed to him.

At Cambridge, with his Anglo-Catholic certainties firmly in place, Robert reacted strongly against Roland, who seemed to sit very lightly to Church structures. 'I saw Roland as too "radical". By that I mean he always went back to first principles. He wouldn't take anything for granted. He related everything to the nature of Christ. That was his measure of everything. I did not see this when I was at Cambridge; I was just provoked by him.'[13] Confronted by Robert's unfailing opposition to his points of view, Roland said to Robert, 'You disagree with everything I say, which is very good for me and very bad for you.'

Robert, however, had a sustained interest in theology and had been intrigued by the phenomenon of religious communities since his first encounter with the Franciscans in Cerne Abbas. He therefore decided that he would study theology at Mirfield College. The college had a name for extreme conservatism in its practice and outlook but was closely related to the Community of the Resurrection (CR), a monastic order for which Robert thought he might be destined. One of the best-known members of the CR was the Revd Trevor Huddleston, who worked in South Africa and was an outspoken critic of the apartheid regime; and the outlook of several of the Mirfield staff had been shaped by the anti-apartheid struggle in South Africa. During his training, Robert gradually rebelled against the college's narrower disciplines, and by the time he left Mirfield he knew that he did not want to join the monastic order of the Community of the Resurrection, but he was ready to accept a posting to an African setting.

However, another influence had impressed him. Robert had been in touch with Roland again during his Mirfield years, and by then Roland had taken up his post as a canon of Sheffield Cathedral. When Robert was ready to leave Mirfield, a rector from a village near Sheffield invited him to go there as a curate. So, Robert went as curate to Rawmarsh, an industrial village which had the name of being 'the dirtiest place in Britain'. At Rawmarsh, he was assigned to a diocesan tutor who would direct his reading and encourage his thinking. His tutor was Roland.

From Roland, he heard of the Little Brothers and Little Sisters of Jesus, who had emerged in response to the vision of Charles de Foucauld. The Little Brothers had a house in Leeds. Every week, Robert would go from Sheffield to Leeds and spend an afternoon with the Little Brothers, talking to them and learning from their experiences of working and living the Gospel. The character of the Little Brothers of Jesus appealed to him, especially their commitment to sharing the life and conditions of manual workers. The small-scale community structure of the Little Brothers interested him also.

Robert also visited Taizé. At that time, the Taizé Community worshipped in a local church and had no building of their own for worship. But, just before Robert arrived, they had received the gift of money and a design for their own church.

'When I went in to see Brother Roger,' recalled Robert, 'he invited me to look at the architectural drawings which were laid out on the table. I viewed the plans and said some approving words about how nice it looked. "Robert!" fumed Brother Roger. "The world over, Man is calling out for Bread! And we give him a Stone!" And with these words he swept the plans off the table, crumpled them into a great ball and hurled them into the far corner of the room. But, as it turned out, the new church was the making of the Taizé Community. Ten years later, and ever since, it has been thronged with visitors.'[14]

By now aware of Roland's gifts, Robert felt drawn to moving over from Rawmarsh to join Roland's training programme, the Sheffield Twelve. But he felt an even stronger commitment to his parish responsibilities in Rawmarsh. However, he used to meet frequently with the Sheffield Twelve trainees in the great big canon's house that Roland occupied, in Sheffield's 'White Highlands' as Robert called it.

When Roland began to make definite plans to establish a

Fraternity, Robert saw the opportunity to join a small religious community free of the weight of a large established institution. With the start of Roland's new initiative in Roslin, Robert was ready to become part of it, although he would not enter fully into its life until he had completed the final year of his curacy in Sheffield.

So, there were three initial participants in planning for the new Community, all priests of the Church of England. In Scotland, they became members of the Scottish Episcopal Church. But, as they prepared to establish their new vision within the complex religious landscape of Scotland, they aspired to be an ecumenical community. This was the adventurous, pioneering element of their venture: the ecumenical dimension. At that time, the only existing ecumenical community was Taizé. But these three Episcopal priests, headed for Roslin, were convinced that the day for denominational Christianity was long past. Any new religious community should aspire to go beyond denominational boundaries. They profoundly hoped that candidates from other denominations would come and join them. They did not want to be dependent solely on the single Christian denomination to which the three of them belonged.

Accordingly, as a signal of their yearning to be ecumenical, they invited a number of senior Church leaders to accept a supervisory role as 'Guardians' of their forthcoming new religious community: from the Episcopal Church Bishop Ken Carey, together with the Provost of Aberdeen Arthur Hodgkinson, and from the Church of Scotland the Revd Robin Barbour. In his fundamental commitment to ecumenism, Roland from his arrival in Scotland had set his heart on securing a link with the Roman Catholic Church. He was delighted to discover that a leading Roman Catholic ecumenist was located only a few miles from Roslin. The Abbot of Nunraw, the Trappist monk Dom Columban Mulcahy, became a close friend of the Community, and though not formally one of their Guardians was a valued and trusted counsellor.

As a final preparation for founding the new religious community, Roland took John Halsey and Robert Haslam with him on two special visits. First, they spent a week on the Ile de St Gildas, a place of retreat run by the Little Brothers of Jesus. And, as they came closer to the day of commitment, 6 August 1965, the Church's day of the Feast of the Transfiguration, they spent four days with the monks at Sancta Maria Abbey at Nunraw. The abbey, established in 1946 in a baronial mansion, and the first Cistercian foundation in Scotland since the Reformation, nestles at the foot of the Lammermuir Hills just 20 miles from Roslin.

Quiet talks with the Abbot Dom Columban were a measured preparation for their new voyage. For they had begun to realise that they were about to leave behind the familiar territory of church life to which they were comfortably accustomed. Like adventurers, they were about to enter an unexplored country with both riches and perils as yet unknown. Recognising that prayer was to be a major component, and indeed the foundation of their communal life, the abbot advised them to be flexible in the early stages of their community, not to govern their life with a strict Rule but to keep their disciplines simple. They therefore agreed that they would begin each day with early-morning prayer, beginning with the hour of silence which was at the heart of the prayer-life of the Little Brothers and Sisters of Jesus. Morning prayers would conclude with the reciting of Charles de Foucauld's 'Prayer of Abandonment', in which the supplicant surrenders himself or herself into God's hands without reserve. There would also be evening prayer, and frequent celebration of holy communion, the Eucharist.

Roland was still priest-in-charge of Rosslyn Chapel. They agreed, however, that their communal prayers would be held in the parsonage, in the room Roland had designated as the chapel which they called 'the Upper Room', echoing 'the upper room' in which Jesus shared the Last Supper with his disciples.[15] Roland described the parsonage as 'the coldest house I ever lived in'; but the room which was the chapel was upstairs, set apart, and it was no trial to them to be at prayer in its stillness. For his own times of quiet, Roland had already installed in the parsonage garden a small wooden shed.

On 6 August 1965, in a service led by the Bishop of Edinburgh, the Right Reverend Kenneth Carey, in a Rosslyn Chapel filled with worshippers, the three Anglican priests made profession of their vows. The Fraternity of the Transfiguration came into being that evening as the three men made their vows to God in the presence of the Bishop of Edinburgh. Roland Walls, Robert Haslam and John Halsey, dressed in monks' habits made from Army blankets, took their vows, committing themselves to what are called the 'counsels of perfection': poverty, chastity and obedience. In dramatic simplicity, they then prostrated themselves before the cross, lying face down upon the flagstones of the floor, their arms outstretched. In that hour, the Fraternity of the Transfiguration came into being.

Thus was established a new religious community. Most people there had never been present at such an event before. At the time of the Reformation in the sixteenth century, the Reformed Churches disbanded the religious orders and closed their monasteries and their convents. Within the Roman Catholic tradition, the orders continued – contemplative orders of men and women such as Benedictines and Carmelites, the Dominican Order who were teachers, and the Franciscans who were devoted to care of the poor, and the new Jesuit Order who had come into being specifically to counter the arguments of the Reformation. But, in the Reformed Church, there were no religious orders for the next three centuries. Then, in the mid-nineteenth century in the Anglican Church, a tide of thinking known as the Oxford Movement stimulated a new interest in the religious life and monastic commitment. The Anglican Church began to welcome into existence new religious orders for men and women.

That August evening in Roslin, however, something new was introduced to the landscape of the Church in Scotland. Here was a new professed religious Community which was ecumenical. This was cutting new ground. Certainly their venture had been inspired by the Little Brothers of Jesus. Why, then, had they not simply joined the Little Brothers? Because the Little Brothers were Roman Catholic, and only a Roman Catholic could join them. This new community was to be ecumenical. It was very daring to set out on such an undertaking. Admittedly they were three Anglican priests, making their profession in an Anglican setting, but they were utterly committed to ecumenical aspirations. The significance of this ceremony was registered perhaps only by those with a detailed understanding of Church history.

The Fraternity's home was the parsonage, and there the day ended with the brothers offering their evening prayers in the upper room. Within a day, however, the resident Fraternity of three became two, for Robert returned to the Sheffield parish of Raw-marsh to fulfil his commitment to serve out a further year there as curate. He would return to Roslin on completion of his curacy.

No sooner had the Fraternity been established than something occurred to occupy their early weeks. The parsonage belonged to the Earl of Roslin, and it had been known that the Earl wanted to sell it. Roland and John had to find the Fraternity a new home. Only 100 yards from the parsonage, further along Manse Road, in the middle of a line of substantial, stone-built villas, stood a very different building. Called the Abernethy Rooms, the building had been given to Roslin for the benefit of miners and their families by Lady Abernethy in 1901. She was one of the Trotter family, local landowners who lived on the Bush estate. A single-storey structure, the Abernethy Rooms were constructed of wood, with an outer skin of corrugated iron sheeting on the walls and roof. It had been designed as a reading room for miners, but in recent years it had been quite neglected. John Halsey recalled that it had a garden with stakes in the ground for quoits, and about 1,000 empty whisky bottles. There were also some interesting trees, Chinese beech, planted by one of the Trotters who by then was a trustee of the Bush Agricultural Centre. Roland and John pooled their savings and raised the £800 asking price for this unusual edifice, and moved into its assorted rooms in the month of October 1965. They chose a Gaelic name for their residence, and had the name painted on a flat piece of wood which they hung over the door: 'Comaraich' which means, 'Sanctuary'. Miss Black the housekeeper, who had come north from Sheffield with Roland, continued to do some cleaning.

So, the new Fraternity chose as its home a dilapidated wooden building clad in corrugated iron, set in a derelict garden. And, of the first two brothers resident in the building, one was the son of a poor working-class family from the Isle of Wight and the other a member of the English aristocracy.

4

The Community Setting and the Worker Priest

The Old Testament Prophet Joel, depicting the character of the Army of the Lord, describes how the warriors respect one another: 'They never jostle each other, each marches straight ahead.'[1] And so it was with the three recruits to the new Fraternity. They were united in their new community, but each one walked straight ahead in his own path.

Roland had been exploring the monastic tradition since he entered Kelham at the age of 17. When he came to organise the pattern of work and prayer for the Sheffield Twelve, he incorporated many of the insights of earlier centuries, for he had already absorbed many of the conventions customary in a variety of religious orders. One of the Church of Scotland members of the Twelve, Kenneth Boyd, acknowledged 50 years later, 'I knew I was being introduced into a tradition.'[2] In becoming one of the founding members of the Fraternity of the Transfiguration, Roland was finally embracing the monastic tradition which had attracted him for many years.

When he went into his little hut and closed the door, he was also entering a place of solitude within himself. There he would fathom the silence and encounter the mystery of being.

Roland was already no stranger to deep silence. But Robert and John were relative novices in the field. Indeed, this new religious community was beginning its life with few of the patterns and practices which long-established religious orders developed to sustain their communal life.

Now, in Roslin, Roland and John had the task of arranging their communal life within the contours and spaces of their new home, in 'the Tin Tabernacle' as it was soon known. They established the house much as it is today, for their original plan has lasted through the years. Entry is through the gate in the wooden front fence – a pliant branch can hold the gate open if there is difficulty getting through. The front door of the house is clearly out of use, with a rambling rose growing over and round it, the name-plate 'Comaraich' visible beside it, slightly tilted. A brick-edged path angles diagonally to the left across the garden grass to the side of the house. What was originally a beech hedge up the side of the garden was left untrimmed, and now the 40-foot beech trees arch over half of the garden. Past the window of the sitting-room, you come to the door. You knock. No answer. 'Hello! Is anyone there?' You can turn the loosely rattling black iron door-knob of the green wooden door and go in.

To the left is the bathroom, to the right the door to the sitting-room. Straight ahead is the door into the kitchen. It's ajar. Often when you come, there is someone in the kitchen making the next meal, but today there is no-one in the house. But so simply do the Community live that they do not lock the door when they go out. Whoever comes in is welcome, and anyway there's really nothing for a thief to take. On the wooden floor stands a plain wooden table, and six wooden stools; plates are in piles along a shelf to the right, the pans and mugs to the left, above the sink; there is a neat box with an array of cutlery, mostly old and not quite straight, but two or three ivory-handled knives. At the end of the table, by the window, is a bread-bin containing one book of Graces and another with extracts from the writings of St Francis of Assisi. Beside the bread-bin is a portable radio. At 8am, 1pm and 6pm, the table company will fall silent for the news headlines on BBC Radio 4.

A gas cooker, a refrigerator and a wood-burning stove complete the furnishings. The walls are adorned with pictures of animals and birds, mostly postcards from friends. On the far wall is a painting of the Last Supper; all the disciples and Jesus himself dressed in the working clothes of twentieth-century labourers. Beyond the kitchen is a small sitting-room where the members of the Community, including the cat, often sit at the end of the day. Bookshelves are filled with a blend of serious theology and modern novels, biographies and philosophy, all accustomed to being wreathed in pipe-smoke.

When you go through into the big sitting-room, you walk on an old, dark carpet. Originally, this room held the miners' snooker table. Under the window sits a large oak dining-room table with its chairs, used for a local Bible-study group and for a celebration meal on birthdays and anniversaries. All round the walls are dark bookshelves with volumes of systematic theology, encyclopaedias, theological periodicals from Churches and religious orders, and books of religious art. An open fireplace is the focal point for a ring of old armchairs. In winter, many visitors have clustered round this fire to gather a little warmth.

Beyond this sitting-room is a small bedroom. A corridor runs left past a recess which includes the never-opened front door. The corridor passes a narrow space curtained off, which is another bedroom known as 'the railway carriage'. And past the 'railway carriage' is the last room, which in the early days of the Fraternity functioned as the chapel. Soon, however, it became another reading room with shelves filled with books. A smell of dampness is in the air here, as there is no fire. Many books are covered with a film of white mould.

'But Roland, isn't this a terrible waste, letting these books go mouldy?' conjectured one visitor.

'You're right, of course,' he said. 'But there are *people* living in conditions like this, being damaged even more. That's really what we should be doing something about.'

When they first moved into the house, Roland and John both had rooms within the building, and the end room was their chapel. But Roland had brought from the garden of the parsonage his little wooden hut, his garden shed, his 'scallop-shell of quiet'. This hut was placed in the house's back garden, to serve as a place of retreat. They named the hut 'Seraphim', after St Seraphim of Sarov.[3] From a local joiner they ordered a larger hut, 10' x 8'. Roland took to going up to the bigger hut, to which they gave the name St Romuald,[4] to read and to work.

Another hut was placed in the garden and given the name St Antony,[5] and it became John's place of quiet. Then there was a hut for Robert. And another for Bishop Neil. In due course, Patty too moved into a hut. 'We all started in the house,' said John, 'but we found it convenient to move out of the house and into the huts.'

Each hut was furnished with a bed, a desk and a light. A selection of shrubs and trees was planted in the garden, signalling the privacy of each space. Soon they began to use the larger hut as their chapel, their place for communal prayer. As the succeeding years drew people to the communal prayers, a second hut was added to the chapel, and the double-hut chapel could hold them all.

As their times of prayer gained significance and became recognised as the pulse of their Fraternity's life, the brothers agreed that the whole of the back garden, now with its various huts, should be designated as a place of quiet. To safeguard the silence, a complete wooden screen was erected. The house, with its atmosphere for communal living, was thus divided from the Enclosure, where silence is observed, except for the communal prayers and liturgy in the little chapel. In the early morning, the Community members leave their huts, the individual cells where they have slept, and make their way to the Chapel for the hour of silence.

The pattern of their lives is guided by their communal Rule. Roland Walls once described it thus: 'The little Rule we live under at Roslin – which is a modification of the Rule of St Benedict – owes a great deal to Brother Roger's Rule for the brothers at Taizé.'[6] Three times a day, the Community meet in the chapel for their times of prayer, which they call 'Offices': morning, midday and evening. A minimum 'Office' would consist of a Psalm, a Gospel reading, Free Prayer and the Lord's Prayer, and a prayer for Grace. Sharing in a communion service will be as frequent as possible.

The daily hour of prayer is complemented each month by a 24-hour silent retreat by each of the members. The members spend this day away from the house, staying in a caravan parked in a field outside the village. In addition, each member makes an eight-day personal retreat at some suitable place agreed by the

Community. There, there will be someone practised at guiding retreats who can offer advice as to what reading or thinking may be most appropriate for the member.[7]

Part of the Rule for the members of the Community is that each day they will say a particular prayer, a prayer which links them to one of the inspirational sources of their communal life. They say the Prayer of Abandonment composed by Charles de Foucauld, the Trappist monk whose life of solitude in the Sahara ended when he was murdered by thieves. The prayer expresses the commitment of the individual's total life.

> Father, I abandon myself into your hands:
> Do with me what you will.
> Whatever you do I will thank you.
> Let only your will be done in me,
> As in all your creatures,
> And I'll ask nothing else, my Lord.
> Into your hands I commend my spirit;
> I give it to you with all the love of my heart
> For I love you, Lord, and so need to give myself,
> To surrender myself into your hands
> With a trust beyond all measure,
> Because you are my Father.

Foucauld's life and death are a poignant symbol of the monastic path. Furthermore, the religious order which arose from his example, the Little Brothers and Sisters of Jesus, was a model to which all of the members of the new Fraternity had learned to look.

None more so than John Halsey. In becoming part of the new Fraternity, John, too, was walking his own path.

A process had begun in John during Billy Graham's mission to Cambridge in 1955. He there experienced an impulse to respond to Jesus' call to his disciples, to leave everything and follow him. It was this encounter with the ultimate demand of faith which first of all propelled him into training for the ministry. But he became aware that he was searching for knowledge of a different order from that which he had gained from books or by fulfilling the duties of a parish clergyman. It had been during his year of training as one of the Sheffield Twelve, in his manual work in the Sheffield steelworks, that he had experienced his clearest sense of what the life of Jesus meant for him. So, he was motivated to model his own path on the pattern presented by the Little Brothers. The inward exploration of the life of prayer and contemplation would intertwine with the outward exploration of life as a manual labourer. John became, in effect, a worker priest.

The worker-priest movement (*prêtres ouvriers*) began in France during the Second World War. From the time of the French Revolution, the urban and rural working classes in France were alienated from the Church. From within the Reformed Christian tradition, the Church made sporadic responses. A notable initiative was the French Protestant Industrial Mission, a small missionary movement founded in 1870 by a Scotsman, Robert McAll, in response to the repression and destitution of workers and their families in the capital following the Paris Commune. Changing its name in 1879 to *Mission Populaire Évangélique*, the Mission continued to focus its attention on the poor of Paris and of other industrialised towns. The intense pressures of wartime exposed the gulf between the Church and the working classes even more clearly. An awareness of this profound estrangement of working people from the Church provoked a response in some Roman Catholic priests.

'Of particular importance was the account of Père Loew the Dominican in the Marseilles dockland, who in 1941 went to work in the docks of his parish. "I concluded it was no good wasting time on paper theories: the thing to do was to buy a set of overalls on the old clothes market, get a job like everyone else, and then at the end of a day's work go off and live with the dregs of the population – the dockers on the ports."'[8]

Such adventurous commitment to expressing the Church's message about Jesus was mirrored in the lives of a number of French priests who were deported to Germany from Nazi-occupied France to enforced labour in German factories. Suppressing knowledge of their priestly status, they shared the fate of the other deported workers and were enveloped in the harsh conditions of labour camps along with them. Some were discovered and arrested, and some died in concentration camps. But one of these 'disguised' priests, Henri Perrin, returned from Germany to France and published his diary of those years, *Priest Worker in Germany*. The diary narrated how Perrin encountered daily the sufferings of people who had no contact with the Church whatsoever. Its publication gave impetus to the Church in France to develop a mission to the working population, 'the proletariat' as Perrin was not afraid to call them. The Archbishop of Paris, Cardinal Emmanuel Suhard, endorsed this drive towards an urban proletarian mission, and a growing number of priests were accepted into the worker-priest movement.

Their engagement in life through industrial employment led many of them to join unions. Before many years had passed, worker priests were found in key roles in strikes and other forms of work-place unrest. The Church authorities became profoundly uneasy at the way worker priests were moving beyond individual pastoral care for their fellow-workers into questioning the economic and industrial structures of society. By 1951 there were 87 worker priests in Paris alone, and the Holy See was anxious that the number of worker priests should not be increased. In 1954, the Vatican moved to suppress the entire worker-priest movement. Of the 100 worker priests still by then in post, one third accepted the decision and returned to parish work. The remainder continued in their industrial lives, and their priesthood ended.[9]

Translated and published in English in 1947, Perrin's diary brought to the consciousness of the Churches in Britain the urgency with which these French priests were addressing the alienation of the Church from working people. In his book, *Britain's First Worker-Priests*,[10] John Mantle illustrates the way in which some people in the Church in Britain recognised a parallel alienation of the working classes from the Church. Ted Wickham in 1949 arranged to meet Henri Perrin in Paris; but, while he saw the importance of what was happening in France, Wickham put his own emphasis on the training of industrial chaplains. In Scotland, as we have seen, the Churches followed a pattern similar to that of England.

Britain's social and political history was very different from that of France, and there was nothing in Britain's wartime experience to compare with what France underwent during the Nazi occupation. Nevertheless, in England a small number of priests, mainly Anglican, mainly married, were so concerned at the Church's neglect of the poor that they were prompted to adopt a strategy similar to that followed by the movement in France which by then had been discontinued, namely the *prêtres ouvriers*. These English worker priests, while remaining obedient to their bishops, moved out of the conventional parish ministry and took secular manual employment. Mantle's book names these individuals, and records that they formed an association named the Worker Church Group. The association drew them all together in annual meetings and developed a theological perspective on their pioneering venture. The worker priests consolidated their commitment to the poor of society by submitting themselves to the treadmill of daily labour. This group was 'the only organisation that would speak for the first worker priests and laity committed to radical identification. Within eight or nine years, a small group would begin to develop a rationale for their total involvement in working life, and would challenge Ted Wickham's methods.'[11]

When John Halsey became an underground worker in the Roslin pit, he was unaware of the Worker Church Group. Like them, however, he had sensed the limitations of chaplaincy as a vehicle for conveying the Christian message to working men and women. Quite independently of these English worker priests, John had committed himself to a life of unskilled labour alongside other working men. For him, this represented his response to the call of Jesus to his disciples.

John would probably have hesitated to articulate this as his motivation. He would have been more likely to offer a self-deprecating interpretation of his actions. He was known on occasion to suggest ruefully that his life could be understood as a series of escapes from burdens: escaping from his social background; escaping from intellectual effort; escaping from institutional responsibility. Yet the truth was that he had set out with great courage upon what was in Scotland an untrodden path, and did so with little support and encouragement from anyone apart from the other members of his Fraternity. The Little Brothers of Jesus were his paradigm, but John knew he had set himself a complex task. 'The Little Brothers have a long period of intensive formation before they join. I did it, "on the hoof" as you might say, with Roland. Roland himself had been through the formation that was provided at Kelham. When I gave my assent to joining Roland in this new Community, I was completely clueless about what might be involved. The religious life was quite outside my experience. I was quite taken aback, for example, at the thought of wearing a habit. Roland explained that we were part of a family of religious orders. I hadn't ever thought of the Little Brothers and Sisters as a "religious order". And indeed they were so much "among the poor" rather than "withdrawn from everyone" that ordinary faithful Roman Catholic church-goers had difficulty seeing them as a "religious order": for they were working in ordinary factory jobs and wore no religious habit in church. Brother Guy from the house in Leeds said that when he and Brother Xavier first moved into their house the neighbours thought they were Mormons!'[12]

John's introduction to the industrial life of Scotland was through the prevailing Scottish Church channel of chaplaincy. But, after a year and a half in this role, as we have seen, he entered into a more direct engagement with the work-place as a coalminer, working as a labourer underground in the Roslin pit.

John had always found physical work satisfying. In the school holidays, he worked on the family's farm. His father encouraged him to learn the ways of farming as a valuable preparation for his future in charge of the estate. John would rise at 4am and milk the cows by hand. At harvest time with all the other farm workers, he would gather the sheaves and arrange them in their stooks. In later years when the combined harvester was introduced, he would help in collecting and stacking the straw bales in the sheds. Much of his time in the Army involved hard, physical work. 'The physical work put me on a level with ordinary working people, from whom so much of my way of life otherwise separated me.' When he joined the workforce in the Roslin pit, somewhere in his mind perhaps was the thought that through taking part in ordinary work he might follow the intention of Charles de Foucauld, who sought 'to shout the Gospel with [his] life'.

At the start of his shift, John joined the other men in the cage, hurtling down 1,000 feet to the tunnels which led to the coal face. John's job was at the junction of the railway lines, bringing the loaded coal trucks from coal face and sending the empty ones back. He had alternately to insert and remove the steel pins which connected each truck to the next. In the cramped and often ill-lit conditions, with heavy metal constantly moving and colliding, there were many opportunities for injury. As a speaker said in 2010 at the Memorial Service for former mine-workers' leader Laurence Daly, 'You can always tell a miner. They're the ones with a limb missing.' John spent three years down the pit, learning the essential business of co-operation among miners and developing a sense of his own identity. He joined the union, the NUM, and before long was appointed as a local union representative. In this capacity, in 1969 he attended a union conference addressed by Scottish miners' leader Mick McGahey and by the president of the NUM, Laurence Daly.

Dom Columban had been quite insistent in endorsing the Fraternity's own wish, namely that the Fraternity should, if at all possible, be self-supporting. The Fraternity were already alert to the value of this policy from their experience in the Sheffield Twelve. While John submitted himself to the demands of his new work as a miner, Roland elected to continue in the post to which he had been appointed in 1963. He lectured in Dogmatic Theology in Edinburgh University's New College. New College housed the University's Theological Faculty, and was also one of four colleges which trained ministers for the Church of Scotland. Roland was first offered the post of Lecturer in Religious Studies at Jordanhill College of Education in Glasgow. But when the opportunity arose for him to be appointed to the University post in New College, the Primus of the Scottish Episcopal Church, Francis Moncrieff, urged him to take it. Membership of the staff of New College had never before been opened to Episcopalians or indeed to Roman Catholics either. With John's weekly wage and

Roland's salary, all bills would be met, and they would distribute any surplus to charitable causes.

As a consequence, when Robert Haslam's path brought him back from Rawmarsh to take up residence as the third professed member of the Fraternity, there was no necessity for him to find paid employment. With Roland and John both in full-time work, the Fraternity decided to position Robert as the constant presence in the house. To Robert, who had spent five hectic years in ministry in a busy industrial parish in Sheffield, the slow pace of life in Roslin's Manse Road presented an almost unbearable contrast.

'When I first arrived, I suffered very much from lack of things to do. I got so bored. I had come from the hectic life of Rawmarsh and now there was nothing to do. Roland kept saying, "You have to BE, not DO!" "Get bored! With God!"'

'But I had absolutely nothing to do. I had a biography of Aneurin Bevan to read. But Roland was out teaching in New College, and John was away working in the pit. And people would occasionally knock on the door of the Frat. They would be asking for Roland.

'"I'm afraid he's away teaching in Edinburgh. Is there anything I can do?"

'"No, thank you. I'll come back when he's here."

'This was such a contrast with how life had been in Rawmarsh.'[13]

In due course, Robert became the Youth Chaplain for the Bishop of Edinburgh – unpaid – and worked with young people in the Loanhead area. This gave him a role in work with which in Sheffield he had discovered he had an affinity.

Thus the founding members of the Fraternity of the Transfiguration addressed the structuring of their individual and their communal life. Anyone who visited the house and spoke with any one of the brothers would gain the sense that, from the very start, they were firmly founded and embodied the assurance of a long-established organisation. Yet in fact, as was natural, the Brothers faced many uncertainties, and their structures took time to consolidate. In particular, it was not clear to them that they had found the best location in which to plant this religious community which was committed to a focus on the poor. Roslin was a rural village, home to many people quite well-to-do. Might it not be best for the Fraternity to move to a more appropriate place, among the really poor?

Robert Haslam spoke of this uncertainty. 'Roland was always suggesting that we were in the wrong place. He was continually suggesting that we should move to this place or that place, and this had a very unsettling effect on us all. I remember I was in the car with him one day, and I said, "We must stop having fresh plans for a new place all the time." Roland agreed. But only a few miles further on he had spotted another place that he thought would suit us better!'

In 1968, Roland talked it over with Bishop Ken Carey. Carey wanted them to go to Niddrie, a pre-war housing scheme on the south side of Edinburgh, where people faced the difficulties associated with generations of poverty, and where there was already an Episcopal church with a small congregation.

John Halsey recalled, 'Mother Mary Clare then came to visit us in Roslin, on a sabbatical tour from Sisters of the Love of God in Oxford. We were sitting at the table at our evening meal. When she heard of Carey's suggestion, she held her knife and fork in mid-air.

'"You'll do no such thing. You stay right where you are. Why is it that, when a tender plant is planted in the Lord's garden, bishops dig 'em up?"

'"But what shall we say to the bishop?"

'"Leave the Bishop to me."'[14]

They shared their uncertainty with Dom Columban of Nunraw. He was as outspoken as Mother Mary Clare. 'If you want to be the same as the poor, you'll stay right where you are. The poor can never choose where they're going to live. They're stuck. Right where they are. You can't identify with the poor if you're moving at your own will to where you want to be.'

Mother Mary Clare was as good as her word. Two weeks after her visit, the bishop came out to visit the Fraternity in Roslin, bearing the letter she had sent him.

'What am I to do about this?' he asked.

Roland suggested, 'Why don't you reply, "Thank you for your letter. I have noted its contents!"'

So the uncertainties departed, and the Fraternity put its roots deeper and deeper into the ground of Roslin.

John's time as a miner, however, was to be of limited duration. Roslin pit was becoming uneconomic, and the Coal Board arranged for its closure in 1969. The mine workers from Roslin were offered transfers to the larger, neighbouring Bilston Glen colliery. But, when the Fraternity looked at their circumstances, they decided that John should not transfer to Bilston Glen but should instead become a support worker for the Cyrenians' Hostel for the Homeless at 20 Broughton Place in Edinburgh. Their friend and colleague, Dominican Father Anthony Ross, had responded to the need for accommodation for young men who had no family support, and encouraged the Cyrenians to open a hostel. But the hostel, which was home to young men with disorderly lives, rootless, homeless and unemployed, was staffed by inexperienced care-workers. The hostel needed to be steered through its escalating difficulties. It seemed likely that John, armed with his experience of four years in the Sheffield parish and three years in the pit, might be the very man to support and guide the young leaders.

What, then, was to become of John's engagement in unskilled manual work, that distinctive realm of the worker priest to which he had chosen to commit his life? Other voices questioned this development in John's working life.

'Andrew Parker and Georges Velten from the *Mission Populaire* in France came and urged me not to desert the industrial scene. But at that time the Community's needs seemed paramount. I didn't see much difference between the two, the Cyrenians and the pit. It was all about the grass-roots, people at the end of the line. The Cyrenian people were all rejects from homes, prisons and mental hospitals. We heard them and sympathised with their viewpoint. What I was doing then seemed very much about the grass-roots. But in the end, five years later, I did go back into industry.'[15]

In those five years, the Fraternity 'increased in wisdom and stature ...'.[16]

5

From Fraternity to Community

Poverty, chastity and obedience are exacting disciplines. Should we live long enough, old age will impose these restraints on most of us. But what would motivate people in the full flood of life to commit themselves to such a demanding path? How many would be prepared to do it?

On the evening of 6 August 1965, when all the seats in Rosslyn Chapel outside Edinburgh were filled with people who had come to bear witness to the founding of a new religious community, two people at least were present upon whose lives the event was to have a profound effect.

One of them, attending the service as a friend of the Very Revd George Martineau, Dean of Edinburgh, was Bishop Neil Russell, who was home in Scotland on a brief visit from his diocese in Zanzibar. The wind of change had blown through Zanzibar in 1964, and a violent revolution had signalled that senior posts in the political structures and in the Church would in future be filled by people with black skin. Neil could see that his remaining time in Africa might be brief.

Before attending the inauguration service, Neil already knew that these three Anglican priests were committing themselves to a shared residential community life. He knew that it was their intention to take unskilled employment, and that they would mark their daily communal life with regular times of prayer and contemplation. The more he learned about their intentions, the more Neil saw the possibility that here was the path for which he had been looking. First of all, it was an adventure. That in itself appealed to a man who had pioneered church work in Zanzibar.

Then, it was a communal enterprise – attractive to a man likely to be bereft of the companionship which had surrounded him in his life as a bishop. Finally, it had a focus on the poor, an emphasis which had consistently motivated Neil in his working life. Small wonder, therefore, that Neil would soon enter into discussions with the Community, pursuing the possibility that he himself might become a member. So moved was he by the three men's demonstration of commitment that evening in Rosslyn Chapel, that on the Monday of the following week Neil Russell came to the door of the parsonage, the residence of the new Fraternity. Once invited in, he spoke to the members of the new community and said that it was his hope and his intention to come and seek full membership of the Fraternity on his return from Africa, whenever that might be.

Neil Russell was born in 1905 in England. His father, a Congregational minister, was English and his mother a Scot. When his father died as a relatively young man, Neil's mother brought him to Edinburgh where there was family support for her, and Neil went to George Watson's School. He worshipped at Morningside Congregational Church. While he was studying at Edinburgh University, he began to worship in Old Saint Paul's Episcopal Church and became an Anglican. He trained for the Anglican priesthood at Cuddesdon, a college known as a nursery for bishops. From 1929 until 1933, he served as a curate at Old Saint Paul's Episcopal Church in Edinburgh, colleague of a legendary figure, the devoted and beloved Rector Albert Ernest Laurie, who died in 1937. Of Laurie, stories abounded: 'of him going down the Canongate at five in the morning to light the fires of bed-ridden old women and make them a pot of tea before opening the church for morning prayers'. Or 'about the clubs and guilds and schools he opened to ease the lives of the poor in one of the most densely packed slums in Europe, however picturesque it was to the eyes of early twentieth-century visitors to the Royal Mile'.[1] It was said that Neil took Laurie as the model for himself and his ministry. Working among the families who inhabited the crowded houses in the towering 'closes' of the city's Royal Mile, Neil developed fine pastoral gifts. He had a sympathy with people whose lives were fraught with problems, and he quickly demonstrated an aptitude for listening to their sorrows.

In 1933, Neil went to Southern Rhodesia as a missionary – but, finding that the Church was closely identified with the white settlers, he stayed for only a year. With the Universities' Mission to Central Africa (UMCA) he went to the Zanzibar Diocese, and by 1943 he was warden of the Church's theological college there. Neil had a cousin who worked as a doctor with UMCA and who eventually became Tanzania's Minister of Health. For ten years from 1948, Neil was in charge of two major inland mission stations in an area which was home to an ethnic and linguistic group of people known as the Zigua. Neil learned their language, Kizikula, and was the last European to do so, as Swahili was taking over everywhere. Next, he served as parish priest in the coastal city of Tanga, where he ran a model parish and was known as a fine preacher. He was reputed to starve himself, and was said to cook and eat grass. Visitors, however, spoke of receiving a good balanced diet at his table.[2] In 1963, he was consecrated as Assistant Bishop to Zanzibar, based in the island. In Zanzibar, he continued his pastoral concern for the poorest in the population, responding to destitution and to the needs of poor families in Zanzibar exactly as he had done in earlier years in the slums of Edinburgh.

In 1964 the revolution arose, and there was massacre and disorder. Estimates of deaths range as high as 20,000. At that time, Neil was effectively the parish priest of the cathedral. There were few Christians on the island, but when the religious leaders met together it was to Neil they turned when someone was required to talk to the revolutionary leaders and to plead for the lives of prisoners. He was the only one who could not easily be imprisoned himself. But, as a consequence of having opposed the new leadership, he was banished from the island. He moved up country to Korogwe and became the chaplain at the teacher-training centre there.

This was the man, by then aged 60, who happened to be in Rosslyn Chapel on the evening of the inauguration of the Fraternity of the Transfiguration.

After his visit to Scotland, Neil made his way back to Africa, where his position as Assistant Bishop of Zanzibar was soon transferred to a black African clergyman. In his years in Tanganyika and Zanzibar, Neil had been outspoken in his enthusiasm for the cause of independence, so he welcomed this development. But there would be no further leadership role for him there. It was time for him to return to Britain. In 1965, he made his overture to the Fraternity of the Transfiguration. On his return to Africa, he committed himself to the Fraternity through correspondence. He made his profession to his local bishop in Tanganyika and subsequently lived under the Rule of the Fraternity.

He returned to Britain in 1968; and, after attending the Lambeth Conference, the ten-yearly gathering of Anglican bishops from around the world, he made his way to Roslin to become resident in the Fraternity. Kenneth Carey installed Neil in the now-vacant role of priest-in-charge at Rosslyn Chapel, and not long afterwards appointed him assistant bishop. So, in 1968, Neil Russell, formerly Assistant Bishop of Zanzibar, now Assistant Bishop of Edinburgh, became a resident member of the religious community known as the Fraternity of the Transfiguration. Having already lived under the Rule in his later African years, he now shared in the communal life. Another garden shed was introduced to the Enclosure – Neil's cell.

The transition to the communal life of the Fraternity was not without its difficulties for Neil and for the Community. Neil was a bishop, and furthermore he had been a bishop in Africa. As fitted African culture, he had been a leader exercising authority in a patriarchal manner. He was striking to look at. His physical appearance was that traditionally associated with an ascetic. To the other members of the Fraternity, he seemed to bear an uncanny resemblance to pictures of Charles de Foucauld. He was tall and upright and sparely made. When not wearing the monk's habit, he would be in dark clothing. His face was thin, the hollow of his cheeks accentuated by his neat white beard. People often remarked on how holy he looked. In Africa, he had been revered.

But in Scotland the atmosphere was very different. The Episcopal Church was small by comparison with the numbers in the Church of Scotland and in the Roman Catholic Church. Furthermore, while a bishop was honoured within his Church, the predominantly Presbyterian character of Scottish civic life still viewed princes of the Church uneasily. In addition, Neil had now entered a community in which the role of leadership was to be exercised through the decisions of the monthly chapter meetings. There was a role for a 'Brother in Charge', but this was simply to ensure that day-to-day matters were efficiently dealt with. Each member in turn would hold that position for a period of three years. There was a further complication: Roland Walls undoubtedly held a key role in the Fraternity. Roland's intellectual ability and his engaging and persuasive manner of address had established him as the community's unofficial leader. This combination of factors presented Neil with difficulties he had not anticipated.

Robert Haslam was always full of fun and laughter, and he regularly tried to pull Neil's leg. Neil did his best to respond well, but strain and uneasy moods resulted. But a more serious stress was present. Robert, reflecting on the consequences of Neil's arrival both for the Fraternity and for Neil himself, spoke of a certain rivalry that developed between Neil and Roland. There were many points of disagreement. Neil had worked in Scotland in the 1930s, as a young priest in the slums of Edinburgh. Now he was in Rosslyn Chapel, frequented by the rich, who had loved Roland when he was there. Neil was not only standing in Roland's shoes in Rosslyn Chapel, but also in Roland's shadow. It made for difficult personal relationships. 'There were serious tensions between Neil and Roland,' Robert Haslam recalled.

John Halsey recognised that Neil was struggling to settle into the life of the Fraternity. One Friday, he and Neil went out to lunch together. In the car coming back, Neil confessed that he was in despair. He was finding it impossible to adjust. When he joined the Fraternity in Roslin in 1968, he was 63. He carried out his duties at Rosslyn Chapel, and he was in demand as a speaker at conferences and retreats. But the intimate communal life of the Fraternity asked of him a range of responses with which he was unfamiliar, and which did not come easily to him. He had difficulty adapting to a completely unaccustomed role as an ordinary, equal member of this close community.

Present along with Neil at that service which launched the Fraternity of the Transfiguration were many of the congregation who regularly worshipped in Rosslyn Chapel on a Sunday. Among these was Mrs Patricia Burgess. The previous Sunday, she had heard that this special service was to take place. An admirer of Father Walls, but knowing little of the event she would be attending, she had come to witness the Taking of the Monastic Vows. Until that evening, Patty had not been aware that the men were in preparation for becoming monks, members of a new religious community. But the intensity of the event made a deep impact on her.

Patty had by then been a widow for six years. She had a young family and was uncertain about what the future held for her. In conversation with a friend, she recalled, 'There was something that I knew I was going towards. I didn't know what it was. Well, it hit me when they took their vows that evening. Rosslyn Chapel was full, and I really hadn't taken in what it was all about. But there was this hymn, "Love Divine, all loves excelling". I had always thought of it as a fairly slushy sort of hymn, but of course it was perfect for the occasion. There is a verse in it, "Finish then thy new creation" – it's tremendous. We were singing it, and I remember at the time thinking, "Gracious me, this feels as though this is exactly what I should be doing." But it was not a sensible thought. I mean, what would you be thinking of? You couldn't do anything about it, because you were a widow, and your family was growing up, and your father was dying and your mother was staying with you.'[3] This moment of insight, however, set in motion Patty Burgess's exploration of the path towards membership of this newly instituted Community. Her journey had begun, of course, long before. Named Patricia Jean Campbell, she was born in 1916, and most of her early years were spent in Edinburgh. Faith and religious practice were part of her upbringing. 'My grandmother and grandfather were both "god-botherers",' she said in conversation with a friend. 'I remember I was only about three when we were leaving Edinburgh for Tidworth and my father's new Army job there, and we had supper late at night. Before we went to the station, we were supposed to sober up to have prayers with Granny and Grandtipa, though I remember giggling all the time. Yes, with them we had a lot of God.'[4]

Patty's church contacts were shaped by her mother, who regularly took her children to Sunday services in churches of different denominations. As a result, although an Episcopalian by family tradition, Patty was comfortable in any church. In 1939, just after the outbreak of war, Patty married Hugh Burgess. She was 22. Hugh's family were in the West Indies, where his father was an estate manager in Grenada. Hugh had been sent to school in Edinburgh. 'He was a lovely man, with a keen sense of the ridiculous!' recalled Patty affectionately more than 50 years after his death. Hugh was making his career in the Colonial Service. He worked in forestry in Nigeria. Patty accompanied him to Africa, living out at the edge of a desert. 'I was only up there for eight months before I came home to Argyll to produce our first child. The commercial families were all perfectly capable of having their families in Nigeria. But for some reason Government families couldn't possibly do that, so I came home to produce Patty Ann.'[5]

Hugh served in the Army in the Second World War, in the Nigerian Brigade of the Royal West African Frontier Force. In the campaign in Burma against the Japanese Army, he was wounded three times. In 1944, he was awarded 'an immediate Military Cross' for conspicuous bravery. At the close of the war, he returned to Nigeria. There, however, partly as a consequence of his war wounds, Hugh became seriously ill. Patty brought him and the three youngest children back to Edinburgh – where Patty Ann, by seven years the eldest, was already staying with her grandparents. Hugh died in Edinburgh in 1959. Patty was devastated, as were the children, the youngest of whom, Peter, was only 7 years old. With the help of her own mother and Hugh's mother, Patty settled with her family in a house in the Pentland Hills, where she tried to build a life for herself and the children. Without Hugh, however, her life had lost its centre, and she was without any sense of direction.

She sought solace and guidance from her Christian faith, and attended her local Episcopal Church, St James the Less in Penicuik. Still in search of her own defining aptitude, she began attending worship in Rosslyn Chapel in about 1963, when Roland Walls was the rector. 'Roland was there, and it was like fresh air. Like a drink of water in the desert. It really was.'[6]

Patty was elated by the service which inaugurated the new ecumenical community, and a few days later she visited the Fraternity in their parsonage. In the house's quiet chapel – 'the upper room' – the brothers said prayers for Patty's father, who she knew was near to death. This encounter with their climate of prayer confirmed Patty's regard for the Fraternity. She maintained her close link with Rosslyn Chapel and with the Serving strand of the new WUSH programme. In 1969, when John Halsey began to work in the Cyrenians' hostel for young men at 20 Broughton Place in Edinburgh, John invited Patty to help him.

The hostel was almost the last refuge for young homeless men who had no stable family life, who were already prey to addictions, and who would try the patience of saints. The young students who acted as volunteer helpers did their best to keep the hostel in order, but their only qualifications were innocence and goodwill. It was evident that the entire enterprise would benefit from the involvement of a woman who had brought up a family. John asked Patty if she would organise the task of taking the hostel's washing to the local washhouse – 'the steamie'.

'I watched John as he went into the laundry room,' said Patty. 'To determine whether it was dirty enough to send to the laundry, he held each piece of cloth in turn to his nose and took a really deep breath.' She shuddered. 'And then I bundled it all up and, with one of the boys from the hostel to carry it, off we went to the steamie.' Week by week, Patty developed skills at washing and drying and ironing in the communal wash-house. The other women who did their washing there grew accustomed to seeing her accompanied by a succession of young men. 'One day, I explained to the women that the boys were from Broughton Place Hostel. "Oh! And we just thought you had all boys!" And they thought that John was one of them – and as it happened I was old enough for it to have been just about possible!' she exclaimed.

Greatly daring, Patty one day asked John, 'John, do you think it would be utterly ridiculous for me to become an official Church worker, a deaconess?'

'Goodness,' replied John, 'I thought you already were one.'

They spoke about it with Roland, who immediately saw that this was a fresh initiative. And so, in 1968, Patty went to Hindhead to train as an Anglican deaconess. When her training was completed, she was received into the Church as a deaconess in a service in Rosslyn Chapel, the service conducted by the rector, Neil Russell, who, as we have seen, was by then a member of the Fraternity of the Transfiguration himself. In Scotland, the Episcopalians had only one other deaconess and she worked in Aberdeen, and so Patty became associated with the Church of Scotland deaconesses in Edinburgh.

Now that she was officially a Church worker, Patty undertook an expanded range of activities. 'I did go round visiting quite a lot. That was the main thing. In a way, that was it. I still remember the first family Roland sent me to see. He said, "Go and have a look at such-and-such a family, and see how they're getting on." And I'm in touch with them still. And there was someone else too. "And go and see so-and-so." Because I think he'd baptised a baby, and they hadn't seen the family since the baby was baptised, and I was to go and have a little look in there.'[7]

One of the Church of Scotland deaconesses, Kay Ramsay, recalls that in 1972 Patty Burgess brought her some news – 'a bombshell', Kay called it. 'She was making the house over to her children. And she was going to join the Community in Roslin. She would live there in Roslin, with her own little hut in the garden. I was taken very much by surprise. I had not known what was going on in her mind. I think she was moved by the call from the Lord to leave her comfortable background behind, and to live a life of poverty with the people at Roslin. I never actually discussed all that with her; it just seemed obvious to me that that was what had happened.'

So, in 1972, Patty took her vows and became a professed member of the Community. At its simplest level, the arrival of Patty provoked a change of name: the men-only title, 'the Fraternity', was transformed into 'the Community' of the Transfiguration. But it was of immense significance that this association of celibate men should be transformed by the inclusion of a woman. Now at the heart of their communal life there flourished maternal emotions and a feminine perspective on all the disciplines which hitherto the brothers alone had designed.

As we shall see, when Robert Haslam was beginning to disengage from the Community in Roslin, he bought a little flat above a fish shop in the neighbouring village of Loanhead, only a 20-minute walk from the Tin Tabernacle. Patty now bought the flat from Robert. As her place of prayer and rest, a garden shed was introduced into her small garden. The shed was partitioned. The wider portion of the shed was for prayer, the Chapel of St Brendan; the narrower was where Patty slept, on the floor.

6

Roland the Teacher

While the other members of the Community pursued their various 'day jobs' alongside their community life, Roland continued to teach.

The role of teacher seemed to have come naturally to him. When he was still just a young student at Kelham College, the teaching staff identified him as a potential future colleague. His intellect and his sensitivity to individual enquiries were already evident. Corpus Christi College in Cambridge eagerly welcomed him as a Fellow and as chaplain for the same reasons.

Many of the 'Sheffield Twelve', who spent a year with Roland as their tutor, testified that what he imparted to them remained a life-long influence. Kenneth Boyd, who became Professor of Medical Ethics at Edinburgh University, said, 'Although I met Roland on only a very few occasions after 1965, I realise, looking back, that our year in Sheffield has been like an underground stream, silently irrigating my life and conscience.'[1] John Oliver, who became Bishop of Hereford, wrote, 'Roland was, quite simply, the best teacher I ever had.'

On Roland's arrival in Scotland in 1962, Bishop Kenneth Carey of the Episcopal Church's Diocese of Edinburgh put Roland's teaching gifts to use without delay. Episcopal priest Brian Hardy observed this when he himself came from his post as chaplain at Downing College, Cambridge, to be part of the team of clergy in the Livingstone New Town Ecumenical Parish in 1966.

'I soon became aware that Roland was a significant person behind the scenes. Ken Carey used Roland quite a lot as a leader,' said Brian. 'Roland was already making his mark as a lecturer in New College. Ken started residential diocesan courses. Each year, we hired Butlin's Holiday Camp in Ayr for a week. These Butlin's weeks were for the clergy, plus two lay-people from each parish in the Diocese of Edinburgh. My brief was to be in charge of the music, and various others were responsible for other aspects. Roland appeared regularly and gave wonderful lectures on the New Testament and on Christian doctrine. He had a wonderful presence. He taught us the most precious gift of laughter. He laughed at everything. He made the most difficult things seem manageable, even the worst things survivable, by laughter.'[2]

Roland's most public professional role as a teacher, of course, was as Lecturer in Dogmatic Theology at New College in the University of Edinburgh. A student in a Scottish university in the 1960s would anticipate that, at the beginning of a course of lectures, the teacher would distribute to all the participants a printed outline of the material to be covered during the term. They would not be surprised if, in addition, they received a set of helpful notes at the end of each lecture. In this way, the student would be able to map the required syllabus and their own progress across the ground. Students taking the more demanding Honours courses would be ready to undertake extensive personal reading in the subject, and to write papers for delivery and discussion at regular seminars, yet they would regard the notes of individual lectures as in some measure the minimum quota of information they would need to acquire in order to pass the end-of-term examinations. They would expect to supplement any 'hand-out' with the notes they themselves took during the lectures.

Roland's approach to lecturing was different. The subject of the course of lectures would be clearly advertised. But Roland's style of delivery and his liveliness of thought would not be confined by any narrow structure. In 1966, I was myself a student for the Church of Scotland ministry, enrolled at New College in the course of Honours Dogmatics. By then in my sixth year of university study, I was quite accustomed to taking useful notes from lectures I attended. Yet I found it impossible to record Roland's style of discourse in any intelligible form of consecutive notes. Roland's train of thought could not be predicted, and its range was unlimited. On the other hand, the poetic imagery in which he spoke was captivating. Historic expressions of Christian doctrine, passages from the Gospels and from the writings of St Paul, cascaded from his scholarly memory. He might give an outline of an important theme of thought, such as the belief that Christ was the Son of God, and he would show how the Church from the earliest times had given itself superior airs on that account. And he'd explode with laughter, saying, 'Isn't it ridiculous?'

When conducting seminars, if discussion was faltering he would interject the incomprehensible phrase, 'What about Thing, then?' This would be the signal for the discussion to take off in a completely different direction. Surprise played a regular part. One afternoon, the Christian Dogmatics seminar migrated from its regular location near the library. The students welcomed their lecturer Roland's invitation to hold the seminar at the Fraternity's house in Roslin. They arrived in sunshine. 'Let's hold the seminar outside on the grass,' suggested Roland. They settled themselves in the front garden. Roland began to guide them through the material for the afternoon's class. One of the students lay stretched out, elbows on the grass, his chin resting in his hands, looking down at the Greek text: The Catechetical Lectures of Cyril of Jerusalem, Fourth Century AD. Walking across the grass, the Community's cat Ninian passed by, quite close to the student's face. Slowly the cat turned, pointed its rear end towards him, and pee-ed straight into his eyes.

Roland did not imitate Father Herbert Kelly as at his own first lecture at Kelham: he did not assert, 'Either God has everything to do with that cat, or He's about nothing at all.' But Ninian's contribution was entirely in keeping with the ethos of Roland's teaching, which was always able to incorporate the unexpected.

Roland's theology was profoundly Trinitarian – that is, whenever speaking of God with particular reference to God the Father, he would balance what he said with reference to Jesus Christ the Son and to the Holy Spirit. He delivered a course of lectures on the Holy Spirit, and again he would carefully indicate that all talk of the Holy Spirit also had indissoluble connections with God the Father and the Son. If there was a predisposed emphasis in his Trinitarian expression of God, it would be towards Christ the Son.

For Roland viewed the Incarnation, God becoming a human being in Jesus, as the heart of Christian teaching and the foundation of Christian life. The object of his contemplation was Jesus the Son of God. As a youth, Roland already understood the significance of the Feast of Corpus Christi. In the body of Christ, so the Christian faith teaches, the infinite God, deathless creator of all things, is united with the finite, mortal human being. In his lectures, Roland gave expression to a theology of the Incarnation. While many students shared my own difficulty in transferring Roland's thoughts into written form on paper, he constantly communicated a sense that he was admitting us to another realm of thought. There was rational argument; there was logic; there was systematic thinking to give structure to the concepts. But the scaffolding of rational argument, which addressed the mind, surrounded a core belief which students recognised must be accessed by the heart.

The scholarly theology, however, was not an abstract exercise. It was continually harnessed to a practical, pastoral intention. One New College postgraduate from the late 1960s recalls having two terms of tutorials with Roland, studying the Early Church Fathers. One day, the student read out loud to Roland his new essay about the convoluted discussion among the Fathers on the subject of the inter-relation of the three Persons of the Holy Trinity, the Father, the Son and the Holy Spirit. When the student reached the end of the essay, Roland sat quietly for a minute. Then he said, 'This afternoon, I have to go to see a lady who is about to be evicted from her house because she keeps a horse in it. On the basis of what you have discussed in your essay, what would you say to her?'[3] In Roland's view, theology had to have an application in ordinary daily life.

In his appearance, Roland did not conform to people's image of a university professor. His clothes were shabby and his shoes were worn out. He continually made reference to the poor as the recipients, and sometimes even as the embodiment, of the Gospel of the love of God. He emphasised the humility of God in Christ, enthusiastically translating a Greek word for this attribute of God as 'the door-mat-iness' of God.

In the Dogmatics Department, he was the junior colleague of Professor Thomas Torrance, an internationally distinguished scholar regarded as one of the most influential English-language theologians of the twentieth century. The third member of the departmental staff was Thomas Torrance's brother James, who later became Professor of Theology in Aberdeen. Roland once joked, 'I had Thomas on this side of me, and James on that side; I used to take what they both said and serve the mixture up as soup for the students.' Roland's own versatility is exemplified by the fact that, although his own scholarship was in the field of New Testament studies, Professor Torrance welcomed him as a colleague in the department of dogmatic theology. Torrance was a majestic thinker across a wide range of theological themes, and wrote landmark theological works on evangelism, ecumenism and the relationship between theology and science. Year after year, Torrance would deliver one or more of his keynote series of lectures. Year by year, he would follow his carefully prepared text, differing in any year only insofar as he had added new refinements or amplifications to his arguments. Roland, on the other hand, wrote no scholarly volumes. 'I'm a talker, I'm not a writer, I know that. My compression when I write becomes unintelligible,' he said.[4] 'When I try to write these things down,' he used to say, 'the words turn to stone.' He knew that his gift lay in the fluency of his conversation.

Although in Cambridge and in Sheffield he had already proved his skill at relating to students, it may be that the role of a lecturer was not what he would himself have chosen. 'He would tell his students that he did not like teaching in an institution, but he did it out of obedience to the Community, whose members urged him to do so.' One of his colleagues on the teaching staff of New College was the Revd Bill Shaw, who later became Professor of Divinity and Principal of St Mary's College, St Andrews. In his student days at Cambridge, Bill was at St John's College. Through a friend at Corpus Christi College, Bill met Roland, who was studying theology on leave from Kelham. 'I was doing Modern Languages,' said Bill, 'and so when Roland was wanting to learn German I taught him some elementary stuff – quite badly I'm sure! Then Roland became chaplain, and we were good friends. Some time later, we were fellow guests at a wedding at which I was best man. But then I didn't see him for donkey's years until he turned up at New College.'[5]

Bill noted that people liked Roland's lectures: 'Yes, people liked them. They were full of jokes!' He saw that Roland was a positive influence on some students in particular. 'They tended to be academically sophisticated, seekers after a way, seekers after a truth. And that seemed enough for him. He didn't pursue his own scholarship.'[6]

It seemed to Bill Shaw that the main focus for Roland was the Community, not New College. He recalled that Roland did not become closely involved with the faculty. 'I don't recall him even coming to faculty meetings. That kind of administration did not interest him.' And he could not remember Roland ever leading one of the mid-morning services of worship which were held daily in the college.

So, while Roland developed a distinctive lecturing style in his New College years, and was a major influence on a significant number of students, it is probably true to say that his chief focus remained his membership of the Community of the Transfiguration.

Nevertheless, in his years lecturing at New College, his voice contributed a fresh and previously unheard sound, namely the mystical theology of the Catholic monastic tradition. Elizabeth Templeton was a student of Roland's at New College, and herself later became a lecturer there in the Divinity department. She came to study theology after studying philosophy at Glasgow University. She had been trained in the school of logical positivism, which had strict principles of verification and falsification, clear criteria for establishing truth. These procedures wrought havoc on the truths of faith, which can seem to be in a realm where such standards of verification cannot operate. 'I was chasing after something [*God*] which I wanted to be true, but couldn't see how it could be true.'[7] She arrived at New College virtually as an agnostic, though wanting the Christian story to be true. She would listen to Roland's lectures. She listened as Roland expounded the doctrine of the Incarnation, Jesus humbling himself to become man, a man.

'I kept asking, "How do you prove it?"

'He just smiled, and chuckled, and said, "It's not the kind of thing you can subject to this kind of questioning."

'He was no help. Yet he was delightful. I began to see him as "a holy clown". He was always saying, "You can't make certainty about any of this."'[8]

Roland's ease with philosophical uncertainty was a brand of theological thinking that was hitherto outside her experience. As it happened, Roland himself did not provide any new template according to which Elizabeth could fashion a renewed faith. However, his assured stance, the warmth and humour of his presence, gave credibility to his responses. And in addition, Roland's faith was known to be sustained in the contemplative community whose life he shared. When a Greek Orthodox scholar, John Zizioulas, joined the New College staff, this species of what can be described as 'mystical theology' received further emphasis, and Elizabeth was able to find in it a sustaining thread.

While there were some students like Elizabeth Templeton who did not find that Roland as a teacher could direct them towards a trustworthy and believable path, there were others for whom he opened doors to new worlds. Particularly notable in this regard were a young married couple from the USA, Brant Pelphrey and his wife Sharon. Brant was a Lutheran by upbringing. By his own account, he moved away from the doctrinal certainties of his evangelical faith and spent some time exploring non-Christian Eastern religious traditions. He served as a US Army medic in Vietnam; and, on discharge in 1971, he and Sharon arrived in Edinburgh. By the time Brant arrived at New College, he was ready to welcome a new direction for his Christian path.

Roland introduced Brant to the historic roots of Christian church life. Brant viewed Roland as 'the source of my own introduction to the spiritual life and theology of the Orthodox Church'. Roland pointed Brant to the example of third- and fourth-century men known as the 'Desert Fathers', and their female counterparts in the monastic tradition. In Egypt and Syria in those centuries, a large number of men and women adopted a life characterised by prayer, contemplation, silence, solitude, attention to the Christian scriptures, and concern for and care of the poor. They laid the foundation of the monastic traditions of the Eastern and the Western Church. Collections of their wise sayings about life and God and possessions and poverty have survived through 16 centuries. Through these subsequent centuries, the Orthodox Church in Greece and Russia valued the example of these 'Desert Fathers'. Brant was captivated when he discovered them, and he found himself drawn to the Eastern Orthodox Church. That Roland was on the New College staff proved invaluable to Brant. For here was a man versed in the writings of the Fathers, who seemed already to embody much of the monastic tradition which was illuminating this stage of Brant's life.

Brant Pelphrey describes the experience of attending Roland's classes in 1973, by which time Roland had been lecturing in New College for ten years. From Brant's account, it seems likely that Roland's style of delivery had developed new features. 'Students never knew quite what to expect in the classroom. Occasionally our professor stood behind a lectern, like other professors, and glanced at his notes – in reality, jottings in a little spiral notebook that he carried in his pocket. Most of the time, however, he walked around the lectern and paced back and forth in front of us; or he sat on a table, or even knelt atop it, chatting with us informally and sometimes closing his eyes. He would lapse into prayer in the middle of a paragraph.'[9] Brant felt that he discerned in Roland a manifestation of the monastic tradition dating back to the Desert Fathers.

To Brant, Roland represented a resource beyond price. Brant recounts how he persistently pursued the man he regarded as his new spiritual guide. Brant continually asked questions in lectures. He sat with Roland at meals and in the intervals between classes whenever possible. He followed Roland out of classes, accompanied him along corridors and up and down staircases, asking, enquiring, listening, noting down and collecting the wisdom which he heard flow in the answers from Roland's lips. Brant and his wife Sharon, with their infant son, took to making the journey out to Roslin, to keep company with the Community there. The practice of hospitality, a constant thread in the Community's life, meant that Brant and Sharon saw at Roslin an expression of the ancient monastic tradition which now so intrigued them. Gentlemen of the road, university teachers, enquiring visitors such as the Pelphreys, all sat at the Community's plain wooden table, eating simple fare. And the members of the Community unobtrusively attended to their daily disciplines of regular prayer.

Brant took note of the pattern and the detail of the Community's life. At one stage, he and Sharon stayed near Roslin for several months, and Brant was profoundly influenced by what he saw as a contemporary demonstration of the way of life pioneered by the Desert Fathers. In the Community at Roslin, he saw a combination of devotional practice and communal living which led him to describe their life as 'a secret seminary'. He saw Roland and the Community teaching a way of life which fulfilled in practice the doctrines that were taught in the university classroom. In Roland he found the intellectual depth, the adherence to tradition, and the spiritual hilarity of a contemporary Desert Father.

For a period, Brant taught theology in the Lutheran Seminary in Hong Kong, and in his book Brant indicates that he took advice from Roland about what syllabus to offer to the theological students in the seminary. He was much influenced by time spent in a Dominican community in Japan, where Zen meditative patterns were integral to the life of prayer.

Brant and Sharon would go on to serve the Greek Orthodox Church in the USA, inspired by what they had learned in Roland's circle. When ordained a deacon in 1999, Brant received a saint's name, Brendan, from his bishop, and as an Orthodox priest he is now called Father Brendan. He and Sharon attempted to replicate the simplicity of the Roslin Community, and its devotional practice, and its commitment to hospitality, in their own life as a married couple with a family. They adopted a theme from the Roslin Rule with a view to establishing a network of such families across the world, a network of 'Tabor houses'. The Community of the Transfiguration took its name from the Gospel account of the 'transfiguration' of Christ, when to the eyes of his three chief disciples he shone with the brightness of the Holy Spirit of God on a Judaean mountainside. Tradition names that mountain as Mount Tabor. Accordingly, Brendan took up the Community's hope that families might adopt what they could of the Community's way of life, and follow a simple Rule as 'Tabor houses'. In his book entitled *The Secret Seminary*, Brendan pays tribute to Roland as a teacher without parallel for his lectures and for his personal spiritual direction over a period of nearly four decades.

When Roland left New College in 1975, he continued to teach, as came naturally to him, in a variety of *ad hoc* formal and informal roles. In his later years, he developed a role as a spiritual guide or, in his preferred expression, as a spiritual companion. He combined a gift for listening intently to the individual voice, with a capacity for assessing the direction and the depth of a person's search. His skill as a teacher had fully matured, and during these years the many people who made their way to the door of the house were proof of the value they placed on speaking with him.

'I remember once sitting with Roland at Roslin, out in the garden at the back of their house,' recalled Dr Monica Jackson, 'and I said to him, "Roland, you have become my spiritual guide." "I don't think I like that word 'guide'," he said; "we're spiritual companions." But he was my guide. He was my Guru.'[10]

Monica Jackson was a child of the Raj. She was born in India, as were her parents and her grandparents before her, coffee planters on coffee plantations. She attended no school until at the age of 11 she was sent to a boarding school in England, run for the children of families who lived abroad. 'Our mother came yearly for the summer holidays, but apart from that we stayed at the school.' During the Second World War, Monica married an officer in the Indian Army and became a professional mountaineer. She organised the first all-women mountaineering expedition to the Himalaya, to a hitherto unexplored part of Nepal. 'In those days Himalayan exploration was in its infancy, and the whole area was blessedly pristine.' On the strength of the book she wrote about the venture, she was admitted to Cambridge as a 40-year-old undergraduate.[11] Discovering now within herself an insatiable appetite for learning, she studied anthropology.

Her father a Protestant, her mother a Catholic, Monica abandoned any Christian affiliation for 30 years. 'I suppose that left a religion-shaped gap within me. This led me to study comparative religion when I was at Cambridge. I developed a passionate interest in myth and symbolism. I read a lot about Hinduism and Sufism.' In her mid-50s, she became a Quaker. Her personal quest for life's meaning led her through psychotherapy – and then, from someone in a religious bookshop, she heard of Roland. 'I loved going there,' she said, 'out to the Community at Roslin. And I was very fond of John and Patty. First of all, it was Roland's sense of humour. I believe passionately in humour. Rabbi Blue said, "Humour is not simply a means of the alleviation of pain; it is a manifestation of the divine on earth." The second thing is Roland's speed of reaction. He was intellectually so quick. He picked up what you were saying in an instant. "It's so exciting talking to you," I said. And he became my Guru.'

Monica went regularly to Roslin, where Roland and she would discuss the interface between science and religion, and she found Roland providing her with intellectual foundation for her continuing reliance on religious faith.

'I ate there at Roslin,' said Monica. 'I used to spend days and days making cakes before I went out there. I would attend the midday service in the chapel. Then we used to have lunch. That was all between 1992 and 2000.'

Monica Jackson was a beneficiary of Roland's capacity to engage with people who had profound questions about life and its purpose. No matter the complexity of a person's background or the intricacy of their intellectual researches, Roland seemed able to understand them and to offer them a path from shadow into light.

Another who recognised Roland's gift of understanding was Elizabeth Templeton. Elizabeth noted, 'Roland clearly had huge intellectual versatility, and could engage with people at umpteen levels. He gave an image of himself once, as a chameleon. That was an accurate self-perception. He could pick up and take on the colour of what was there in the environment.'[12]

Roland used to visit the Holy Isle, Lindisfarne, in support of the small gathered religious community there. On one of his visits in 1996, a young man was staying for a few weeks, resting after the exhausting distress of marriage breakdown. The young man, a doctor, had experience of madness in his own family, and now feared that he himself malfunctioned so seriously that he could never have a proper relationship with anyone. He had concluded that he simply was not fit for it.

He listened as Roland spoke to the Lindisfarne Community. Puffing at his pipe, Roland talked about Unity, Christian Unity and the unity of the individual. And when he'd finished speaking, Roland said, 'If anyone would like to talk to me more about any of this, I'll be outside, sitting on the steps.' The young man went and spoke with Roland. With Roland then offering him an open invitation to visit the Community in Roslin, this was the first of many conversations. 'I called Roland my "Guru". But he didn't accept a title like that. So, how do I describe him? Not "Guide". Not "Father". Was he a Teacher? Going to Roslin was like making contact with myself. It was so easy to talk to him.'[13]

The young doctor undertook further training as a psychotherapist, and went on to work with some of the most seriously disturbed children in British society. The encounter with Roland enabled him to find himself. 'I could talk with Roland about things. He was completely with me. Not as a Friend. But just listening and talking. It was as if there were three people there; me, Roland and God, in the room, when we talked.' The long process of self-discovery brought rewards for the young doctor: 'Here I am, married, with three kids and a garden. I never could have imagined it.' In his garden there is a garden shed, set aside as a place of quiet and prayer.

Roland's career as a university lecturer drew to a close in 1975, but his role as a teacher continued without interruption for a further 20 years. Indeed, we might say that the 1980s, after he became a Roman Catholic, were the richest of his teaching years. For his diaries of those years indicate the huge number of invitations he received to address monasteries, convents and gatherings of priests throughout Britain. Once, he was invited to address a conference of chaplains to the United States armed forces. On another occasion, he addressed a conference of university chaplains, and in the following years many of those chaplains invited him to address groups in their university.

In addition, he remained a valued resource for individuals seeking to clarify their own understanding of Christianity and to make their belief explicit. But in two situations, as we shall see, he set out to offer a course of theological studies for people working in specific Christian contexts.

7

The Religious Life: a Sign

'We've learned the importance of "place",' said Roland. 'Once the village knew we were going to stay here – actually, when they knew that we were going to die here – they accepted us completely.' Initially, as we have seen, Roland himself and the Fraternity with him had been unsure of where they should be located. Clear, strong advice, however, from the Abbot of Nunraw and Mother Mary Clare of the Sisters of the Love of God, stilled their initial uncertainties. Thereafter, the Fraternity settled to a simple daily and weekly pattern of life in the Roslin house, establishing routines which gradually developed but which in the main remained unchanged for over 40 years.

A woman who through a friend first made contact with the Community in 1968, only three years after it had been founded, reflected, 'It was so settled that I assumed it had been there for decades.' Brant Pelfrey, only a few years later, sensed that same air of permanence in the Community. 'As a student, I thought that Fr Roland had deliberately imitated the ancient style of community life in the arrangement at Roslin. However, in reality, the modern Community had slowly arrived at a pattern that had been used by Christians centuries before, quite on their own. They did this by passing through a number of stages, sometimes painfully learning lessons of what did and what did not work.'[1]

John Halsey recalls that one day in 1968, when the members of the Community were gathering together for the monthly meeting called 'the Chapter Meeting', Roland came in and announced, 'I've laid an egg!'

Early in the morning, Roland had risen from his bed and written out a Rule for the community.

Since the time of St Benedict, a comprehensive written expression of the aims and practices of a religious community has been known as their 'Rule'. When he founded a monastery at Monte Cassino in AD 500, Benedict guided the communal life of the monks with his comprehensive Rule. The Rule of St Benedict, often summed up in the two Latin words *Ora et Labora* – 'Work and Pray' – has since provided a basic pattern of life for many religious communities.

'The egg' laid by Roland for the Fraternity of the Transfiguration did itself draw on Benedict's Rule, though Roland's was simpler and more compact.[2] It begins by presenting the vision which guides the Community:

Your vocation is none other than the call of God, who wills you to live to the praise of his glory – the light of that glory he has revealed in the face of Jesus Christ.

God in his mercy has called us sinners to witness to the fellowship of the mystery of Christ. See your calling as a token of the calling of everyone.

The Rule goes on to describe how the Community are to be witnesses: 'Your function within the Church and to the world is to be a sign.'

Then, in the most direct of terms, the Rule indicates three ways in which the Community is to personify the sign.

First: to be a sign of Christ in his detachment from all to belong to all – a sign of Christ's poverty by which he made all men rich, a sign of Christ's chastity that he might become the Brother of all and the Father of the poor, a sign of Christ's obedience that he might give to everyone his true freedom.

Secondly: to be a sign of our baptismal promises whereby we have renounced the vain pomp and glory of the world, and all the sinful desires of the flesh so that we will not follow or be led by them, and have promised to keep God's holy will and Commandments.

Thirdly: a sign to all people of the life to come, in which our life does not consist in the abundance of things which a man possesses, in which we neither marry nor are given in marriage, in which no-one who has loved their life will keep it.

A visitor to the house in Roslin would quickly become aware of the major themes of the communal life: prayer, work and hospitality. As their life engaged with each of these themes, the members of the Community themselves embodied the sign which they existed to portray.

Daily there was communal prayer at the beginning of the day, at midday and in the evening. The day began early with an hour of silent prayer, the opportunity for each member of the Community to contemplate 'the glory of Christ as we allow the transfiguring of ourselves and this world in the light of His glory'. The Rule says firmly, 'The hour of adoration may never be omitted except for grave reason.' To visitors, even those who are regular in attending to the duties of their own religious tradition, this hour of silent contemplation could constitute quite a dividing line between themselves and the members of the Community. Twenty-first-century living has little space for silence. In public worship, it is rare to experience a silence so long as the two minutes of Remembrance on Armistice Day. But the practice of silent prayer of contemplation is one of the distinguishing marks of the Roslin Community. Members of the Community, according to their inclination and as their other duties allowed, extended their time of contemplation beyond that single hour. Each day offered opportunities for silence. Every month, each spent 24 hours on their own either in the Enclosure or in the hut, another garden shed, which in 1969 they placed out in the nearby Pentland Hills. This new wooden hut was erected in a copse beside the Army's firing range, and it was located near an old farmhouse which had an outside toilet and cold running water. In addition, each year, they spent a week on retreat in some appropriate religious community where silence contributed to the process of self-examination. Their contemplative experience was consummated in the frequent celebration of the sacrament of Holy Communion, the Eucharist.

This was the communal framework of prayer for Roland teaching at New College, for John working in the Broughton Place hostel, Robert in his youth work, Patty in her pastoral visiting, and Neil in his work in the parish and the diocese.

Robert, as we have seen, was not required to take paid employment, as John's wages and Roland's salary provided sufficient money to support the Community's simple style of life. However, Robert developed a role in working with local youths, and his sense of humour contributed to the Community life. 'I remember the atmosphere in the Frat,' he recalled. 'We were constantly in stitches with laughter. With Roland there, bringing in all kinds of people, the most extraordinary situations would arise. One time, staying with us for a few days was a wandering soul who came from Bolton. Roland also brought a distinguished church visitor, and we were all in the chapel. In the time of open prayer, the man from Bolton gave quite a long prayer for Bolton Wanderers Football Club, who had just lost an important match. He prayed that the supporters would be helped to get over their sorrow at losing.'

One Sunday, Roland and Robert were leading the service in Rosslyn Chapel. They were wearing their monks' habits tailored from old Army blankets, and over the habit they wore a white gown, an alb, cut and sewn from old calico sheets. 'As we made our way out of the sacristy into the aisle of the Chapel,' recalled Robert, 'I said to Roland, "Roland, we look like two double beds." John Halsey could see, as we came down the aisle, that something was happening, as we desperately tried to keep our faces straight and maintain the dignity of the service.'

Seeing Robert spending ever-increasing time on his youth work, Roland suggested that perhaps Robert should redirect his focus. 'Roland came up with the idea that maybe I should try being a hermit,' smiled Robert in recollection. 'He took me out to look at somewhere beside Nine Mile Burn at the foot of the Pentland Hills. There would be some arrangement for a place for me to live. I remember standing there, surveying the desolate wastes of bog and heather, and thinking, "I don't think this is for me." In the Frat we had a saying, "It is more important to be than to do." I could see the value of just being; but I had a need for doing, as well.'

This revealed to Robert that after three years in the Fraternity it was time for him to move on. A legacy from an aunt enabled him to purchase a tiny flat in nearby Loanhead; and he took a job with the Midlothian County Council youth service. Gradually distancing himself from the Roslin Community, two years later he left for Cumbria, where he bought a farm in Eskdale and became a goat farmer. 'I owe the Community a lot,' he said, looking back. 'Particularly living with Roland. I was influenced by the way he saw everything in theological terms. He is the only person I have ever known who always thought theologically.'

Robert's life progressed in fascinating directions, but his Roslin episode was over.

In their working lives, too, the members of the Community were a sign. For 18 months, John Halsey continued to give support to the young leaders in the hostel in Broughton Place. He began by travelling into Edinburgh each morning, returning in the evening. But, at the end of the first week, he detected that because he remained merely a day visitor, the young residents of the hostel and the young leaders viewed him as an outsider. 'Either I'm going to have to give this up,' John told the Community, 'or I have to move in.' Roland, who was teaching in Edinburgh, saw that he too could live at the Broughton Place hostel. So, he and John took to staying at the hostel from Monday to Friday. They saw this as a pattern pioneered by the Little Brothers. The Little Brothers had retreat centres as a general resource for the scattered communities, and what they called 'working houses' where the working brothers lived. Broughton Place would be a 'working house' and Roslin the 'mother house'. 'The first thing I did on moving in', said John, 'was to make a little "upper room" in a cupboard with a skylight. I put in a carpet and a small stool: it was a little place of quiet where I could pray the Office.' There was no accommodation for Roland in the main building, so he slept in what had been the outside toilet, a building which stood in the back garden. Naturally, they referred to him as 'the Loo-tenant'.

This left Neil Russell with the key responsibility for the house in Roslin through the week. A number of students from New College would come to stay, but there was a growing recognition that the Community had become very scattered and that the communal life of the professed members was not receiving appropriate attention. So, in 1971 they made a decision that they would draw themselves back into Roslin 'and wait on the Lord'.

Miss Black was still their housekeeper; and a lady from Roslin, a Miss Gray, also came to do cleaning. Each of them rather wished to be their only daily help. To keep the peace, it was arranged that one would come only in the mornings, the other only in the afternoons. But, having decided to draw all the members back into the house, the Community made new arrangements. Miss Black the housekeeper retired, as did her part-time colleague Miss Gray. As they drew themselves back into Roslin to wait on the Lord, the Community themselves now took over the housekeeping and the catering.

Patty bought the little flat in Clerk Street, Loanhead, from Robert, who had just left for Cumbria. Patty quickly made friends with the young people of the street. As soon as she moved in, before she had any furniture and when the floor was still her only bed, the young ones were inquisitively at her door. They were complaining that the local youth club had recently closed, so Patty suggested they could come to her house. 'So I said, "Well. You could come here." That was jolly rash of me. "One night a week, you can come here." So we arranged for Monday at half past seven.

'And I said, "Now, you'll have to leave any tools – any weapons you have, you'll have to leave outside. And if you want to go to the loo, you can be there for three minutes, but you're not to lock the door." And there was one thing more. I said, "And everybody's equal. Nobody's to shout at other people and say that they're poofs or whatever. You know. And if they were, so what?" So that was how they started to come.'[3]

But, when the Community decided to focus more closely on their communal life together, she moved for a time into the house in Roslin.

Patty visited people from the congregation of Rosslyn Chapel, and also travelled to visit young people in Polmont Borstal and in the women's prison, Corntonvale, in Stirling. In addition, she offered herself as a volunteer at Rosslynlee, the local psychiatric and geriatric hospital.

'What would you like to do?' they asked her.

'What's the job nobody wants to do?' she responded.

'The teeth!' came the immediate answer.

So, Patty went round the geriatric wards cleaning the sets of false teeth in the jars on bedside tables.

The Community 'waited on the Lord' for a short number of months. Then, utterly unexpectedly, a flock of strange creatures alighted on Roslin and stretched the imagination and the intellectual resources of the entire Community for nine months. Of this there will be more later.

But, by 1975, the Community agreed that the time had come for John to return to industrial life. He went to the Jobcentre and within a few weeks found employment as a labourer in a paint shop that was part of a garage in Edinburgh. There were about 30 men on the shop-floor, seven of them in the paint shop. As a newly employed labourer, John was at the bottom of the heap. 'I felt like the little dog listening to his master's voice on old HMV records.'[4] The atmosphere in the garage was universally tense, with a sense of suppressed fear. This tone was set from the very top. Management and workers all viewed each other with apprehension, suspicion and distrust. Everyone was harshly ordered about by their superiors.

On his first day in the work, during the morning tea-break, John asked his new workmates, 'What about a union in this place? Is there a union, or what happens?' The atmosphere at once became highly charged. It eventually emerged that in another branch of this garage some men had tried to start a union and had been fired on the spot. This workforce where John now found himself had no intention of risking the wrath of management by any mention of a union. So John learned his labouring tasks, polishing vehicles after the panel-beaters had straightened the damage and the painters had resprayed them.

John bided his time. He had worked there for two years when the management over-reached themselves, demanding that the workers sign an agreement to do two nights' overtime or else face dismissal. One of the painters had a friend who was a lawyer. At tea-break the lawyer was smuggled in, and such was the shared fury at this illegal demand that nearly all the men joined the union. Management were not pleased. There were running disputes with management for three months, at the end of which time the shop-steward was sacked. 'The outcome was', said John, 'that I was put in as shop-steward because no-one else would take the job.'

John raised the issue of contracts of employment, which all employees were supposed to receive. This was a protective measure for employees of which the firm claimed to be unaware. And, in the end, all employees were issued with contracts. On one occasion when an employee was unexpectedly made redundant, John called a walk-out. When they returned to work, the workforce maintained an absolute silence about what they had discussed, which in itself seemed to cause panic in the management.

John did not accord with people's stereotype of a union activist. He was neither a firebrand nor a rabble-rouser nor an anarchist. Yet, as he explained it, he was able to sustain the position of shop-steward only through his membership of the Community. John would explain to the Community the problems the men were facing, the dilemmas and difficulties which confronted him as shop-steward. Their understanding and support were essential prerequisites for his often difficult and confrontational role. 'There would have been no union membership in the works if I hadn't been there, and this wouldn't have happened if I hadn't belonged to my community.'[5] The essential connection between the Community and John's work is expressed in the Community's annual report in the chapter minutes for 1985:

John's work at the garage continues. The fact that this provides little that is newsworthy or sensational does not lessen the conviction shared by the Community with him, that a place of hum-drum work in the secular world is certainly no less a place where God can be served and contemplated than a monastery, a church, or a job that might appear more obviously useful or interesting. We see this as an integral witness to the Community's vocation.

John was continuously employed in the garage for 18 years. Daily in all weathers, he cycled to and from his work. With unfailing fidelity, he attended to the details of his job. It was said that no-one could put such a shine on a resprayed vehicle as John. He continued in his post as union shop-steward; and, although membership of the union dwindled, he would meet weekly with the senior manager and thus was able to keep the workforce aware of any forthcoming developments. When he was just 60, he retired from work on health grounds, suffering from severe rheumatism in his hands.

Brother Neil was priest-in-charge at Rosslyn Chapel, and attended to the needs of the congregation. He took his share in the duties of the housekeeping, and also at cooking – which was not always to everyone else's satisfaction. Neil would pride himself on having fed everyone very economically on lentils. But, if Neil was cooking, John Halsey was not the only one known occasionally to slip quietly from the house late in the evening to enjoy a fish supper from the village chip shop.

Renowned for his African experience, Neil was often called upon to lead retreats and quiet days in the Diocese of Edinburgh. He was also consulted by individual priests about confidential matters in their congregations. His helpful intervention in a difficulty was recalled 35 years later by a grateful priest.

'In 1975, my wife Susan and I were assigned a council house in Edinburgh's huge, newly built Wester Hailes housing scheme. My job was to found a new Scottish Episcopal Church congregation there. Bishop Neil was wonderful. At the time, the Episcopal Church was running into money problems. With churches in Wester Hailes, Craigmillar and Pilton all costing them money, some people were demanding, "Why are we wasting good money on loss-making little churches in the housing schemes?" Bishop Neil always made the point that the Gospel was good news for the poor. He said to them, "We must keep making available to the poor, the joy, the simplicity and the compassion of the holy Gospel." He was a great ally to the housing-scheme churches.'[6]

However, Neil pined for Africa. Unexpectedly, in 1979 the bishop who had succeeded him in Tanzania invited him to come for a three-month visit. He received a warm welcome. 'Places I'd left 30 and 40 years ago welcomed me back as if it were only a short time.'[7] A further invitation followed. 'The bishop invited me to end my days among them – or, as one priest I'd ordained said, "We want you to lay your bones here." But my parting words to the bishop were, "I think that with our small numbers [in Roslin] there is only the remotest possibility that my Community will agree."

'But when I came to Roslin, before I'd touched on the matter, Roland said, "Neil, we've decided we must send you back to Tanzania."'[8]

So, Neil returned to Tanzania, where he was appointed priest at Makuyuni, a village where there was a small church built of mud and sticks and with a grass roof. He lived there in a simple hut until his death in May 1984. He was buried before the altar in the little church. In 1992, the congregation of Old St Paul's Church in Edinburgh raised money to build in Makuyuni a new church of concrete blocks. In this new church, Neil was buried before the altar as he had been in the old one.

In his years at Roslin, Neil, who was at heart quite a solitary man, struggled with the demands of communal religious life. Yet, when his friend George Martineau was dying, long after Neil had returned to Tanzania 'to lay his bones in the African earth', George said that he had never seen Neil happier than he was in his Roslin years.

A good friend wrote, 'He was a much-loved priest, and in many ways true to his Congregational principles: he regarded authority with suspicion.'[9]

The Community also sought to be a sign in the generosity of their hospitality. Their table welcomed whoever came to the door at mealtimes. And the house was known to gentlemen of the road, wayfarers, who told each other that they could always find a night's lodging there.

'How did you hear of us?' Patty asked one such travelling man.

'I heard about you down in Dover.'

It seemed that such travellers know of places of welcome on their paths all through Britain. They knew that if they travelled up the east coast they would find a bed at the Abbey of Nunraw. From there, it was an easy day's journey to Roslin and the

Community of the Transfiguration. Often, one or more of these visitors would be present at the table for a meal. Patty learned from Nunraw that the travellers had once been discussing moving on to Roslin, and were speaking of the woman there whose name was 'Patty'. 'Or is it "Batty?"' they were said to have asked.

Rosemary Lee stayed at the house for some months in search of her future. She would in due course become a Sister of the Love of God and spend more than 20 years in that silent, enclosed order in their convent in Oxford. While she was at Roslin, Rosemary's mother came to visit, staying overnight in Roslin's Original Hotel. That night, she came for the evening meal at the house. The electricity was off, so the table was lit by candle-light. Mrs Lee later recalled the faces round the table, some scholarly, some ascetic, some worn with life's trials; all etched in light and dark. 'It was like a picture gallery,' she said. 'Roland was a Rembrandt. Neil was an El Greco.'

'Yes, there would be all sorts,' said Patty. 'Men of the road, and bishops, theologians and people just out of Barlinnie prison. Just whoever would turn up.' The arrival of travelling men sometimes heralded difficulties, of course. Sometimes their wandering ways involved an excessive consumption of alcohol.

'Yes,' said Patty, 'and you would have people there like Big Peter, who when he was very drunk was prepared to break all the windows in the house. I remember the first time. It was November. And actually it didn't seem to matter. Because it was no colder, because it was November. It was just that the windows hadn't any glass in.

'After Peter had come often enough, he knew he was always welcome unless he was drunk. At the beginning, people could come, liquor or no liquor. Then we realised we really had to say to them, "Go and sleep it off, and then you can come back tomorrow morning." Latterly, after years, Peter came back – the first time he had come back after he'd had a go at not drinking. He brought a couple of chairs for the house, because Roland had been so good to him, talking to him when he was saying a lot of nonsense. Where did the chairs come from? Who knows?'

People with psychological difficulties might come and stay for months, because they found the atmosphere so accepting, and there was enough flexibility to accommodate their anxieties and their sometimes strange ways. Roland had a brother, Gordon, who suffered with psychological problems. Often, Roland did not know where Gordon was. But, from time to time, Gordon would come and stay for some months. Another man, who had undergone drastic treatment, a pre-frontal lobotomy, in his teens, came by invitation and stayed contentedly as part of the Community for over five years.

The hospitality of the house included members of the Community being available and accessible at any time. One woman remembers being sent in the night to look for Roland when the husband of a friend was drifting into a psychotic episode. 'It was after 11 at night when I knocked at the door of the Tin House. I was asking for Roland. The man who came to the door took me away into the back garden, under the trees and into what seemed the darkest corner. There he knocked on the door of a shed. Inside was Roland, reading in bed. But at once he got up and dressed, and I took him away into Edinburgh to do what he could for my friend's husband.'

How is a life of this character to be evaluated? How can its significance be measured? Probably the first Church of Scotland minister ever invited to be the spiritual adviser, the Visitor, to a religious community was the Revd Duncan Finlayson, who was then principal of St Colm's College, the Edinburgh training centre for deaconesses and for overseas missionaries. He remembered coming out to Roslin each year on 6 August, the day of the Feast of the Transfiguration, for the service for the renewing of the Community's vows.

'It was a tremendous experience for me, to receive their vows. I remember the first time I did it. We were out in the hut, "the chicken hut" – their hut chapel. I read the Rule to them. It made a big impression on me. But, because I'm Highland, it took me quite a long time to read it. The next year they said, "I think we'll dispense with the reading of the Rule this year"!'

Duncan went on, 'It was remarkable, the Rule. It spoke of the kind of issues that they as a Community represented. One instruction was very immediate. The Rule states, "We are not to seek publicity." And this is the answer to the question that I kept asking myself, "What is this man giving up?" And, "Is this a waste of his life?" They could be doing all sorts of things – Roland, Archbishop of Canterbury; John, goodness knows what. But the Rule told them, "You are to be a sign."

'Beyond the things you could understand, just having been in contact with them you found that they were exactly that: a Sign. It was not just that they looked after the poor and needy, though the Rule set down that for them. No. It relates to the business of the seconds, minutes, hours and days of your life. They are not just lived things; but they are given.

'We saw a pouring out of these lives. Lives poured out like that somehow signify a positive, not a negative.'[10]

Confirmation of the significance of the Community came from Jean Vanier, founder of L'Arche, an international federation of group homes for people with developmental disabilities and those who assist them. L'Arche is widely recognised as honouring the special gifts of people who have frequently been dismissed as having only special needs. Vanier himself has had a huge influence on Western culture's way of viewing people with such apparent difficulties. Whenever he came to Scotland, usually to visit the L'Arche house in Inverness or the one in Edinburgh, he would always visit Roslin to meet with the Community.

He affirmed the important aspects of the Community: 'These three things I would say: how close it was to the Gospel; its beautiful poverty; and the reality of the ecumenical bond – because I believe there's no other way forward.

'Every time I went to Edinburgh, I went there. I was with Roland at the Eucharist often there. So, for me, it was like a light shining in the darkness. And I believe that there is a kind of mystery – that the little has to remain little. Then it is and remains a sign; not a solution. So I just felt a very deep communion with them. And, as I say, every time I was nearby I went to see them. I felt at once that it was one of the few authentic realities that exist. What else can I say? Except that ... they have been a sign of what the Church can become – of what the Church is, but people don't know it.'[11]

8

Enquirers Visit the Community

Jean Vanier, warmly commending the Community of the Transfiguration, said of it, 'The little has to remain little. Then it is, and remains, a sign. Not a solution. A sign.'

'But they were trying to grow,' said the visitor.

'They *hoped* to grow,' affirmed Jean Vanier. 'Hoping, certainly. But the word, "trying"? No.'

Jean Vanier was quite definite about that. But, with delighted, intermittent laughter, he went on, 'They were open to growing. But under conditions which would make growth very unlikely, indeed impossible! When I say "the conditions would make growth unlikely", I mean it would have had to be a growth in poverty – a growth in both poverty and in insecurity. Well! How can you create growth in insecurity?'

He paused for a long time, and nodded silently in approval of their having remained little.

Indeed the Community did hope to grow. From its inception as 'the Fraternity of the Transfiguration', the brothers hoped that the community would attract like-minded people to join them. A considerable number of men and women, hearing of the new community being formed there, came to the house at Roslin to see if they were suited to the pattern of a communal religious life.

The first was Peter Hipkin. In November 1965, three months after the Fraternity was established, Peter came to stay in the house. He was one of the six members of the Sheffield Twelve who had lived and worked in Sheffield with Roland in 1959 and 1960. John Halsey was another of the Twelve that year; and Robert Haslam, though not one of the Twelve, was their close friend. Thus Peter knew all the current members of the Roslin Community.

From his year in Sheffield, Peter had returned to Westcott House to complete his training. He then went out to South Africa, where he was ordained deacon in 1961 and priest in 1962. When he came to Roslin, he was already familiar with the Little Brothers of Jesus. He was eager, therefore, to take unskilled work. He was employed as a care assistant in Rosslynlee, the nearby hospital for people with learning difficulties and psychiatric problems. It seemed for some months that he was likely to join the Fraternity. In the end, however, he did not join, but instead returned to South Africa to work with the Anglican Church. He maintained his contact with Roslin, drawing support from the friendship. In common with many Anglican priests involved in the anti-apartheid movement, however, Peter found that these turbulent years in South Africa's history made immense demands. He left South Africa again and returned to Britain. He worked in Birmingham as a care-assistant in a psychiatric hospital. By then he had become a Roman Catholic, and he seemed in some ways to prefer the duties of a care-worker to the responsibilities he had carried as a priest. He kept in touch with Ted Longman, another of the same year's contingent of the Sheffield Twelve, who was a parish priest in Birmingham; and Roland went there to visit Peter. A short time later, Peter went back to South Africa, and contact with him was lost.

In 1967, Humphrey Bradshaw came, asking to become a member of the Community. He became a 'postulant'. That is, he entered the first stage of the process which would lead to membership of the Fraternity. Humphrey was a Scottish Episcopal priest who shared the work of the parish of St Barnabas in Edinburgh with a colleague, John Maitland Moir. Moir was later received into the Orthodox Church and at the time of writing is, as Archimandrite, a much-respected figure in the Orthodox Churches in Scotland.

But Humphrey was the first to leave St Barnabas, and he moved into Roslin just before Christmas 1967. He immediately began to share in the devotional and communal life of the Community, and was settling well to the pattern. However, at that point, Roland did not have any time to spend helping Humphrey to shape his life in the Community, for Roland had his New College duties and all the Christmas events associated with being curate-in-charge at

Rosslyn Chapel. When January came, Roland knew that he must sit down with Humphrey and create the plan for his formation as a member of the Community.

'We must have a talk about it all,' said Roland to Humphrey.

'It's all becoming quite clear to me,' responded Humphrey.

'No, no! Not too quickly now,' Roland remonstrated.

'But it is clear to me,' insisted Humphrey. 'It is quite clear to me – that I must get married!'

So, only a month after coming to join them, Humphrey left the Community again. He married, and remained an Episcopal priest and worked in the Borders.

A young trainee for the Church of Scotland ministry, Peter Millar, had known Roland through his studies in New College. Attracted by the Community's commitment to prayer and to solidarity with the poor, he wondered if this might be a path for him to follow. He moved into the house, was allocated a hut in the Enclosure and began to share in the pattern of daily life. But, in a matter of weeks, he concluded that this was not, after all, a life he could sustain for long. He proceeded to ordination into the ministry of the Church of Scotland and worked in a demanding urban parish in the east end of Glasgow. Then he married, and he and his wife went out and worked with churches in India for many years. Later in Scotland, as members of the Iona Community, they designated their home in Inverness-shire as a Columban house, offering hospitality to people whose lives were in crisis.

The ecumenical aspirations of the Community received a boost with an enquiry from Raymond Lloyd. Raymond had studied theology in Zurich and then served as a Baptist minister in Wales. He heard about the Community at Roslin and went to visit them. '"Ah", said John Halsey, "We thought, an Ecumenical member, a Baptist brother!" But our Ecumenical hopes were to be a little disappointed. For, by the time he did come to join us, Raymond had already become an Anglican!'

Raymond joined the Fraternity as 'a Novice', a beginner committed to learning the disciplines of the religious life. He faced a dilemma. Having already worked as a Baptist pastor, should he move forward to full profession as a member of the Community, or should he go for ordination as an Anglican priest? The Fraternity discussed the situation and decided that Raymond really should go first to Coates Hall, the training college of the Scottish Episcopal Church. While attending the courses of lectures at Coates Hall, he lived in the Community at Roslin. A man of many accomplishments, Raymond could cut hair and was an excellent practical nurse. Forty years later, the Community still remembered what a very good cook he had been. There were other memories too, of protracted Baptist-length sermons for example, when on occasion Raymond was on duty in Rosslyn Chapel.

In 1968, Thomas Merton died. The significance of this contemplative Trappist monk, prolific author of works of poetry and theology, was already widely recognised; and Raymond chose to write his dissertation on Merton and his insights. Raymond was ordained in 1972 in the Glasgow Cathedral of the Episcopal Church. He went on to become a significant member of the Anglican Franciscan order, taking the name Brother Ramon.

A young man named Vincent Kirk stayed in the house at Roslin for a time. He had been a resident in the Cyrenians' hostel at Broughton Place when John Halsey was working there. Vincent was gay, which in that era could often lead to hostility and violence. Knowing that, away from the hostel, Vincent was often bullied, Roland took him under his wing, and Vincent eventually moved into the house at Roslin. On one occasion in Edinburgh, Vincent was attacked and was very badly knocked about. He put in a claim for compensation to the Criminal Injuries Compensation Board. The grant took a long time to come through; and, as he looked forward to receiving it, his expectations grew and grew. He looked forward to being able to travel. When the compensation money was finally paid, he started his travels by making a journey to Aberdeen. Roland arranged for him to stay with his former colleague James Torrance, by that time Professor of Systematic Theology in Aberdeen. But very sadly, while he was in Aberdeen, Vincent took his own life.

After Patty Burgess joined the Community, a number of women visited the house in Roslin on voyages of enquiry, tasting the life of the religious community without necessarily intending to join. Among these was Rosemary Lee, daughter of an Anglican vicar. Rosemary was a primary-school teacher who had given up teaching in order to become part of the life of an organised community. At first she looked for a lay community without religious affiliation. Advised, however, by her vicar to look at religious communities, she went in 1978 to Lindisfarne, the Holy Island off the Northumberland coast. While there, she encountered Roland, who was on one of his regular visits as friend and spiritual guide to the people who stayed on the Holy Island. Roland invited Rosemary to Roslin to talk about her search, and at the Community's invitation she spent six months in Roslin taking part in the communal life. At the end of the six months, the Community advised her to move out for a short while, in order to see from a distance if Roslin was for her. Rosemary found work as a nursing auxiliary in a large Northumberland psychiatric hospital. Later that year, 1979, the Community invited her back to Roslin for a special service in which she made a profession as an Associate of the Community. As an Associate, she worked in the hospital for three years altogether, all the time maintaining her daily Roslin prayer discipline in the hospital chapel. Roland invited Rosemary to come to Roslin again, on an occasion when Mother Mary Clare of the Sisters of the Love of God in Oxford was to be visiting. Rosemary subsequently went to Oxford and within a short space of time entered the Novitiate of these Sisters, to the surprise of her family and her friends. For the next 20 years, Rosemary observed the strict disciplines of silence and contemplative prayer which constituted the character of the enclosed order. She was released from her vows in 2002; and, having developed a life of contemplation and service, she worked in a variety of homes and hostels in the south of England. She was to return to Roslin in 2008 in circumstances which we shall in due course discover.

Nancy Allison came to Scotland in 1968 from the USA with a degree in theology, at a time when women could not be ordained to the Anglican priesthood. Initially she was employed by the Iona Community in their Clydeside centre in Glasgow and then on Iona. Then she became a teacher and house-mother in an approved school for girls under the protection of the courts. After that, she spent nine years as a tutor in New Testament and Theology in St Colm's College in Edinburgh, where the Church of Scotland trained men and women for the diaconate and for missionary service overseas. In Edinburgh, she went to church at Old St Paul's Episcopal Church. Feeling drawn towards a vocation in the religious life, she began to visit the Community at Roslin to speak with Patty and with Roland. She found the atmosphere of the Community wonderfully welcoming but was astonished at their way of life. In disbelief, she said to the Revd Duncan Finlayson, principal of St Colm's, who was also the Visitor to the Community, 'They live in chicken huts! And chicken huts that no self-respecting chicken would be seen dead in!' Although the religious life had a growing appeal to Nancy, she did not consider entering the Community in Roslin.

In 1979, however, Nancy returned to the USA and entered the Order of Saint Helena, a traditional religious order within the Episcopal Church, spending eight years there. In 1988, she was ordained deacon and priest by the Bishop of Upper South Carolina and served parishes in North and South Carolina until retirement.

Reflecting many years later on Roslin's place in the development of her self-understanding, she said, 'My most enduring memory of the community was sleeping and praying in those chicken coops. There was something about that cramped, bare space, with only lantern light, that made the demand of God so much more real. I am a procrastinator by nature, and I think, now, that I would not have moved ahead to enter the Order of St Helena, nor moved from there to the Episcopal priesthood, without the hours I spent in silence with the community at prayer. They followed the example of Charles de Foucauld and the Little Brothers and Sisters of Jesus. Everyone in the community was highly educated, yet they made their life the life of ordinary working-class men and women. I found it a powerful witness to the Gospel.'[1]

While it was of the very nature of the Community to welcome and give hospitality to such visitors and enquirers, they also gave attention to the contemplative aspect of their own life. They had their wooden hut in the Pentland Hills to which they and others could go for retreats. But they knew it would be helpful to have a place at greater distance, to which the members could go for longer periods.

They learned of a possible location for just such a resource. It was situated in the Firth of Clyde, on the Isle of Cumbrae, just off the west coast of mainland Scotland.

On Cumbrae, on the outskirts of the island's town of Millport, stands the smallest cathedral in Britain, the Cathedral of the Isles, the Collegiate Church of the Holy Spirit. The Community saw the precincts of the cathedral as an ideal location for a permanent place of retreat. The cathedral was under the care of a trust, one of whose trustees was the Earl of Glasgow. The trustees were pleased at the thought of the precincts being employed in what they saw as a suitably spiritual endeavour. The Community organised for themselves an Enclosure at the cathedral, in the former rose garden. They set a wooden hut at each of the garden's four corners, with another in the centre as a chapel. Thus it became a place of peace and contemplation for the Community.

With a birthday gift from his sister Margaret, John Halsey bought seeds to plant in the cathedral field, among them tobacco seed. There was an unusually fine summer in Cumbrae. An American visitor said he had not seen better tobacco growing in his home state of Virginia. Roland and John harvested the leaves and dried them. Cut and pressed and stored in large tins, the tobacco provided them both with pipe tobacco for more than a year.

One afternoon in 1973, a lady from the nearby village of Polton came to meet with the Community in Roslin. Roland had baptised this lady's baby. Now she brought her brother. He had come to visit her and spent the day talking without interruption, and she did not know what to do with him. The only thing she could think of was to bring him over to see Roland. So here he was, Michael Hollingshead. He was bearded, quite dishevelled, and his long hair was all over the place. He had been working in the USA, at Harvard University with Timothy Leary. Leary and he had been running a special programme at Harvard. They had been experimenting with giving LSD[2] to prisoners, and monitoring its effects. It seemed that they were hoping that with this new drug there would be a chance of altering the criminal mind-set. But the people running the experiment had themselves become converted to the frequent personal use of LSD. So, Michael arrived at Roslin and spent the afternoon chatting with Roland and John. He spoke of the spiritual doors that opened through taking LSD. Then off he went, saying that he was going south. Within just a few minutes, the police were at the door:

'Have you had a visit from this man?' they asked, showing a photograph of their recently departed visitor.

'He's just left us,' they replied.

'Do you know where he has gone?' the police continued.

'He didn't say.'

'Interpol would like to see him.'

A year later, he returned to the house in Roslin. He came to the door, this time clean-shaven and short-haired. He had spent the intervening months in custody. It so happened that the Community were planning to go to visit the Buddhist community at Sam-ye Ling, down in the Scottish Borders; so they took Michael with them. He said he had a friend staying there. When they arrived, who should open the door to them but Michael's friend Robin. Robin had a girlfriend there in Sam-ye Ling, and she was related to the Earl of Glasgow, who with his fellow trustees had so recently granted the Community access to the rose garden of the Cathedral of the Isles. Another friend of Michael's named David, a young man from the USA via Kathmandu and India, was also at Sam-ye Ling that day. He was at once ready to join the Roslin Community, as his time in India had fired him with enthusiasm to be in 'a brotherhood'.

Always on the alert for signals to guide the shaping of their life, especially at this time when they had decided to 'wait on the Lord', the Community were in no way discomfited at the next development. Michael Hollingshead and his friend Robin and a number of their friends from Glastonbury and from the New Age Community in Findhorn came to stay at Roslin, about ten people in all. With some accuracy, we can call them 'the Hippies'. Some of them lived in the house, others in their travelling bus which was parked in Manse Road outside the gate. The Community carried on with their times of prayer and silence, and the Hippies circled round it all, fitting in here and there. These new arrivals felt that they had gained access to a spiritual dimension of life through the use of hallucinogenic drugs. Now they wanted to make a link with others who had a different path to the spiritual realm.

The Community sent John Halsey to Cumbrae with the Hippies, to see if something might come of the dialogue between the Community and the Hippies. Reflecting on the episode many years later, Patty said, 'The Hippies seemed to be anxious to try to start living some sort of life. I'm not quite sure what sort of life. Because actually when they came to Cumbrae with John, they didn't really do anything very much at all. But it was a good thing to do, to give them a chance to see how they would get on.' John took up residence in a hut in the rose garden. The Hippies meanwhile settled into the cathedral annexe, which they insisted on calling 'the Ashram'. They lived what can best be described as a disorganised life.

On behalf of the cathedral trustees, the dean of the cathedral, the Very Revd George Douglas, maintained contact with them all. It was quite difficult for him to negotiate with the Hippies. Two of the Hippies, however, were attracted by island life. They really wanted to settle on the island and to get jobs. The dean could negotiate with these two about the matters he wanted to raise with all the Hippies. But the other residents in the Ashram didn't want to organise or be organised. On the contrary, Michael Hollingshead wanted to have his own kingdom, an enterprise he called 'the Free, High Church of the Isles'. At its centre would be 'acid', LSD. Acid would be a kind of sacrament.

One day, the earl and his wife came to visit. The earl's wife found her cousin sitting on the steps of the annexe, 'the Ashram', having the nits picked out of her hair by her boyfriend. This cameo brought the delinquent communal life of the Hippies into focus. The earl, an ex-Naval officer, told the Hippies that their time on the island had expired. As if issuing an order to the ratings, he told them to leave at once.

The Hippies did not receive this news well. They locked themselves in the annexe. There was no way they would leave.

A few days later, they were seen coming out of the annexe in a long line, with gardening tools – spades, hoes and rakes – on their shoulders. They were striding out, it seemed, to work the land. What could this be? Next, off the ferry came TV cameras and reporters and photographers from the press. Here were these poor, hard-working members of the cathedral's harmless commune, being put off the island by the wicked earl. Despite ingratiating themselves with sympathetic media, the Hippies found that they were no longer welcome within the cathedral precincts.

So, back to Roslin everyone trooped, the Hippies in their bus. At Roslin, Neil had been holding the fort, and some students from New College had taken up residence in the house and the huts. There was no room for the Hippies – and before long, in resentful mood, they prepared to depart.

> One moment in annihilation's waste,
> One moment of the well of life to taste,
> The stars are setting and the caravan
> Starts for the dawn of nothing, Oh make haste![3]

Having spent several months testing themselves in the kindly but demanding company of the Community of the Transfiguration, the Hippies climbed aboard their bus once more. The stars having set on their Cumbrae sojourn, the caravan started for the dawn of a different day.

A year or so later, two young men independently approached the Community to see if they could come and test their call to the religious life. Neville Long was South African. Before he came to Scotland, he had worked in Birmingham in personnel management. Peter Walters was brought up as a Roman Catholic and was educated in a school run by the de la Salle Brothers. He had studied Chinese at university. By the time he came to Roslin, however, he had already become an Anglican.

By the time Neville and Peter arrived in Roslin, the Community were making growing use of the retreat centre they had established on the Isle of Cumbrae. The Hippies had departed, and an atmosphere of tranquillity was more easily attained. One of the two newcomers would go to Cumbrae with Roland, and then John would go to Cumbrae with the other. Neville stayed for about a year but then withdrew from the Community altogether to pursue a different life. Peter continued his engagement with the Community and explored the possibility of entering into full membership. But, after 18 months with the Community Peter decided that his future lay elsewhere. He left to become a social worker. However, he developed early-onset dementia, and he died in 2005 at not much more than 50 years of age.

When Roland and John were busy over in Cumbrae with the Hippies, Bishop Neil was the permanent figure in the house in Roslin. Often, however, Neil would have duties in Edinburgh associated with his work as assistant bishop, and so there was a difficulty in maintaining the rhythm of the Community's prayer disciplines, the Morning Office, the Midday Office and the Evening Office. At this time, therefore, Patty moved from the flat in Loanhead over to Roslin. Thus Patty became the mainstay of the daily discipline of regular prayer, while the others fulfilled this commitment whenever they were in Roslin.

Among the enquirers came another visitor, this time one who was already engaged in the religious life. Harold Palmer was an Anglican Franciscan, a lay brother, when he first visited Roslin. Harold visited the Community from time to time, and always participated in its daily life of prayer, contemplation and hospitality. The community at Roslin sensed a companionship between their own venture and that in which Harold was engaged. Harold's family had a connection with land held in trust, in the hills above Alnmouth in Northumberland. In 1968, he established himself there as a hermit at 'Shepherd's Law'. His retreat house became a resource for individuals, and at different times Roland and John went there on retreat. In addition, the Roslin Community used to encounter people who wondered if they were destined for the solitary life of a hermit. They would send them to Harold the Hermit, who was glad to let them discover for themselves whether that life was for them or not.

Much later, Harold would recall, 'I reflect that Roland's example, and the prayer of the Community in their fragile steadfastness, was so important in my own life. And there was the friendship of John, Neil and Patty, and the many rich characters who congregated in the corrugated house, from shop-lifters to gentry, who remain to people my mind.'⁴

Harold recognised that his friendship with Roland and the Roslin Community had deepened as a consequence of one particular encounter. 'It was not until the Hermits' Conference at St David's in the autumn of 1975 that I entered into Roland's friendship and counsel.' The conference to which Harold refers was a turning point for the Roslin Community also.

The Community's first ten years saw them develop for themselves a pattern of life which organised and sustained them, a pattern which visitors found both welcoming and compelling. Yet the members of the Community themselves were aware that their Community was small, and still quite new, and also quite different from any other religious community known to them. Certainly they had close links with the Little Brothers and Sisters of Jesus and with Taizé, with Nunraw Abbey and numerous other religious communities. They knew that they were part of a major Christian religious tradition. But, at this point in their development, they were not altogether sure of their exact location in the landscape of the religious life. The assurance of the Community in its later years renders it difficult to imagine how it could in earlier times have known any uncertainty about its identity. Yet John Halsey recalled how significant and how reassuring it had been for them all when Roland relayed to them an unexpected word of affirmation.

In 1975, Mother Mary Clare of the Sisters of the Love of God organised a conference at St David's in Wales, on the topic of 'The Hermit Life'. Brought together were people who had taken the path of solitude and entered into the depths of the meditative life. Among the speakers were eminent and highly regarded individuals, recognised and revered within their own religious families as profoundly wise and experienced in the contemplative life. Among these were Abbé André Louf, a Cistercian monk who was the abbot of his monastery; Anglican Sister Benedicta Ward, one of the world's most knowledgeable writers on the legacy of the

Desert Fathers and Mothers; Canon Donald Allchin, a leading Church of England theologian, a close friend of Thomas Merton, and warden of Fairacres, the Convent of the Sisters of the Love of God; Archimandrite Kallistos Ware, already at the age of just 41 the leading English scholar of Orthodoxy;[5] and Roland himself. Roland spoke on the Biblical background to the hermit life.[6] When Louf gave his paper, he told how at the beginning of Christian monasticism everything was on a very small scale. He showed how this happens at all times of renewal, where people spontaneously respond to the needs of the day. Small groups of committed people emerge. And he said, 'There is a thirst today for a new form of monasticism.'

After he had heard Roland speaking both about the solitary life and about the Community life which the Community were endeavouring to live out in Roslin, he and Roland went for a walk. Roland told him about Roslin, about the old house, the hospitality, the huts and the solitude. As they walked together, Louf was in tears, realising that what he had prayed for was actually happening. He confided in Roland that for years he had been praying for communities to come into being who would focus on contemplation and prayer. More than once he had sought to leave his monastery and begin such a small community himself, but his brothers would not let their abbot leave. 'And here it is!' he said. 'You and your Community are doing exactly what I have been praying for.'

'Roland's encounter with Dom André Louf brought a deep affirmation,' said John Halsey. 'We gained an assurance that our venture was worthwhile, and that our small size was itself a valued part of the whole tradition of the religious life. The Eastern Orthodox Church from the earliest centuries recognised the value of the small religious community, the "skete" as it was called. We now had a real sense of our identity, which had been lacking hitherto.' For some years after the conference at St David's, the Community referred to itself as 'the skete', even though the significance of the term was lost on the majority of the Community's friends.

In that same year, another enquirer was welcomed, and he set himself on the path towards membership of the Community.

John MacDermott, affectionately known as 'John Mac', was originally from Wigan in Lancashire. He lived there with his mother,
who always looked after him and was very protective. When she
died, John came to Edinburgh. He came in search of a gardening
job which he had seen advertised but which did not materialise.
John Mac, unmarried, lived in a succession of digs and boarding houses. He attended an evening course of adult Christian
Education classes in New College, where Roland was one of his
teachers. He first arrived on the scene at Roslin when John Halsey
was giving support to the Cyrenians' hostel in Broughton Place.
John Mac stayed in the Church Army hostel nearby. When the
Church Army hostel closed because of dry rot, he was in various
digs. But he was always left stranded. He stayed at Roslin a few
nights when he had nowhere else to go.

John Mac wanted to belong somewhere, and the welcoming
door of the Community meant a lot to him. As Patty recalled, 'he
wanted to have a go at being part of the Community'. A room
was found for him in the house, and he moved in. He expressed
an interest in making a commitment to the life of the Community
of the Transfiguration, and the Community affirmed the possibility of this. After John Mac had made his profession as 'a Novice'
and expressed himself ready to undergo the formation to prepare
him for full membership, Roland tried to give him instructions on
what he should do.

'This is what we do ...,' Roland would say, outlining how the
Community did things.

'No you don't,' John would respond. 'You don't always do
that.'

Roland soon knew that he hadn't a hope of instructing John
Mac in anything, but that John would always go his own way.

John Mac insisted on taking his turn at cooking. His cooking
was always out of the ordinary. He would serve the Community
with potatoes baked for only half an hour, with the earth still on
them. Other items would appear on the menu, all served in an
unusual order.

John Mac was by this time in his late 50s, and he had never
before lived in such a close community. He was in completely

unfamiliar territory. Patty was living in the house in 23 Manse Road, and the tiny house in Loanhead was available to become home to Bishop Neil, John Mac and John Halsey. John Halsey's private space was Patty's small wooden hut in the back garden, his place for prayer and his place to sleep. Neil and John Mac shared the bedroom. In the cramped contours of the little bedroom, a partition was erected to designate what space was for Bishop Neil and what for Brother John Mac. It was clear that pressures were building up.

In 1977, on the day of the Feast of the Transfiguration, 6 August, the Community met with their Visitor, the Revd Duncan Finlayson. Even 35 years later, Duncan Finlayson could recall how the three senior brothers asked if they could see him alone. 'Well, they sat me down and said, "We have a problem," and what would I advise. So, we thought about it all and the difficulty they were having with the way this gentleman did things, and I gave them my advice. They took not a blind bit of notice of anything that I said, of course. They dealt with it in their own way. But they found it difficult, because they were such tolerant people. There was something lovely about seeing these very holy men coming to the end of their tether.'

In the end, the Community recorded in the chapter minutes: 'We resolved that there was a hope of the continuation of John Mac's Membership of the Community in a non-residential capacity.' The Community bought a caravan on the local caravan site. It was not a luxury caravan: it was quite old and at a price they could afford. 'The Church Wagon', they called it. The caravan became home to John Mac, and he sustained his share in the communal life through coming regularly to meals in the house and prayers in the chapel. The Community supported John in his wish to study, and they encouraged him when he enrolled for a degree course with the Open University. Over a period of several years, he attained all the required grades and was awarded a degree of Master of Arts. Patty accompanied John Mac to the graduation ceremony in Edinburgh's McEwan Hall. When his name was called and he rose to collect his degree, a resounding cheer arose, for he had become quite a personality in the courses. Forward he went, a bright red cravat at his neck, and Roland's academic gown flowing around him.

Day after day, the Community maintained at the house in Roslin their discipline of prayer and work and hospitality. Visitors of all kinds arrived and departed: wayfarers, scholars, clergy of many denominations, men and women from religious orders, people with delicate mental health, others on pilgrimage to different communities. Receiving this continuous sequence of visitors drew heavily on the personal resources of each member of the Community. The place of retreat on Cumbrae fulfilled an important function. While the trustees of the Cathedral of the Isles were thankful at having banished the Hippies, they continued to extend the warmest welcome to the Community of the Transfiguration. Roland and John appreciated the remoteness of the island and the quiet atmosphere of the cathedral rose garden. From the peace of their place of retreat, they drew strength for the other aspects of their communal life. But the tranquillity of their Cumbrae connection was not to last.

9

Cumbrae and the Community of Celebration

The Community of the Transfiguration was by now firmly established in its additional home on the Isle of Cumbrae. The members continued to use their small huts in the cathedral rose garden for times of retreat and solitude.

With the departure of the Hippies, the Provost of the Cathedral of the Isles was glad to offer the premises of the College of the Holy Spirit as accommodation to another pioneering if more conventional enterprise, a team from Youth With a Mission. Known by its abbreviated title, YWAM, this organisation was founded in California in 1960 by a young married couple, Loren and Darlene Cunningham. They had a vision of a world-wide movement of young people afire with faith and proclaiming faith among others. Non-denominational, non-profit-making and dedicated to harnessing the energy of young people for the purpose of evangelism, YWAM swiftly grew from small beginnings into the world-wide movement its founders had hoped for. At the time of writing, it has an estimated 20,000 workers in 171 countries. The team who worked on the Isle of Cumbrae occupied part of the North College and regularly brought young people from the mainland to spend days or weeks in training for their outreach activities. As together they shared the resources of the remote cathedral site, the Community of the Transfiguration were on the friendliest of terms with the YWAM leaders and with their young visitors from the industrial central belt of Scotland.

During the two years in which YWAM were based on Cumbrae, the leaders were delighted when Roland accepted their request to spend time with them, reflecting theologically on their faith and their work. Roland drew on his gift for expressing familiar subjects in new and invigorating ways. He established a course of Bible study and contemplation, meeting with them weekly when he was on the island. From these simple meetings, the leaders drew inspiration for their personal lives and for the work in which they shared.

Eventually, however, the remoteness of the island and the complexities of reaching it by train and then sea-ferry meant that the YWAM team decided they must relocate their work to the mainland. Their initial two-year lease of the premises at the cathedral was not renewed.

The bishop, however, was keen to put the accommodation at the cathedral to good use. He learned of potential new tenants, an Anglican religious community whose qualities seemed impeccable, and whose origins and practice seemed especially appropriate to the cathedral and to the College of the Holy Spirit. They were called 'the Community of Celebration'. With their musical outreach teams, 'the Fisherfolk', they had already earned a name for their gifted contribution to Church life and musical worship on both sides of the Atlantic.

The Community of Celebration grew out of the activities of the Church of the Redeemer in Houston, Texas. Redeemer had been a faltering Episcopal congregation in the district of Eastwood in inner-city Houston, Texas, when the Revd Graham Pulkingham was appointed rector in 1963. In 1964, Graham felt that he experienced a spiritual conversion through the prayers of David Wilkerson, a New York preacher renowned for his ministry to street gangs in Brooklyn, as narrated in his book *The Cross and the Switchblade*. With a new energy following his dramatic encounter with David Wilkerson, Graham led the transformation of the Church of the Redeemer from a threadbare little organisation scarcely able to survive, into a vibrant Church community in which people experienced personal renewal and where they dedicated themselves to communal disciplines of service and saw themselves as expressing mutually the love of Christ for the world. The members of this revitalised Church community were in no doubt that their vigour was a direct consequence of the Holy Spirit of God at work in them. They felt themselves to be people under the influence of the Holy Spirit. There was fervent worship, with singing from a thousand voices; there were healings; there was speaking in tongues. The Church of the Redeemer gained a reputation for being the leading Church of its time, and in 1971 CBS-TV aired an hour-long programme about it. In the following year, 'The widely-read *Guideposts* magazine chose Redeemer as "Church of the Year".'[1]

By 1971, the Redeemer membership already counted more than 1,400 active participants, more than one third of them living 'in community'. Graham Pulkingham himself, by then a preacher with a dramatic presence and a scintillating use of language, was a supremely confident leader. He was at the centre of the Church households' developing programme. Those in the Church community lived together, not as family units but as 'households' – gatherings of families and individuals numbering from 15 to 25 or 30 people. They shared salaries and worked hard to transform their low-income communities. Leadership of the Church households was exercised by the rector Graham Pulkingham and a small number of elders. And new ideas and new policies were introduced by the rector as he felt the Spirit moving him.

The Episcopal Church of the United States was invigorated by the charismatic contribution from Redeemer. In 1971, it seemed to Graham that it was time for him and the Redeemer community to take the new life of the Holy Spirit to the home of the Anglican Communion: to England. Cuthbert Bardsley, the Bishop of Coventry, invited Graham to come to Coventry and to lead some days with the clergy of his diocese. Graham confided in him, saying he had a vision that God would bring him to work in Cuthbert's diocese. A year later, Bardsley invited him to come with a group from Redeemer to spend three years in the Coventry Diocese. On this invitation, Graham launched out from Houston with a household of 25 people and arrived in Coventry near the end of 1972.

Remembering this significant migration from Redeemer, one of the original household said, 'We arrived in 1972, and early in

1973 there were 25 of us all living in a little bungalow called The Smithy, and we went to St Michael's Church in Potter's Green just outside Coventry. We were so overcrowded in The Smithy that some of us would work all night and sleep during the daytime, because there were not enough beds for us all to be able to sleep at the same time! And we were always leading singing events in the Cathedral and in parishes round about.'

Soon they were at the very centre of 'the Charismatic Movement' in England, sponsored by a recently founded Fountain Trust. As their numbers grew, they sought larger residential premises. They moved to Berkshire, to a 40-roomed house which formerly had been a convent of Anglican Benedictine nuns, Yeldall Manor. They went there at the invitation of the Benedictine monks of Nashdom Abbey, into whose care Yeldall Manor had come. By this time, the musical skills of the Community of Celebration, their voices and their instrumental talents, were sought after by many church groups. Three separate groups of the Fisherfolk travelled to lead worship at conferences and other Christian events all over England and also in Europe and the USA. 'The Community was by then over a hundred people, working with the local parish.'[2] The original household from Redeemer in Houston had been augmented by people from Britain, Canada and Sweden. Graham had made contact with another, smaller Christian community in Dorset. Sir Tom Lees and his wife Faith had established a religious community in Post Green, in buildings which had been in the Lees family for generations. Faith Lees sensed that her community was at a point where it was ready to come into close relationship with the Community of Celebration.

At this point, Graham received an invitation from Richard Wimbush, Episcopal Bishop of Argyll and the Isles. He invited Graham to accept the post of Provost of the Cathedral of Argyll and the Isles in Millport, and to bring the Community of Celebration to take up residence in the adjacent College of the Holy Spirit. From Berkshire's Yeldall Manor and from Dorset's Post Green, an advance party of the Community of Celebration arrived in Millport in February 1975. They made the North College ready for their companions, with YWAM still occupying the

South College. 'There they had landed, an island of American Episcopalians surrounded by an ocean of Presbyterian Scots.'[3] As other groups arrived from the south, their numbers increased, and they began to establish their new patterns of life.

The new residents were taken by surprise to find the well-established presence of the Community of the Transfiguration. In particular, the fact that the Transfiguration had their four wooden retreat huts located in the cathedral's rose garden led to Graham Pulkingham confronting Roland.

Graham was particularly unsettled by the Community of the Transfiguration's apparent lack of concern about its own future. Roland had described the Transfiguration Community to some of the Celebration members as being like a little rubber duck bobbing about on the waves, by comparison with the great ocean liner which was the Community of Celebration. Graham was clearly uneasy at having to share any space on the cathedral premises with people from the Community of the Transfiguration.

'What is your policy about children?' asked Graham of Roland, as if he feared that the children of the Celebration community might be lured away. These two men were both strong individuals, and they were both leaders. Graham seemed uneasy at sharing the space even of the rose garden with another Community, and he was not willing to yield ground to Roland.

John Halsey recalled, 'Our relationship with them through the rest of that session showed that the island was too small for both communities. So, we removed from the island and thought of closing our Cumbrae end all down. But our Warden, Mother Mary Clare of the Sisters of the Love of God, had other advice for us. In prophetic words, she said, "No. Keep a foothold on the island. In ten years they'll be gone and you will be there still!"'[4] Accordingly, the Community purchased a small house on Cumbrae, in George Street, the quiet back street of Millport. They called it 'the Snoopy House' in honour of the kennel of Charlie Brown's dog in the famous comic strip 'Peanuts' by the US cartoonist Charles Schulz. Despite the cool relations with the Community of Celebration, people from Roslin would still spend occasional weeks on retreat in the Snoopy House.

Having once withdrawn from their huts in the cathedral rose garden, however, the Community of the Transfiguration had no wish to disturb or annoy the new residents of the Cathedral of the Isles. The Community of Celebration continued to contribute to the wider Church through their composition of music for worship. To their acclaimed song-books, *Sounds of Living Waters* and *Fresh Sounds,* and recordings, which they had produced in their days in England, they now added a further volume, *Cry Hosannah!* and a companion album. The royalties from book sales and musical recordings brought a considerable income for several years. In addition, they purchased the local bakery in Millport and added its revenues to the common purse which financed their Community's life. They continued to live their well-organised community existence, hard-working within and beyond the cathedral premises, prudent and thrifty in expenditure, and with communal worship at their centre.

For a year or so, there was no direct communication between the Community of Celebration and the Roslin Community. There were two people, however, who remained close to both communities. Brant Pelphrey, the American student at New College who thought so much of Roland, paid regular visits to Cumbrae and the Community of Celebration. He consistently spoke well of Roslin to the Celebration people, and of the Celebration people to Roslin. A man called Kevin Bean frequently visited Roslin, and he was close to Graham Pulkingham. When he was at Roslin, Kevin would praise the Community on Cumbrae: 'These are very gifted people; you really should get together with them.' At the cathedral, he would praise Roland to Graham: 'This man is a saint and has incredible wisdom and understanding. You should get to know him.'

On a brief return visit to the USA Graham was relating to a bishop the vigorous life of the Community of Celebration. The bishop praised the hard work and the worship. 'That's not bad', he said, 'for a two-legged stool.' Graham asked what he meant. 'I don't see the place in your Community's life for silence, prayer and contemplation. A religious community will not endure without this aspect.'[5] Graham pondered this observation, and when he returned to Cumbrae he introduced the issue into discussion within the Community.

Eventually, when Roland was spending a week on retreat at the Snoopy House, he walked up to the cathedral to talk with Graham. After they had had a cup of tea, Graham invited Roland to come to the cathedral library. Most of the Cumbrae Community members were gathered there as Roland and Graham spoke together. One of them recalled, 'I can still remember it. It was a wonderful occasion. They were over by the window, the two of them. They shook hands. People were moved to tears by it. Maybe they embraced. I can't remember. No. I think they shook hands.'

Graham invited Roland to address the gathered members. A published account preserves that singular moment.

'People sat in every available space. As Roland sat down he said, "I think this is an absolutely remarkable group of people." They were warming to him already, encouraged that this man with a reputation for being a giant of the faith should think them remarkable.

'"Do you know why?" he continued.

'They thought. "Is it because of our worship life? Because of our theological understanding? Or what ...?"

'Roland turned to Graham and pointing at him said, "Because you have been able to live with this appalling man all these years!"

'He brought the house down because, of course, to live and work with a prophet like Graham can be hard work indeed!'[6]

This meeting signalled a turning point in the relationship between the two Communities. Roslin remained wary of the Community of Celebration. But Graham welcomed the introduction of Roland into the pattern of life in the cathedral. Here in Roland, on the very doorstep, was a man of genuine and profound contemplative character, able to offer access to what Graham had come to recognise as a missing element in the Community's life.

This step opened the door to a new relationship. When these two were reconciled, people began to go to Roslin on retreat. Some began using the Community of the Transfiguration's huts for quiet days. Roland started a theological course. A small group of Celebration members met to plan the course with Roland, and thus to educate the whole Celebration community. Graham recognised that Roland was a major theologian. Five members of Celebration sat down with Roland to draw up a suitable course. Their Community at that time numbered about 50. With little delay, a sixth member arrived at the classes, Pat Allen. Pat was a long-standing member of Celebration. She had grown up in the USA in a family who followed the religious traditions of the Southern Baptists. The fervent atmosphere of the Church of the Redeemer, the exuberance of the musical side of its worship, and the warmth of its household fellowships, had made it possible for Pat to leave the strict Biblical certainties of her family church and to become an Episcopalian and a fully engaged member of the Redeemer. She was enthusiastic at each stage of the developments in the Community of Celebration which had brought them to England and now to Scotland. Already, Roland's words about the importance of silence in prayer and contemplation had touched a chord in her. She joined the theology course.

The course got under way and ran through into 1980 and 1981 and 1982. The Community arranged work schedules so that the students could attend, in spite of their own demanding work schedule. The Community had the farm to run, and the guest house, and the bakery. And that was in addition to the musical and worship side of the Community of Celebration's work.

By this time, Roland had withdrawn from teaching at New College in Edinburgh University. Here on Cumbrae, he drew up a course covering Church history, Biblical theology and Bible study. Not attempting to turn people into academic theologians, Roland nevertheless wanted to help the members of the Community of Celebration to reflect theologically on their own experience. They soon discovered that, in contrast to the experience of their childhood years, this learning process under Roland was not competitive. They worked co-operatively and with mutual encouragement. Clearly, Roland recognised the remarkable commitment and devotion within the members of the Community.

One of the Community members later went on to do a three-year course in theology at university. 'But nothing that I learned in those three years had the influence on me that those meetings with Roland had,' he said.

Roland's presence alongside the Community of Celebration also opened the awareness of the Cumbrae Community to the significance of the poor. An essential element of the life of the Community of the Transfiguration, explicitly articulated, enshrined, in their Rule, was an association with the poor. They understood Jesus to be actually present in and among the poor. The Cumbrae Community noted that, when Roland was on Cumbrae, he was often visited by tramps and by people with nothing. His own appearance tended to confirm his companionship with the poor – one of the Celebration Community recalled, 'He could look as if he'd just stepped out of a rubbish-bin.' In their earliest years in the Church of the Redeemer in Houston, the Celebration Community had had a sharp focus on the needs of the poor in the inner-city district of Eastwood. But the busy musical years in England and in Scotland had diluted their attention to the poor. Roland and the Transfiguration gave new impetus to their recognition of the importance of the poor in the proclamation of the Gospel.

The Isle of Cumbrae is situated in the Firth of Clyde, on the approach to the nuclear submarine base in the Holy Loch. Members of the Community of Celebration went on marches and demonstrations to express revulsion at the global deployment of nuclear weapons of mass destruction. The Community of the Transfiguration is indissolubly bound to the nuclear issue by the fact that the Church has since early centuries celebrated the Feast of the Transfiguration on 6 August. On that very date, 6 August, in 1945, the Allies exploded the first nuclear bomb over Hiroshima. The new contemplative dimension which Celebration were discovering through Roland drew them deeply into this urgent reality. One of the English members of Celebration writes, 'Although the Community [of Celebration] had always had a special concern for those in need, prayer and contemplation under Roland Walls' guidance moved this beyond pastoral concern into a deeper understanding of the social and political dimensions of the gospel.'[7]

By now, Pat Allen was finding within herself a need for greater solitude, for opportunities to be on her own. This was in order, as she would say, to listen to God in prayer and through the Bible. With the help of Roland, she began to discover in herself a vocation to the contemplative life. The Community of Celebration welcomed Roland's readiness to guide Pat in her search. Pat was a richly gifted member of the Community. An accomplished pianist, a song-writer with a wonderful soprano voice, she was an outstanding member of the Fisherfolk, who were invigorating the public worship of congregations in Britain, Europe and the USA. On Cumbrae, she was a hard-working member of the team who ran the local baker's shop, and very popular with the customers. She was the regular accompanist for the choir, and she was much in demand for giving piano lessons. She was a most valuable contributor to the corporate life of the Community. Consequently, her gradual withdrawal from her accustomed activities caused distress to many of her companions. More and more of her time she gave to silence and quiet prayer, contemplating the life and death of Jesus. Yet, in her continuing wish to share in the Community's life, she set up a quiet room in the South College, simply furnished, with a shelf of books on prayer and meditation. At first just one or two, but then more, people began to take a quiet day, a day of retreat, in the room which Pat had prepared.

In the quiet room, Pat placed a small basket of broken shells she had collected. Beside the basket stood a card with these words:

> If you find a shell among these broken ones that you especially like, please take it. They hold a certain beauty not found in whole shells. Their brokenness exposes their interior. With them nothing is hidden. We, like them, are broken people. And yet our brokenness, like theirs, is a very precious gift. It exposes the true source of our life and living, Christ himself. Don't hide your brokenness. It is the gift of your own uniqueness.[8]

As Pat progressively withdrew from the communal life, she took to living in one or other of the retreat huts in the rose garden. There she endured the wind and rain of the summer and the snow of the winter. Eventually, she moved to a room in Millport before setting out to stay with Sister Patty Burgess of the Community of the Transfiguration in that Community's little flat in Loanhead. Pat Allen lodged with Patty Burgess for a year as she came to a fuller understanding of her sense of direction. She was received into the Roman Catholic Church in a service in Loanhead, and shortly afterwards set course for Jerusalem, drawn there by the city's place in the life of Jesus.

For the next 15 years, she lived as a hermit not far from Jerusalem, offering her solitude and her prayers as the sum of her life. In the often violent political atmosphere of those years in Israel, her hermitage continued to be sheltered in the grounds of a convent. When she became seriously ill, she was cared for by the sisters until her death in November 2011. In May 2012, a memorial service was held for her in Millport, in the Cathedral of the Isles, to which friends came from Cumbrae and other parts of Scotland, from England and the USA, and from Sweden and Germany.

The advent of Roland and contact with the contemplative life of the Roslin Community impacted more on Pat Allen than on any other member of the Community of Celebration. Yet, through Pat's own influence, and through Roland's continuing engagement with the Community on Cumbrae, several other people were moved to explore their own aptitude for a monastic life.

Very many of those who spent time as members of the Community of Celebration knew it as a richly positive experience. Sadly not all, as later became clear. After ten years on the Isle of Cumbrae, a variety of factors influenced Graham to bring the Community's occupancy of the Cathedral of the Isles and the College of the Holy Spirit to an end. A new Bishop of Argyll and the Isles had been appointed, who was not so much in tune with the Community of Celebration as his predecessor had been. It was not certain that the Community's lease of the premises would be renewed. The Community now had a smaller number of members, and its musical creativity was diminished. The association with the Church of the Redeemer in Houston had weakened, and Redeemer no longer remitted donations to support the work of the Community of Celebration. In addition, Graham was unsuccessful in his request that Sir Tom Lees of Post Green should make his ancestral buildings and lands over to the Community of Celebration. Graham sent out a request to the Community's supporters and friends, asking them to contribute to a target figure of $1.1 million to sustain the Community's work in Scotland.

A new opportunity presented itself, however, in an invitation from Alden Hathaway, the Bishop of Pittsburgh, asking the Community to relocate and to continue its work in Aliquippa, a small town in Pennsylvania. The Community sent Graham, together with Bill Farra from the leadership team, to review the possibilities of this proposal. On their return, and after discussion in the Community, it was agreed that the time had come for them to make this new commitment. It seemed to the people of Millport that it was a sudden decision. It was a decision which removed up to 35 people from the already small local community, and it gave rise to much disappointment and sorrow. But, at Pentecost in 1985, the Community of Celebration brought to an end its ten years on Cumbrae and launched into the new phase of its life in Aliquippa.

Sadly, in the USA, a complaint was lodged against Graham about the conduct of a pastoral relationship. The details were set out in a book by a journalist who had at one time been a member of the Community of Celebration.[9] When the facts of the case were intimated to Hathaway, the Bishop of Pittsburgh, in 1992, he suspended Graham Pulkingham from his ministry, pending a Church enquiry into the allegations and accusations.

Wide publicity was given in the press to the fall from grace of this man who had been held in the highest esteem by Church and civic leaders, and who had led the Charismatic Movement in Churches in the USA, in England, Scotland, Australia and South Africa. The following year, before the Church authorities had advanced the case towards a hearing, or arrangements had been made for damages or reparations to be paid to people who had been adversely affected by Graham's actions, there ensued a further act in the drama. With his wife Betty, Graham was shopping in a supermarket in Burlington in North Carolina. A deranged gunman entered the store to settle a score with his former girlfriend, and opened fire from a point near the Pulkinghams. Two women were shot dead before the police arrived and shot the gunman dead. In the intensity of the action, Graham fell to the floor. He had suffered a heart-attack which was to prove fatal. He died in hospital not long afterwards.

At the time of writing, the Community of Celebration still exercises a ministry in All Souls parish in Aliquippa, Pennsylvania. But the death of Graham Pulkingham constituted a sad epilogue to the phenomenal Cumbrae years of the Community of Celebration. And to those positive achievements the Community of the Transfiguration had made its own valuable contribution.

10

The Jewishness of Jesus

Simon Hughes, a young Baptist piano teacher, was intrigued when he first encountered Patty Burgess of the Community of the Transfiguration. She was speaking in the Episcopal Church in Dalkeith on the evening of the World Day of Prayer. Simon could not help noticing that she was wearing, as a skirt, a small carpet inside out. Here was a contemplative nun addressing the ecumenical gathering, dressed in what might once have been someone's prayer-mat.

But it was not only the way she dressed that captivated Simon. His interest was caught by the topic on which Patty was speaking. She explained that each Friday evening, in the Christian Community to which she belonged, they observed some of the rituals of the Jewish Sabbath. The detail which impacted most vividly upon him was the covering of the knives.

'Why do the observant Jews cover the knives? On the Sabbath, their thoughts are of peace and harmony,' said Patty. 'The knife is seen as a weapon of war and violence. So, the knives are covered to remove from sight any visible token of the violence of the world. The Sabbath bread is then broken apart by hand, and pieces are given to everyone present. It is a way of giving a sign of peace.'

In Judaism, the day is not from midnight to midnight but from sunset to sunset. Thus the Sabbath, which is Saturday, begins at sunset on Friday night. So, every Friday evening, the Community members, and any guests who happened to be with them, sat together round the plain wooden table in the kitchen, in imitation of the pattern which devout Jewish families follow on the Sabbath eve. The Community's Sabbath observance was not limited, however, merely to the covering of the knives. They adopted other elements of the Sabbath ritual. First, they would light two candles to welcome the Sabbath, and offer a prayer of blessing on the Sabbath. Then came a prayer of blessing focusing on the cup of wine and a prayer of blessing on the bread, and recalling God's deliverance of the Hebrews from their slavery in Egypt.

The decision to celebrate each Friday evening as a Jewish Sabbath meal, and the Saturday as a Sabbath day of rest, was made following discussion at several of the Community's monthly chapter meetings. Since the founding of the Community in 1965, they had consciously and deliberately invested a 'Sabbath' element in the pattern of their life. The Hebrew word *Shabat* means 'cessation' or 'time of rest'. Each day, there was the hour of Silence. Each month, there was a full 24-hour retreat, and annually the eight-day retreat. So, the introduction of Sabbath prayers on a Friday evening was simply an extension of an already valued arrangement.

By celebrating the Friday evening as the beginning of the Sabbath, the Community elevated Friday evenings to a new and significant role in their week. Their communal life of prayer, work and hospitality had an unremitting tempo, and there often seemed no opportunity for relaxation. The introduction of the Sabbath, therefore, gave a celebratory atmosphere to the Friday evening, and in addition it underlined the dedication of Saturday as a day not for work but for recreation.

It was not the need for a rest, however, which motivated the Community to introduce this development. No. It was part of a deliberate strategy to explore the Jewishness of Jesus. In Britain, it had proved perfectly possible to profess the Christian faith, and to believe that Jesus is the Son of God, and faithfully to recite the 150 Psalms, without really noticing that Jesus was a Jew. The Community of the Transfiguration were daily chanting the Psalms and reading the Gospels; and, as the years passed, the realisation gradually dawned that they had not given sufficient attention to the simple truth that Jesus was a Jew, his mother a Jewess. Although in their daily reading and their meditative study of the Bible they had acknowledged Jesus as belonging to first-century Israel, they were unreflectively in thrall to the age-old Christian theology which held the Jews responsible for Jesus' death. Through the centuries, the Christian Church has persistently seen the Jews as 'deicides' – killers of God – and on these grounds has repeatedly been hostile to their presence in Christian communities and Christian countries. Again and again, the Church was adamant in its opposition to Jews, endorsing their expulsion from one country after another in the name of the Christian Christ, Jew though he was. It was almost as if the Crucifixion had uncoupled Jesus from his Jewish heritage and delivered him into the Christian Church.

There is no record of the occasion which brought this realisation home to the Community at Roslin, or of the individual member who drew attention to it. In the mid-1970s, however, the Roslin Community did come to recognise that they had effectively ignored the Jewishness of Jesus. They saw an urgent need, now, to investigate the connection between the Jewish Jesus and the continuing Jewish community of today. Not only did they introduce these weekly Sabbath celebrations, but they also began a course of purposeful reading. As a means to learning how Jews understood themselves in the last part of the twentieth century, the Community began to read novels by contemporary Jewish writers.

They were well served by the first writer to whose works they were directed, Chaim Potok. Potok was born in the USA in 1929, the son of Polish immigrant parents. From a strict Orthodox Jewish upbringing, Potok excelled at English and in his rabbinical studies, and became a rabbi and a writer. While it would be a mistake to identify Potok himself too closely with the central character of his first major novel, *The Chosen*, nevertheless the time and action of the narrative cohere closely with the details of Potok's own life. *The Chosen* is set in the mid-twentieth century, in New York City. This story of two friends takes place over a period of six years, beginning in 1944 when the protagonists are 15 years old. It is set against the backdrop of the historical events of the time: the death of President Roosevelt, the end of the Second World War, the revelation of the Holocaust in Europe, and the struggle for the creation of the state of Israel. The book's storyline introduces the Gentile reader to several important themes in twentieth-century Judaism. The narrative includes a portrayal of the strict disciplines of life in an Orthodox Jewish family; it displays some of the different strands of the Jewish tradition – the Talmudic path of studying the Law, and the Hasidic expectation of mystical contact with the spirit of God; and it demonstrates the significance, for post-Holocaust Judaism, of the creation of the state of Israel. All the members of the Community of the Transfiguration became absorbed in reading this and other novels of Potok, and began to recognise the affinity of these Jewish intellectual and spiritual struggles with their Community's own quest for an authentic religious life.

In a later novel, *My Name is Asher Lev*, Potok explored the conflict between tradition and individualism, and the tension between religion and art. This book seems to embrace much of Potok's own life and character. Asher Lev of the book's title has grown up in New York and been brought up in a Hasidic family, focused on the Jewish spiritual traditions which flourished in Eastern Europe in the late eighteenth century. Asher Lev's childhood is set in the 1950s, a time of the persecution of Jews in Soviet Russia under Stalin. Asher Lev's brilliant artistic gift is anathema to his profoundly religious father, and the Hasidic community regard art as at best a waste of time, and at worst as sacrilege. Asher Lev knows that his mother has been through terrible sufferings, grief at the loss of her brother, and fears for her husband on his travels into Eastern Europe. There comes a time when Asher Lev is moved to paint his feelings for his mother's long, solitary suffering. 'His search for an artistic motif reveals none powerful enough in his own tradition, and so he turns to the central theme of suffering in the Christian tradition: crucifixion. In the eyes of most Jews, crucifixion instantaneously triggers images of rivers of Jewish blood because of the thousands upon thousands of Jews who died all down through the centuries on account of the charge that they participated in the slaying of Jesus. But Asher Lev knows no other symbol can give full expression to the feelings that he has about his mother's long torment.'[1]

Even though he knows it will precipitate a breach with his father and the whole Hasidic community to which he has belonged,

Asher Lev paints his supreme work of art, expressing there the suffering of the Jews and the sufferings of his own mother. And the painting is a crucifixion, 'The Brooklyn Crucifixion'. The family and the Hasidic community ask him to leave. Asher goes away, not wanting to inflict further pain on the ones he loves.

In the eulogy he delivered at Chaim Potok's funeral, his friend Rabbi Jeffrey Tigay said, 'Chaim's books opened a window to the Jewish soul for Jew and non-Jew alike'.[2] And indeed his books were effective for the Roslin Community in revealing to them the Jewish soul.

From other authors, the Community learned about the Jewish tradition of 'the Just Man', the 'Tzadik', 'the righteous man who suffers'. The Talmud says that at least 36 of them – anonymous 'just men' – are living among us in all times, and it is for their sake alone that the world is not destroyed.[3] A persistent motif among the Jews in times of persecution and suffering is the appearance among them of someone who seems to transcend the cruelty and violence of the time. This man, often not recognised until after his death, moves among the suffering men, women and children dispensing kindness and encouragement, reflecting with wisdom on the goodness of God. And in due time this Just Man himself falls beneath the blows of persecution, sometimes taking the place of someone who, but for the Just Man substituting himself, was himself doomed to violent death. This is the theme of *The Last of the Just* by André Schwarz-Bart.

The book was published in English in 1960. Schwarz-Bart the author was the son of a Polish Jewish family murdered by the Nazis, and he based the story on a Hebrew legend. Schwarz-Bart imagines the story of the Levys, one family in which the role of the Just Man was hereditary. They have suffered death down the ages, beginning with the massacre of the Jews of York in England in 1185. In later generations, this wandering Jewish family suffers at the hands of the Spanish and Portuguese Inquisitions; they are expelled from one area after another; the Cossacks add their contribution; and, when we come to the late nineteenth century, the family leaves its home in Zemyock in Russian Poland and settles in Germany. At this stage, there are three generations of the family, all Just Men in the making. (Unsurprisingly, one reviewer of the novel criticises its gender-chauvinism.[4]) The saga ends with the story of a schoolboy, Ernie Levy, the last of them all, who perished in an Auschwitz gas-chamber while comforting a terrified flock of orphaned children. Ernie being without descendants, the world is now one Just Man short of the saving 36.

The piercing insights of these authors illuminated for the Roslin Community the sensitivities of post-Holocaust Judaism. The authors wrestled with the huge questions of human existence, its purpose, the origins of hatred, the fragility of each human life and the mercurial nature of hope. It was inevitable that the Community of the Transfiguration would soon begin to discover, beyond even the nightmare quality of what they already knew, the depths of suffering and horror that lay within the history of the Holocaust. They found some writings of Elie Wiesel in a volume published in 1974: *Night, Dawn, The Accident – Three Tales.*[5] In the first tale, *Night*, Wiesel recounts how, as a youth of 14, he was rounded up with all the other Jews from his village of Sighet in Transylvania and transported with them to Auschwitz in cattle trucks. Within hours of the family's arrival at the camp, his mother and sister were taken off to be gassed and incinerated. Elie and his father were imprisoned in a long hut with 100 others in preparation for an unimaginable future. This youth, already a mystic seeking to hasten the coming of the Messiah by his prayers and his fasting, saw everything he had loved, everything he had lived for, consumed by the fires of the crematorium. In the darkness, the ashes of his sister and his mother and a thousand others flew from the tall chimneys into the clouds of the night sky, his faith with them.

The testimony of Wiesel and of other Holocaust survivors entered the consciousness of the Community of the Transfiguration, and their outlook was thereby permanently transformed. The Holocaust became for them the defining image, the touchstone, of the undeserved mortal sufferings of the poor. It was to affect almost everything that the Community did thereafter.

In 1980, a friend of Roland and John Halsey wrote a book about the causes of the Holocaust, implicating the Church in the centuries-long process of creating a climate of hatred towards the

Jews.[6] Alan Ecclestone was known in his day as the most radical and challenging of Church of England parish priests. For 27 years he was the vicar of Darnall, an industrial town at the edge of Sheffield. Ecclestone was attuned to the plight of the very poor. Even through the years of the Cold War, he maintained his membership of the Communist Party and sold the Communist newspapers the *Daily Worker* and the *Morning Star* outside the local factory gates on a Friday. His wife Delia sold the Communist papers outside the church after the Sunday morning service.

Painstakingly in his book, he analysed the way that over the centuries the Church had developed a theology which held the Jews to blame for the death of the Christians' Saviour. He traced how the Church had endorsed and promoted anti-Semitism in earlier centuries, and he saw that the Church in the twentieth century connived at and acquiesced in the Nazi persecution of the Jews. 'The train-loads of Jews on their way to the death camps passed through countrysides dotted with Christian spires.'[7] For the Community of the Transfiguration, Ecclestone's book articulated a theological critique of the Churches' complicity in anti-Semitism and the Holocaust. Furthermore, Ecclestone called upon the Christian Churches to recognise the connection between the fate of the Jewish people in modern Europe and the crucified Jew who appears in the Church's stained-glass windows. He went so far as to say that Scripture's images of the bruised and battered servant of God,[8] and the crucified Christ, are to be recognised in the crisis of the Holocaust. 'I am compelled to believe, by the Scriptural faith for which we are indebted to the Jews, that the iniquity of us all, including the specific iniquities of Christians like myself, was laid on the Jews. I am an onlooker at the crucifixion.'[9]

So highly did the Community regard this book that they wrote inside the front cover, 'Not to be lent out to Anyone!' The book helped the Community to recognise the Holocaust's critical significance for the Christian Church and for the Church's understanding of itself.

With the passing years, the Community grew in their understanding of the Jewishness of Jesus, and increasingly they registered the cruel inhumanity manifested in the Holocaust. In their daily reciting of the Psalms, they now found themselves compelled to listen with Jewish ears: to imagine the Jews in the death camps reciting the Psalms of gratitude while enduring unimaginable privation; to picture the Jews awaiting execution while appealing to the merciful Lord for help which did not come. This daily acknowledgement of the Holocaust was accentuated in other ways. The Community gathered some of the ashes from their fireplace, placed them in an empty tobacco tin, and laid the tin on the floor below the crucifix in the chapel. These ashes were symbolic of the millions who had perished in the Holocaust. In addition, as we shall see, other tokens of the Jewish experience were placed in the little wooden chapel, at the focal point of their times of worship.

Writings by other Jewish survivors deepened the Community's engagement with the Holocaust. Such books were a constituent part of the Community's diet of reading. The Community in 1985 watched the nine-and-a-half-hour documentary film *Shoah*. 'Shoah' is the Hebrew word meaning 'the Holocaust'. The film was edited from 350 hours of filmed interviews with people connected with the Holocaust. The interviewees were survivors or bystanders or perpetrators of the programme to eliminate the Jews of Europe. The film demonstrated that the plan to exterminate the Jews required some people to be actively applying the policy, and many others to acquiesce in it without resistance or complaint. The overall effect of the film was to confirm that far more people than would admit it knew of the attempt to destroy the Jewish race.

As their reading programme continued, the Community were transfixed by a 25-page story by a Lithuanian Jewish writer, Zvi Kolitz, first published in 1999.[10] Purporting to be a diary found in the ruins of the Warsaw Ghetto, the story presents Yosl Rakover, a Jewish man defiantly confronting the God in whom he has always believed. Even though he can see that God is allowing his Chosen People to be savagely destroyed, Yosl Rakover warns God that nothing will stop him believing in Him. 'You have done everything to make me lose my faith in You, to make me cease to believe in You. But I die exactly as I have lived, an unshakeable believer in You.'[11]

The Community's concentration on their Jewish theme imparted an added dimension to their prayers and to many of their actions. Roland felt very strongly that, liturgically in their pattern of worship, the Christian Church ought to recognise the Holocaust at the same level as Christ's death on the cross at Calvary. He proposed that the crucifixion of God's people should be observed liturgically in Holy Week.

Then in 1983, while the Community were still advancing in their exploration of the Jewishness of Jesus and in their engagement with contemporary Judaism, a young man arrived at the house, ready to enter the Community as a novice. His name was Jonathan Jamal. Son of an Anglican vicar, he was a Christian, and he was a Palestinian.

'I first met Roland in 1976,' said Jonathan.[12] 'My mother brought us all up for a week on Iona. It was a week on the topic of 'Prayer and Politics', and it was led by Roland. We spent a whole week in the abbey. My young brother Ben Jamal said of Roland, "He looks a right tramp". I never for a moment thought that one day I'd be in the Community.'

Jonathan wanted to belong to a community. He made approaches to a series of religious communities before coming to ask advice from Roland and the Roslin Community. They advised Jonathan to go and spend a year with the Anglican monks of Crawley Down in West Sussex, the Community of the Servants of the Will of God. He stayed there until October 1982 but sensed he was not going to be at home in a denominational community. He hoped to find one able to welcome a wider range of traditions, an ecumenical community. So he applied to Roslin, and in January 1983 he arrived; and there he would spend the next 14 years of his life.

Jonathan shared in every aspect of the Community's religious life, including the Sabbath prayers on the Friday evening. With other members of the Community, also, he took his place attending the regular meetings in Edinburgh of the Council of Christians and Jews. The Council aimed to facilitate relationships between the Churches and the synagogues, and to encourage greater mutual understanding. The Community of the Transfiguration were already alert to the tensions still arising from the establishing of the state of Israel in 1947 and the ensuing displacement of a million Palestinians from their homes. But their interest in the Holocaust overshadowed the Palestinian issue. With Jonathan now in their midst, the Community had a heightened awareness of the way that the government of Israel set limits on the freedoms of the Palestinians in Israel.

Still in pursuit of a closer relationship with the Jewish community, Roland went to visit an Edinburgh rabbi to discuss the possibility of the Roslin Community standing with the Jewish people on *Yom Ha Shoah*, Holocaust Memorial Day. Roland explained that, on Friday evenings, the Community were saying the traditional Sabbath prayers. He spoke of the Community's engagement with contemporary Jewish literature, and their shame at the Churches' complicity in the Holocaust, and their desire to embrace the Jewishness of Jesus. 'But you are just playing at this,' responded the rabbi. 'The problem lies in your Book, the New Testament.' And, as for Roslin being associated with the Jewish community at the commemoration of the Holocaust, the rabbi – on whose study wall hung a large contemporary map of Israel – was unenthusiastic.

Around this time, Jonathan's father, the Revd Khalil Jamal, sent to the Roslin Community a book by David Gilmour, *Dispossessed: The Ordeal of the Palestinians 1917–1980*.[13] 'Roland read it,' said Jonathan, 'and it shook him.' Gilmour's detailed presentation of the history confirmed the Community's apprehensions about the plight of the Palestinians in Israel. 'The Community began to think that perhaps I was sent by God,' Jonathan recalled. 'But at that time I knew very little about my family's background in Palestine.'

Spurred on by the Community's interest, Jonathan learned from his father about the history of his family's place in Palestinian Christianity. His father was from an ancient Christian family who proudly traced their roots to their conversion through the preaching of the Apostles in Jerusalem at Pentecost, 50 days after the resurrection of Christ from the dead. In the earliest centuries of Christianity they were part of the Eastern Orthodox Church, and in later centuries they were part of the Melkite Catholic Church.

In the 1800s, that Church excommunicated the family for something not at that time permitted, namely reading the Bible at home. The bishop of the Anglican Church in Jerusalem welcomed them, however, and Jonathan's great-grandfather Khalil Jamal was the first Arab to be ordained a priest in the Anglican Church. Here now was Jonathan, a fifth-generation Anglican from Palestine, entering the ecumenical Community of the Transfiguration.

The Community fully acknowledged its debt to the Jewish people as the cradle of Jesus Christ the Saviour and Messiah. They also sought constantly to express an ever-deeper compassion for the victims and survivors of the Holocaust. In addition, they acknowledged the significance of the establishing of the state of Israel in the time immediately following the Holocaust. However, the Community could not extend the same spirit of compassion to the policies of the government of the state of Israel towards the Palestinian people. Thus, with the arrival of Jonathan Jamal, there grew, alongside their horror at the Holocaust, an understanding of the suffering of the Palestinian people.

In 1985, Roland visited the Holy Land with a group from the Edinburgh Roman Catholic parish of St Ninian's. While he was there, he met with Father Elias Chacour of the Melkite Catholic Church. Chacour, a Palestinian Christian, was already an outstanding prophet of peace in Israel, working for reconciliation between Palestinians and Israelis, Christians and Jews. His book *Blood Brothers*, recounts how, when he was a child, all the family were put out of the family home and land in 1947 by armed Israelis, and became refugees in their own country.[14] Thereafter, Elias Chacour trained in Paris and was ordained in the Melkite Church. He undertook practical measures to build schools and hospitals for the Palestinians; he articulated the call for justice for the Palestinians who had been robbed of their homes and their land; and he emerged as a rare voice of hope and reconciliation. He and Roland found a common spiritual language.

In 1987, Scottish Churches House in Dunblane hosted a conference on the future of the Holy Land. Elias Chacour spoke from the Melkite Catholic Church in Palestine. Roland was the representative speaker from Scotland, and he gave an impassioned endorsement of the Palestinians' call for a just settlement for their refugees. Such contacts illustrated the Community's commitment to the Palestinians' cause in Israel/Palestine.

The Community had entered on a voyage to discover more about the Jewishness of Jesus. As their journey continued through the years, they discovered that their compassion had grown wider and deeper through the way they had entered into the darkness of the Holocaust. Now that experience delivered an unforeseen harvest. Their intensified compassion for the poorest and for the abandoned was able now to embrace the Palestinians, who were being so brutally treated by the Holocaust's children.

11

The Chapel

In many respects, the Community's premises are unique. Of no part is this more true than the chapel. There is a door in the green wooden screen which divides the front garden from the place of silence, the Enclosure. You must lift the latch, and push. But the door sticks. You have to push it hard to gain entry. A path of uneven paving stones leads you up through the long grass, past silver birch and beech, to the door of a wooden hut. Among the trees, one, two, three – altogether five – other smaller huts are located round the periphery of the garden. All are painted green, and roofed with mineral felt. This one, twice the size of the others, and erected at a total cost of £243, is the chapel.

Here is to be found the essence of the Community's life.

When you enter, the air carries a scent of candles and of the wild flowers in a vase. In front of you stands a tall reading desk, an open prayer-book on its sloping shelf. A low wooden bench stands along each side wall. A small table, the altar, is visible at the far end of the chapel.

Is there another chapel like this? With twigs and branches tapping on the window, and the scraping of birds' feet as they alight and walk along the roof?

Let me give you to Roland, as he looks at the features of the chapel and talks about them to a long-time friend of the Community, Lesley Reid.[1]

* * *

This little chapel has been here since 1965. It was built by 'Coffin Jock', who lives at Eddleston. I went to him and asked, 'Coffin Jock, do you make anything bigger than a coffin?'

He said, 'Yes.'

So I said, 'Would you make me a hut, ten feet by eight?'

And that was the first part of the chapel. Then we thought of putting another hut ten by eight and cutting a way through. So, here we are with two ten-by-eight huts. A local joiner who's been a friend of ours came and did the second one.

When you come in, your eyes go to the east end of the chapel, where there hangs one of the most important Christian works of art. It's called the Crucifix of San Damiano. This is a copy of it. This crucifix has a very curious history. The original was painted probably by a Syrian monk in the ninth or early tenth century. We have no idea how it got to a little church two miles from Assisi, at what is now known as San Damiano's. It was almost certainly brought as a piece of loot from the Crusades. The ordinary soldier took up anything he could carry and brought it home, either to sell it or to give it to his local church. A lot of Crusading loot came back to Europe.

That crucifix is famous for two reasons. The first is that it spoke to Francis of Assisi! As a young man, Francis lived a self-centred life. He was the leader of a gang of rich, laid-back hippies, and with a bit of self-regard he wanted to become a knight, and he'd been on a couple of expeditions inside Italy in the Wars of the City States. He has already had one conversion whereby he had renounced his family, famously standing naked before the bishop when his father was bringing him to court for having misused all his goods and sold them – a very expensive son. Now he comes into this ruined chapel and kneels before this crucifix in absolute emptiness, asking, 'What am I to do?' He has come to the end of his youth, and now in manhood he thinks he must give up everything and serve Christ. But he didn't know what to do. So there he was before the cross. And in the vision or whatever it was, the Christ on the cross turned his head to Francis and said, 'Francis! Build my Church!'

Francis looked around, and of course the church was in ruins, and he thought he had to rebuild the church he was in. So, he went and sold some more of his father's cloth, sold the horse he was riding, and came back with the money and rebuilt the church of San Damiano.

But it took him a lifetime to learn what that crucifix and its words meant – what Christ had meant with 'Build my Church.' Because the Church was in ruins. It had become an enormous institution, with pomp and ceremony on all sides; priests and bishops and cardinals wearing goodness knows what, and the Emperor Constantine who had taken the Lord's religion and turned it into a state religion for the Empire in 325. By the time of Francis, Innocent III was the pope. And young Francis comes into the picture with the words of the Christ of the crucifix always in his mind, 'Build my Church'. It is all in ruins.

That crucifix, by a Syrian monk, presents the humanity of Christ. His body is central. It is not a crucified body. It is a risen body. He hangs on the cross, but he hangs as the risen Lord. Now that crucifix has become one of the most famous crucifixes in the world. And it hangs now in San Damiano – and here's the second thing about the crucifix.

When he was rebuilding that ruined church, Francis one day had the biggest problem of his life. A high-born young lady, Clare, aged 18, escaped from her home at midnight on Palm Sunday 1212. She rushed down to Assisi, to the Portiuncula to the little patch of land where they were building huts to have the Brotherhood, to join this new movement. What was he going to do with her? It could have become a scandal. So, he took her to a couple of Benedictine places, where she became a sort of servant-girl. Then he asked her, 'Would you like to go up and stay at San Damiano? It's not quite ready yet, but it would do.' She liked the idea, and there she remained for the rest of her life. She had a little group of women, 'Poor Clares', and they stayed there in that little church. And that crucifix is still there, in Assisi. And here, as you can see, that crucifix is the centre-piece of the chapel.

I'm 82, and I have lived and seen this wonderful flow of the icon into the Western Church. The icon is a particular Christian form of art – just like plainsong is the form of Christian music, so the icon is the form of conveying to us transcendence, a beyond-ness. In the West, we have recently – well, as recently as the past 800 years or so, we've majored on a particular form of art, statues. And, as a result of the Reformation, we've had a great division between those who can't bear them and those that fill their church with them. But now it is all different. If you go into a modern Catholic church, you'll see something so inoffensive that other denominations, Reformed people, can manage it. You'll see a little painting, not attracting your attention unless you want to give it.

So, this is a gift of Eastern Christians to the West who on the whole had lost this. The Russians, the Greek Orthodox, the Armenians, the Copts, they all have icons. What is so special about an icon? Because they are in two dimensions; because the unsayable beyondness must be in silence, and must be something that happens to you as you stand before it. You've got to stand before the window of heaven and look through it before you can see the worshipful God, or the venerable mother, or the holy saint.

Icons are 'happening places'. So, we have them. And we would never have statues, because we have to be ecumenical and make a home for Protestants and Catholics and Charismatics – the lot – and for people who don't know where they are. We knew that from the start this place must not be offensive.

We place the icons in the corner, because they think that a line has no thickness. So, you put the icon in the corner, and there are the two dimensions there, and behind it is this indefinable line which leads you through the immeasurable, unsayable sign of beyondness, beyond space and time. The line of the corner.

So, here round the altar is the Christ giving us the Eucharist, there is the mother and the child, and all round we have the saints.

And there in the middle is this icon, the most famous icon of this century. There was a marvellous film about it. Andrei Rublev painted it in the fifteenth century. I could go on about this for ever. He took Genesis 18, when Abraham saw three young men coming when you'd never visit anybody, at noon. They'd just had a little slight meal and gone back to their tents to sleep. To Sarah's annoyance, I'd think. She was furious that Abraham asked them to stay for a meal at that time of the day – no-one would think of turning up at that time of the day.

'Come and refresh yourselves! I'll go and kill a goat and we'll set it down to you.'

And Sarah's just coming out of deep sleep, and he says, 'Sarah, we've got three guests.'

'Oh, Godfathers, what do you want me to do?'

'I'll get the goat, and you make some cakes and we'll put it in front of the three young men.'

'You're crazy, crazy! Why didn't you tell them to go and just lose themselves?'

And then, while Sarah's getting all this ready and swearing under her breath, she hears Abraham being told, 'And, of course, in a year's time your wife'll have had a son.'

At 84 or something! She thinks, 'That's a lot of nonsense!' And she laughs.

One of the angels, the young men, says to Sarah, 'You laughed.'

'I didn't laugh,' she said, because she knew there was something more going on – she was very embarrassed.

'Nay, but thou didst laugh,' he said.

And so, when her son was born, she called him 'Laughter' – 'Isaac' means 'laughter'. The impossibility of what was being told her, but also the laughter, at the sheer complete nonsense of God when He comes – He always upends the complete life for her, and for everybody.

So, there's the Rublev icon. The Three. And, if you notice, the Father is being looked at by the Son, whose whole interest is in the Father, because he does his Will. Here is the Father looking at the Spirit, who is stretching his hand out to bless the bread. So, it becomes the body of the given Son. And there is a fourth place there. For you. Everybody standing before it is invited to join the Three. You could pray in front of that icon and never finish thinking what it is all about. So, that is our central piece, placed between the upright sides of the altar.

So, there we are. That's good.

Now, what about all these other old dears, then? There's a nice one over there. That's St Siluan, an Orthodox monk, who was just a humble labourer. The abbot of the monastery on Mount Athos got so fed up – he only died in 1938 – he kept on saying, 'Why do you all come to see this old labourer? He's a nobody. What do you all come and see him for?' One of the visitors spoke up and said, 'Yes. But he's a man of God.' So, the abbot was rebuked for criticising the numbers of people who came to see that old man in his lifetime. Siluan.

The Sisters of the Love of God in Oxford gave us that one. Isn't it beautiful?

And look at this one those Sisters gave us. This, at the time they gave it to us, was one of the few icons of Saint Julian of Norwich. See, she has a hazelnut in her hand, and she lives in a tiny little hermitage, and she found it very difficult to get through the narrow door into her place there in Norwich.

So, there's all these friends of ours. All friends. When I pray alone in here, I sometimes think, 'Oh, perhaps I would like to go – which I don't now do very much – go to some big congregation and see all the people and be with them.' But you get the answer every time when I feel like that. They're all saying, 'But we're all here!' The icon people are all here. When you put up an icon, you are saying, 'You are a special friend of mine.' And they will all be there. It is an extraordinary experience. From the icon, you know that it is not just a picture of them, or a reminder. It is a form of presence. This has become clear. One of the most incredible things I find in living the hermit life now, with all this solitude of the huts and everything, one of the things that comes on you is the Communion of Saints. So, the icon prayer is extremely important to me, to us as a Community.

Now look there: there's the little crib. For Christmas. It was Francis who started all that. At Greccio, there were lots of peasant people coming about. He had the idea that, if they had a little representation of what Christmas was about, they would love it. So, he got a cave near Greccio and got someone to bring a real ox and a real ass and a real baby, real everything, and they all came at midnight Christmas Mass, and celebrated the midnight mass in the cave. And it spread like wildfire. As soon as they heard that Greccio had a crib, they all wanted one. And now there's hardly a

Christian church of any description which hasn't got a Christmas crib.

Is that right? Look at that!

Now, I must show you this. Here, below Mary and the child? A sad thing. Along came an Italian man in tears. We made him a cup of tea. And in his tears he told us, 'My son has just died. After ten years in a coma. He was only a boy. Only 18.' I think it was a car crash. He was very angry with God, the father was. And we've had him as a friend – he comes regularly, especially at Christmas and Easter.

'I don't like to go to the ordinary churches, because it reminds me of what I thought about God and the Church when I was so angry. But do you think I could find a place in your chapel to put a photograph of my son?'

'Look,' I said, 'put it there, just under Our Lady the Mother of God. She will understand you, she will understand him. She had a son who was taken, when he was 33, from her.'

So, he put it there. And every Christmas, as he did just now, he brings a little memorial gift of flowers. We've known Bruno, his father and his wife for 15 years now. And it's so good to have that little corner there.

Once this place becomes God's house, you can do all sorts of things with it; people can bring all sorts of things. I could go on and on about all the things that have been given to us.

And here, see? Here is a book of the Gospels, bound in green, on the altar. The Gospels. Lest we move away from where it all started. The Gospels. Central. And it's a fact that, at every Ecumenical Council, including Vatican II in St Peter's, the Four Gospels are put on the altar. Because, whether they do it or not, they're supposed to be in absolute line with what's in there. But, 'Bah ...!'

Now, that volume with the Gospels came to us from a nurse, a matron, of the Saint Columba's Hospice. What a very good memorial from the marvellous place where they look after the dying. So, that was gratefully received from St Columba's.

Then we have these hand-made wooden candle-sticks here, yes. But look! Here's a menorah – a seven-branched candle-stick. Now that was amazing, that was. We had a young man here who was born into a Jewish family. His mother wasn't a Jew. She was an Anglican Christian. He had been brought up, really, without anything; because they'd said, 'Oh well, let him choose for himself when he can choose.' Well, the boy grew up, a marvellous person. And a good priest told him to go to Medjugorje, the place where Our Lady had been appearing. He went there, and he prayed in the little church where the visions had been taking place. And he came home converted to the Christian faith. That was a joy to his Anglican mother – but, to his non-practising Jewish father, er, not so. Now he had to think about what to do with his life. He was in his early 20s. The priest told him, 'You'd better go to Roslin for a month.' So, from Medjugorje he came up here.

He said to me, 'What do I do?'

'Well,' I said, 'wait on God. Wait. Wait. Wait,' I said. 'You may have to wait years, I don't know. Wait for as long as you need to, to hear a word from God.'

Well, after he'd done this a month, I said to him, 'Are you any nearer hearing anything?'

'Nope,' he said.

'Well, we'll have to do what they did in the Acts of the Apostles.'

'What was that?'

'They put some names in a bowler hat,' I said, 'and then prayed and took one out.'

So, he wrote down on separate cards the things he thought he might do. And he placed them face down on the altar.

'Now,' I said, 'we've got a very hard job to do. And it might take us a very long time, many hours in here. Are you prepared to stay here till something happens?'

So, we were there for about three-quarters of an hour.

And I said, 'Hey. Are you ready?'

'No, I don't think so.'

'Well, we'd better have a bit longer.'

So, after another quarter of an hour, I said, 'Rod? Are you ready now?'

'About as ready as I'll ever be,' he said.

'Put out your hand, then, and take one of them cards, and look at what it says underneath.' And so he did.

'It says "L'Arche".'

So, do you know? That young man got up at breakfast and said, 'I'm going.'

'Going where?'

'Oh, Trosly.'

And off he went to see Jean Vanier at Trosly. He stayed and worked there for years.

His Mum was so pleased to see how his life had gone, that she said, 'What can we give them at Roslin, to say, "Thank you"?'

'Oh, you can't give them anything. They don't want anything. People are forever giving them things. They loathe it, because they've got everything they want, or need, that's the whole point. Their house is full of books and things people leave, and they get so mad.'

And she said, 'Don't be so silly. There must be something.'

Then he remembered what I'd told him. I'd said, 'Everything in these last 35 years has gathered in this tiny chapel. And it's perfect. But it would be completed by a menorah, a seven-branched candle-stick, that we can use for the glory of the Lord, and re-affirm our commitment to the Jewish people that God has laid on us as a community.'

So, he went back to his Mum, and she got him this menorah. Perfect.

But it still wasn't complete.

We can now go on to the final extraordinary thing. If you lift up the menorah – just gently from the roots, the middle – you'll find a stone underneath. If you take the stone ... It is the middle of an extraordinary story. This stone was brought back by a priest friend of mine who was going to Poland. He said, 'I'll pray for you at Cracow' – where he was going – 'but I'll bring you something back from Poland.'

After his holiday, the priest came to the house.

'Here we are!' he said. 'I've brought you my present from Poland.'

I was pleased, and I thought, 'I wonder what it is.' Because he's quite wealthy, and it would be a nice present.

He held his hand out, and he opened it like that. It was a stone.

'What is this?' I asked.

'It's a piece of Poland,' he replied.

'Where from?'

'From between the rails at the terminus at Auschwitz.'

Well, by this time we've had about nearly 20 years of some commitment. It's extraordinary how it began. But this now just sums it up completely. We keep this under the base of the menorah, the seven-branched candle-stick. Auschwitz. The place where the evil of man obliterated, for the Jewish people of all people, the vision of the Love of God. And so the Presence of God comes, growing out of the misery, and as it were overcoming the misery. This is the menorah, the sevenfold sign of 'the shekinah', 'the presence of YHWH', the God of the Jews and our God. So, that is very central to us, in front of the icons of the Blessed Trinity.

Well now, if I told you the story about this next thing, you couldn't believe it. I couldn't believe it myself. But it brought us this beautiful Jewish prayer shawl.

And we keep the shawl here, in this chapel. We use it at the Benediction.

Now look at this next one. Last year, I went to stay with the Franciscan Friars near Cologne, with my Spiritual Son, Johannes. On the last day, he took me to the airport.

And he said, 'We're an hour early. Is there anybody or anything you'd like to see in Cologne?'

'Oh,' I said, 'there's one place I'd love to see before I die.'

'Where's that?' he asked.

'The Carmel,' I said, 'at Cologne, where Edith Stein was a nun.'

So we found it, and we went into the chapel. It must have been about 10 in the morning. And the little place beyond the porch was free for people to say their prayers. But the nave of the church and choir of the nuns' chapel was locked. And you couldn't get any further than this little bit. But you could see the high altar, and across from it on the left there was an altar to the memory of Edith Stein, with a big picture of Edith hanging above the altar.

So, I prayed towards the Edith picture. As I did so, I thought of her courage in leaving the security of the Dutch convent, to which she'd gone under advice from her order. They had sent her to

Holland to escape Hitler's mob. But she was born a Jew, and she wanted to share the fate of the Jews, so she left the shelter offered by the convent. And, as a consequence, she was captured and transported from Holland and consigned to Auschwitz along with her sister. And she died there, on August the 12th, 1942.

Well, as I prayed, thinking about all the Jewish stuff that had been happening here at Roslin, I had the beginnings of – I do not know if my eyes were closed or open – it was like a video, that's all I can say – it filled my sight ... There was a train, drawing up at Auschwitz, an extraordinary thing, drawing up at Auschwitz. A man's rough hand pulls the door of the cattle truck open. And there, standing with their sandalled feet in human excrement, were Edith and her sister, looking terrified, both of them, bewildered. Terrified, the poor souls, as they were forced out of this truck on to the ground. I saw this. Now I began to cry. First of all, just tears. Then something happened that had never happened to me before in my life. I was taken over by an absolute sobbing fit that simply would not stop. And my dear friend, my dear young Franciscan friend, was next to me and said, 'What is it?' But I couldn't explain to him; I couldn't speak. It went on and on till I thought a doctor might have to be called. I couldn't stop crying, but I couldn't let my friend know what was going on. And then he tried to comfort me, but of course he didn't know what was happening. Then slowly, after quite a long time, gradually it began to calm down. I was quite exhausted at the end of it all. And I said to him, 'Look. I've seen something I couldn't believe I would ever see so clearly.' And I told him about it.

Now he, Johannes, has just been moved to a priory at Cologne, and he has let the Carmel know that this happened to me in their chapel at Carmel. And now there is a bond between this funny little chapel here, and the Cologne Carmel, where the Saint of Auschwitz was.

Every day, I try to read a part of the Kovno Diary of the Lithuanian Ghetto, the most detailed account day to day from 1941 to 1945, about how they treated Jews in the death camps and in the Ghetto. Day by day degrading them by every little issue that came with the Gestapo in Kovno in Lithuania. Reading that every day, and then praying out of that. I don't know ... I do that five days a week, because I don't think I could do it every day. It's appalling. Appalling. What would it be to abandon yourself to God under those conditions?

I read de Caussade immediately afterwards.[2] And I'm trying to put together the marvellous 'abandonment' spirituality of that Jesuit priest of the seventeenth century with this extraordinary thing.

How would I be? How would I abandon myself to God in the midst of all that terrible stuff? Now all this has got to be done. And it has got to be done here. Because Our Lady, a Jewess, for the sake of her Jewish son ... After all, we're surrounded by it – the whole thing is Jewish. We don't like to know that.

There's no Gentile stuff here. The whole thing is about how God spoke to his people through Jews. And we'll never get over it. Because we're anti-Semitic to the core. I find myself, when I'm called to this extraordinary special little job, having to clear out the dregs deep down in my soul, of anti-Semitic stuff that's been put there by layers and layers of Christian culture, Gentile culture. And it's there in the Church. And we've got to know that. I mean, Hitler grew out of a country, whatever, Austria, good gracious me, a committed Catholic country. He'd been through all the ropes of Christian stuff. But he stands on top of a whole pile of muck of Christian Churches. And this is what we've got to deal with. The whole of this means prayer.

And I'm no good at it. It's one thing I'm not much good at. I sleep during prayer. I wander. I even make only short times available to God. And yet here he is, calling me and this Community into this extraordinarily difficult prayer.

So, let us finish up with this picture of Edith Stein. Here we are in this little community – it's always little, it's feeble, it's going to die, it's about as feeble as it can be. It's like a pigeon's feather, blown about by the wind into the muck in the end. I mean, we're just nothing. Thank God, in one way. But it's all so strange. The whole thing's strange.

I said to a woman I met in Geneva, when I was on some Church business, Council of Churches, in 1962, I said to dear Ilse, dear Ilse, a German woman, a Jewess, who was Lutheran by upbringing, Anglican by practice, and Orthodox by spirituality – she was an ecumenical person in herself – so, I said to Ilse who worked for the Council of Churches, 'Ilse, I've got something in my heart I don't know what to do about.'

'What's that?' she asked.

'Well, I don't know, but I've been told, I think by the Lord, that it's no good just doing a professional job on this Gospel, being able to teach it or to preach it, and talk about God, professionally. I need to live it, and I can't do it on my own. It can only be lived in community – in family and in community. It's there that the Spirit works, to get the thing out.'

'That's true, that's true,' she said. 'And the Orthodox would say that. Yes. You can only live it in the communion of the saints and in the community of the Holy Spirit who joins you to the Father and the Son.'

It was marvellous, what she said.

'So, what does that mean?' I asked her.

'Well, you could make your community out of a parish.'

'No,' I said. 'I've got to put myself into a position where something can form which won't be me, but God will send people.'

She looked at me, and she said, 'There's only one person you can go to. There's a monk on Patmos, an Orthodox monk. And you must see him.'

I knew I would never have the money to go to Patmos. But, to cut a long story short, it was the time when I was leaving Sheffield to go on my ridiculous quest to Scotland. And some well-heeled friends in Sheffield said they wanted to send me on a holiday, 'to anywhere in the world'! Wasn't that marvellous? Patmos was in reach!

So, George and Muriel took me to Athens and put me on a boat to Patmos.

So, when I got to Patmos, I found myself at their monastery with a lot of garrulous monks. Goodness knows when they sleep – they seemed to pray all night and talk all day. Never seen such a garrulous lot. I had a word with the abbot, and asked him, 'Have you got a hermit on the island, called Father Amphilochius?'

'Oh yes. A holy man. He's very old, now. He's 81.'

'Would he be able to see me?'

'Why don't you go down to the convent? They have him to tea on Tuesdays.'

So, I went to the convent, and the abbess said, 'You'll need a translator, because he speaks modern Greek very fast and you won't understand a word. But one of our Sisters has just come back from England, where she got a First in English at Oxford. She can be your translator. After he's had his tea with us, Father Amphilochius can speak with you.'

On the day, this marvellous young nun said to me, 'I'd better warn you. Father Amphilochius hates talking about God. He thinks you can't talk about God for very long without saying ridiculous things.'

Quite right.

'And he hates religion. He hates talking about religion. But be on your guard. During the conversation he will say something to you which you've come for. He'll know what it has to be. And it will be yours for life. Once you've heard it, you'll never forget it. People come from the ends of the earth to see this man. And they take back with them something that will live in them for the rest of their life.'

So, I was very excited. I went in, and he started talking.

'So, you're from Scotland? Does Scotland have fir trees?'

'Oh yes, very many.'

'Well, do you know that the wind in a fir tree sounds different from the wind in any other tree? Do you know why that is? Do you know how they plant them? Do you know where to plant them? Do you know why the Greek islands have fir trees? And they had a lot more in the old days before they cut them down and burned them.'

My goodness, he went on and on and on. And we had the second cup of tea. And my mother told me that, after you've had your second cup of tea, you leave. You mustn't stay after you've had a second cup of tea. So, I got up to go. And I was thinking, 'I've come all this long way, and he hasn't told me a thing! What has all this been about? I must be so bad he wouldn't tell me a thing.'

I was in a bit of a sweat. But he waved me down. So, I sat down again. He looked at me with those blue eyes of his and his great big beard – he looked like Saint John himself.

He just said to me, 'Saint John was near enough to his Lord to hear his heart beat.'

So, I just knelt down and received his blessing.

Now, I told this to two Catholic men, very 'West of Scotland' sort of triumphal Catholic men, who had come here one day. And one of them illuminated that text, and we have it hanging there. Look at it there, eh? So, when this place was founded, I already had a text from which in the end all this grew.

So, here is this little chapel which will one day fall apart. After all, it's just a couple of wooden huts. But the Lord will use it in his own way, goodness knows. I'd like it to be a little memorial somewhere in the Edinburgh region, for the Holocaust. I don't know. We mustn't think about that. We have no control over our future, over the future of anything we have used. We just have to let God make use of whatever it is.

Is that right?

So, there it is.

* * *

The chapel has made an impact on most people who have visited it. John Peet was one. John was brought up in Edinburgh and trained as an electrical engineer. After a management course, he became an executive in an engineering firm in Leeds. Made redundant in 1984, he wondered if he might have a vocation and went to Rome to study for the priesthood. But, after four years, he sensed it was not for him. He travelled back to London, having had his fill of clericalism. He caught a bus from Victoria Station to Leeds. Back from Rome with nowhere to go but his cottage near Bingley.

'I took my seat on the bus,' recalled John, 'and what should happen but this? A habited nun came and sat beside me. Her companion, another nun, sat on the seat the other side of the aisle. I thought, "God, what are you doing? I'm going to have to speak to this nun." I got talking to the nun, and I told her my story. By the time we got to Wakefield, she said, 'I think there's someone who might be able to help you. Father Roland Walls. He lives in Roslin, outside Edinburgh in the Community of the Transfiguration.' The bus stopped in Leeds, and they parted.

John's mother was still alive then in Edinburgh. He went to visit her, and cycled up from Carlisle. It was a dreadfully wet three-day journey, and he decided to call in at Roslin. He asked in the village and they said, 'It's along Manse Road.'

'I went in,' John said, 'and I remember entering this kitchen. A Little Sister of the Poor was sitting there, and two chaps smoking pipes, and another woman. I looked round and said, "I'm looking for Roland Walls." A chap who looked a little like Popeye the Sailor-man, in a blue boiler-suit, said, "I am he. Come and sit down and have tea."

There were evening prayers in the little chapel. The contrast with Rome's riches, and with St Peter's, that was made by this little chapel ...'

Roland and John went for a walk, out past the offices of the Roslin Institute for Animal Husbandry. 'I remember Roland's laughter. As we approached the Roslin Institute, he said, "You see, that's the Vatican." Then he turned to the field full of pig-sties and said, "This is where community really is. Amid all the poverty and mess." Roland seemed to understand where I was. I'd come back from Rome, and had not become a priest. I must have had a sense of failure. But nothing in what Roland said ever made me feel that he thought that.'

John Peet already had friends in L'Arche, and was thrilled to discover the Community's close friendship with L'Arche and with Jean Vanier. Within months, John had become company secretary of L'Arche UK, and soon afterwards was appointed General Secretary, a post he held for 16 years.

'Scarcely a week passes without me thinking of the little chapel and the experience of prayer there. Roslin has always been there, within reach. Reminding me that I need to be quiet, that I need to have time each day, each week, each year, for God.'[3]

12

L'Arche

In the late 1970s, the members of the Roslin Community were exploring the Jewishness of Jesus. At exactly the same time, the Community made contact with another enterprise which would affect them profoundly. In 1979, Rosemary Haughton, a Roman Catholic lay theologian and a pioneer founder of therapeutic communities, invited John Halsey to address a conference she was organising at Spode House, a Dominican conference centre in Staffordshire. She had heard of the Roslin Community through her son Benet, one of her ten children, who had been a care-worker in the Cyrenians' hostel in Broughton Place with John. Rosemary and her husband Algernon had established a community called Lothlorien near Moniaive in Dumfriesshire, and the conference was examining what it means to be a specifically Christian community.

John had never given such a talk before. He gave it the title, 'Prayer and Politics'. He spoke about the life of their religious community, explaining how they shaped their daily life around their times of prayer, and how their door was always open to welcome strangers to their table. He then described his work in the garage, showing how its demands and pressures involved him in responsibilities within the Transport and General Workers' Union. He concluded by saying that, in his view, the contemplative life and engagement with politics belong together. John's detailed description of the community's prayers and the labourer's life in a busy garage, all spoken in his quiet voice, quite captivated the audience. The other main speaker was Anthony Gibbings, leader of the L'Arche Community in Liverpool. Having heard John's presentation to the conference at Spode, about the contemplative life integrated with work in unskilled employment, Tony invited John to attend and speak to a gathering of L'Arche Northern Europe which was to be held in Inverness later in the year.

John already knew of L'Arche. He knew of it as a visionary enterprise, dedicated to improving the lives of people with major mental or developmental disabilities. He knew that its vision had begun to become a reality from its foundation by Jean Vanier in 1964 in Trosly-Breuil in northern France. Jean Vanier, a French Canadian, was already by that time a highly regarded theologian and philosopher. Searching for his own vocation, Vanier had paused on the threshold of training for the priesthood. Then, guided and influenced by a French priest, Père Thomas Philippe, he became aware of the life of oppression endured by people with major physical and mental handicap. Jean Vanier began the Community of L'Arche more by instinct than by planning. Into his own small house he welcomed two men who had major disabilities, Raphael Simi and Philippe Seux, and enabled them to participate to the full in shaping their shared life. They named their house 'Foyer de L'Arche' – L'Arche meaning 'the Ark' – Noah's Ark. Before long, Jean Vanier was invited to take charge of a much larger house for disabled people in the same village, a foundation known as Val Fleuri, the Valley of Flowers. He soon discovered that, while L'Arche was a wonderful place of growth and healing for the people with intellectual disabilities, many of whom had suffered in dehumanising institutions, to his surprise it was also a place of personal growth for him. The people he had befriended had much to teach him about what is most important in life. This awareness of the mutuality of relationships and the humanising gifts of people with disabilities was soon seen as fundamental to L'Arche. L'Arche came to be spoken of as 'a university of the heart'.

When Jean Vanier took his first step, inviting the two men with their disabilities to share his home, it was by no means clear to him how the enterprise would develop. A biography of Jean Vanier puts it thus: 'Jean Vanier lays claim to being conscious of only two things at the beginning of L'Arche, two things which he would not have been able to put into words at the time: one was that what he was doing was irreversible; the other was a somewhat ambivalent feeling about possible growth.'[1]

However, the movement grew with astonishing speed, with new communities of the same character being established in a wide variety of places on different continents. At the time of writing, there are around 140 such communities in 40 countries on five continents. In all of these L'Arche communities, people with disabilities and those who assist them live together in homes and apartments, sharing life with one another and building community as responsible adults. Jean Vanier's initiative in forming the first L'Arche community was driven by his own Christian faith, and the chief resource for his inspiration remained the person of Jesus, and the Gospel of John with its portrayal of the power of the Holy Spirit.

L'Arche Inverness was at that time the only L'Arche community in Scotland, and the invitation to address the meeting of L'Arche Northern Europe, at Reelig Glen outside Inverness, propelled John into an unaccustomed public role. Numbering between 50 and 60 people, the audience consisted of core members of the communities – the people with handicaps, in the terms of the time – together with leaders including Jean Vanier, and assistants from six countries. 'I don't like speaking to large numbers,' said John in recollection, 'but it was strange. With them I felt a rapport. At once I felt accepted, welcome. It was the same sort of atmosphere we tried to create at Roslin. In this hall there was a good proportion of disabled people, "core members", who wouldn't be able to follow at one level, but I sensed that they were with me. Jean Vanier said, "Yes, we don't always know about communication. We think it's a person delivering a message. But really it's more like a concert, with audience participation."'

Once more, John captivated his hearers by his simple relating of daily events, his working life interwoven with his life in the religious community. One of the L'Arche Lambeth assistants, Marguerite Millar, remembered the impression John's talk made on her. It gave her a new perspective on the Church and on belief.

'As a young person new to L'Arche, for me personally John's talk was amazing. I was hearing from John new things about the

Church and about God. And the things I was hearing were so surprising, so unstuffy. There were people praying in huts … in a garden … and in Midlothian. And there was an open door, a place of welcome… And this man, he worked in a garage … All these surprising things were laid out. His words were inspirational for me, and helped me to deepen – in choosing the core values of L'Arche.'[2]

Even 34 years later, Jean Vanier could still recall that meeting in Inverness when John spoke to them all. 'I was deeply moved by John, by his story, and the vision.'[3] It was Jean Vanier's first encounter with the Roslin Community. He at once recognised their kinship. So began their rich and mutually supportive association.

Attracted by what they had learned of Roslin from John, assistants from L'Arche began to come to Roslin on retreat. They would spend one or two days there, sharing in the Offices of prayer as and when they wished, and talking with Roland and John and Patty. There were marked affinities between L'Arche and Roslin. On the very simplest level, the two communities were almost exactly the same age. L'Arche was founded on 4 August 1964, the day when Jean Vanier welcomed the two men into his house and it became home for them all. The Community of the Transfiguration was inaugurated in the service in Rosslyn Chapel when the three priests made their profession on 6 August 1965.

Both communities grew out of a sense of communion with Jesus of the Gospels. Jean Vanier's sense of direction had been hugely influenced by his friendship with Père Thomas, a Dominican scholar, and he developed a love for the Gospel of John. Roland's life-long love of Scripture had been crystallised in the blessing he received from Father Amphilochius on Patmos, hearing that 'Saint John was near enough to his Lord to hear his heart beat.'

Their devotion to Jesus led both communities to focus on the poor and neglected of society. In pursuit of this intention, they both adopted a very simple, basic style of life from which no-one was to feel excluded. In the case of L'Arche, the core members were drawn from among people who were poor, in that they carried major intellectual and developmental impairments. Yet these core members consistently revealed, to the assistants who shared their life, the strength of their grasp of life's value. At Roslin, the Community lived in the simplest fashion, in conditions as poor as those of anyone in Scotland. The Community at Roslin thus made it possible for the poorest people to feel comfortable in their house by denying comfort to themselves. In the words of Rosemary Lee, 'People sat there together, wayfarers and professors and people of all denominations, with Roland making them all laugh. Such a place would need to choose poverty as its way of life. Gaining a certain degree and level of comfort separates us from all others staying below it. A place like Roslin, poor enough to be able to welcome the really poor, isn't created and sustained without sacrifice. The relentless choosing of poverty, out of love, in response to God's love, undergirded all that Roslin gave and meant to so many.'[4]

As L'Arche grew in size and influence, the leadership developed a comprehensive programme of meetings, to ensure a common sense of direction and purpose throughout the organisation. John Halsey's intuitive understanding of L'Arche and its atmosphere meant that he was regularly invited to help with leading these conferences and weeks of training for L'Arche communities. The gatherings took place in various centres in England and Scotland. In 1984, L'Arche held an eight-week renewal course for long-term assistants, people who had been assistants for five years or more. They held it in Drygrange, at that time a Roman Catholic seminary near Melrose in the Scottish Borders. John and Patty and Roland together visited for half a day, and it was the first opportunity Roland and Patty had had to meet Jean Vanier. The encounter confirmed the bond between Roslin and L'Arche, and it was decided that Jean Vanier would visit Roslin at the earliest opportunity.

Two years later, the opportunity arose. On 19 October 1986, Jean Vanier, accompanied by Marguerite Millar and two of the core members, drove down from Inverness to Edinburgh through the first light snowfall of the year – 'Our Lady's Mantle', as the first snow has been called. They had arranged a public meeting that evening in Edinburgh, to launch the prospect of a new L'Arche house in the Edinburgh area. But their first call was at

Roslin. They shared in worship in the chapel, and then they had lunch. Marguerite Millar recalled, 'Then came the key moment. That was when Jean Vanier and Roland and John and Patty went and had a chat in the little room off the kitchen. The outcome was that they would pray for the establishment of a L'Arche, 'within walking distance of the Roslin Community'.

'So, where do we go from here, then?' the Roslin Community asked.

'Well,' said Jean Vanier, 'Your community is founded on prayer. So is L'Arche. So, I suggest you set up a prayer-group of local people from Roslin, to see if it is in the Lord's will for there to be a L'Arche here. Not in Edinburgh. But here in Roslin, within walking distance of your Community.'

The Community drew up a list of local people, Church of Scotland members and Episcopalians from Rosslyn Chapel. They visited them and invited them to meet in the house on Advent Sunday. There they all agreed to keep the prospect of a Roslin L'Arche in their prayers; they would meet again only when there was a new development to discuss. News of this initiative, however, brought interest from a variety of people. Soon, in parallel with the group who were praying for the coming of a Roslin L'Arche, there was a group of very capable activists in Edinburgh, including a businessman, Des Farmer, who worked with his brother, Tom Farmer, founder of the KwikFit vehicle repair chain. Gradually, it became clear that a new L'Arche would be founded not after all in Roslin, but in Edinburgh. To some, it was a disappointment that it would not be, in any practical sense, within walking distance of the Roslin Community. But the coming of the new L'Arche was itself a cause of great pleasure and hope.

On 6 August 1990 Jean Vanier came to Roslin again. The Community of the Transfiguration were celebrating their 25th anniversary. This event coincided with the plenary meeting in Edinburgh of a world-wide organisation called Faith and Light, based on the same principles of respect as L'Arche. This organisation had been founded in 1971 by Jean Vanier and Marie-Hélène Matthieu. It is a cross-denominational Christian charitable association, built to help those with learning disabilities and their friends and family, by meeting together for friendship, prayer, celebration and sharing. At the time of writing, there are approximately 1,648 of these communities, organised into 50 provinces in 79 countries. In August 1990, Faith and Light were holding their four-yearly plenary meeting in Edinburgh, in the university's Pollock Halls of Residence. Jean Vanier and the leadership team of the organisation went out to Roslin for prayers in the chapel on the evening of the 6th, the Community's 25th anniversary. The anniversary service was an ecumenical occasion, and to have the leaders of Faith and Light present that evening gave tangible confirmation of the close links among them all.

By that evening, the complex organisational process of forming a new L'Arche community was virtually complete, and the first L'Arche Edinburgh house was about to open with Nicki Ewing as leader. Nicki, with her parents, had played a major role in bringing L'Arche Edinburgh from vision to reality. Nicki had spent several years with L'Arche Lambeth; and that evening, 6 August, she came to the service in Roslin straight from the London train.

The L'Arche house was named 'The Skein'. 'Skein' is the word for the flight-formation of a line of wild geese, a familiar winter sight in the Scottish skies. The wild goose is said to be the Celtic Church's symbol of the Holy Spirit. The Skein was the fulfilment of many years of prayer and organisation, in which the Roslin Community had been intimately engaged. The bond with L'Arche was for Roslin a singularly substantial relationship. Although they themselves were a tiny community, they found in the much more extensive community of L'Arche an ethos in which they were utterly at home.

In those days, John Halsey was still working as a labourer in the garage. He had maintained regular contact with what remained of the worker-priest movement in England, the group then calling itself the Worker Church Group. In the minutes of the chapter for 1985, the Community recorded:

We are grateful for the continuing support and stimulus in this whole area by the links [John's] job gives with the Worker Church Group – itself a mixed bag of mustard seeds with an ever-growing variety of members spanning the whole range of sex, denomination, work situation, and doctrinal perspective.

The Worker Church Group, incorporating such variety of experience and standpoint, changed its name to 'the Shop-Floor Association'. Annually, John would attend the association's conference and continue his discussions with the others in attendance, including Andrew Parker. John himself saw no conflict between his union activity on the shop-floor and the contemplative and sacramental endeavour of the religious community. But there was increasing friction at the annual Shop-Floor Association conference over whether or not it was acceptable for there to be some form of religious observance. John discussed with the Community his reservations about the direction the Shop-Floor Association was taking. He saw them as embracing an ideological, Old Testament-based commitment to solidarity with the working class, but resistant to any language which they would judge as exclusively belonging to people inside the Church, and positively hostile to the notion of worship. Simultaneously with strengthening his engagement with L'Arche, John was becoming increasingly alienated from the Shop-Floor Association's standpoint. In 1990, the Roslin Community decided that John should withdraw from the Shop-Floor Association, and John wrote to Andrew Parker to advise him of this step.

This marked a decisive rift between Andrew and the Roslin Community. There had always been tension between Andrew Parker's ideological activism and the Community's conservative, contemplative character. It issued finally in a deep estrangement. Andrew continued his quest for the political cutting edge of Jesus and his Gospel, publishing books of Biblical scholarship in illustrated cartoon-style format. But his involvement with the Roslin Community and its prayers was over.

The opening of L'Arche Edinburgh's house 'The Skein', however, unlocked a new realm of activity for John. He had very great respect for the work done by the assistants, but could not imagine himself in any role in relation to the core members. Marguerite recalled, 'The marvellous thing about John Halsey is his way of seeing things. When L'Arche Edinburgh began, he would say, "But we are not living the life you are." He viewed our work as beyond his capabilities. He was hesitant, and thought there was no way he could accompany people with disability. But, within a short time, he had built a very strong relationship with Tom, one of our core members, who had a severe hearing impairment.'

When Tom was ill and likely to die, John wrote 'A Letter to Tom'. Tom recovered and lived a further ten years. But, when Tom died and his ashes were buried in the Enclosure garden at Roslin, John's words were read out, still so apt even though composed ten years earlier. This extract from John's address conveys Tom's character and illustrates John's ability to accompany someone with disability:

Dear Tom,
There was always a distance between us
at any rate for me – which I felt acutely,
the distance between Roslin and Leith
between my background of privilege and yours of suffering
between your silence and my chatter.
I feel such a distance now as you slip away.
Yet you dispelled the distance in a flash – bang – ZOOM !!
A flash of immediate recognition.
That broad grin with a shout and a great HUG
(like hugging a porcupine, though I've never done that!)
You were so full of LIFE – energy – affection
(sometimes rage, it must be admitted)
expressed in so many ways.
Your fiery colourful painting
the haunting music on your mouth organ
and those badges you wore
and the paraphernalia you carried strapped round you.

From its beginnings in France, L'Arche had a strong centre in Roman Catholic Christian faith. As the movement grew and spread, L'Arche responded to the prevailing faith culture of each new country it entered. In coming to Scotland, so strongly marked by the Reformation, L'Arche recognised the need to give a welcome to people of all denominations. Indeed, so sensitive to this issue were they that in the early years of L'Arche Edinburgh there was even discussion of whether theirs was necessarily a Christian community at all.

Anthony Kramers became the second leader of the Edinburgh community in 1992. 'A particular grief for me,' he said, 'coming as I do from a Roman Catholic background, was that there was no Eucharist, no Eucharistic fellowship, no sharing in the bread and wine at the Lord's table.' But he knew that, in an ecumenical setting, this sacramental meal raises the issue of unity and division. While some denominations invite all other professed Christians to share in receiving the bread and wine of Communion, the Roman Catholic Church imposes a strict discipline. Only Roman Catholics 'in a state of grace' may receive Communion from a Roman Catholic priest. And the Roman Catholic Church forbids its members to receive Communion from anyone other than a Roman Catholic priest when guests at a service led by another.

There was a human inclination just to go ahead and do it, to make people welcome, and to disregard the bar which is in the Roman Catholic discipline. But to do that would create acute problems for people who felt bound to maintain that discipline. What they saw as the alternative was to hold a dialogue with the authorities about it, demonstrating that L'Arche presented a special situation.

The Community of the Transfiguration had been required to address the issue over many years, as we shall shortly see. So, the contribution from Roslin on that problem was inspirational. As time went on and the discussion progressed, the L'Arche Edinburgh Community was able to agree with the local Roman Catholic authorities that there could be 'occasional Eucharistic hospitality'. On the understanding that it was occasional, and was not a defiant flouting of the rules, they were free at special times to welcome everyone to the table. Even once a year, such Eucharistic hospitality to communicant members of other traditions could be a witness to unity.

The bond between Roslin and L'Arche Edinburgh was such that Marguerite Kramers (née Millar) was probably right when she said, 'I like to think that L'Arche Edinburgh really is within walking distance of Roslin. Not in an actual, geographical sense. But in a "journeying" sense.'[5] And this sentiment was reinforced when the second L'Arche Edinburgh House, which was opened in 2010, was given the name, 'Creel Ha", the name of the house at 21 Manse Road, Roslin, next door to the Community of the Transfiguration.

John Halsey was always conscious that he did not function as a single individual but was continuously part of his religious community. In the garage, at his labourer's job and in his union work, he was representing the Community. The same obtained in his engagement with the Shop-Floor Association: he was representing the Community. Similarly, in his role with L'Arche Edinburgh, he saw himself as representing the Community. Anthony Kramers recognised the communal associations of John in his relationship with L'Arche: 'We saw John as the active pastoral ministry of Roslin to us. John was ideal for that, whereas Roland was ideal as a contemplative partner, with Patty in a similar role, too. For John always said, "We come as a Community".'

Marguerite Kramers expressed a very similar understanding: 'With the three of them in the Roslin Community, the Community had three facets. Each was a facet. Roland was the Community for some. John was that for L'Arche. Patty was the Community for others again.' So, although John was the one most directly in contact with L'Arche, Roland and Patty had an equal delight in the close ties between the two Communities.

We have looked already at the affinities between the two Communities, Roslin and L'Arche. However, there were also some major contrasts. When Jean Vanier took the step from his first small Foyer de L'Arche to taking charge of the larger institution for disabled people known as 'Val Fleuri', he could see that he had entered an entirely new realm. From the small house and the simple domestic needs of the three companions, himself, Raphael and Philippe, he had now assumed a range of responsibilities which would require both assistance and scrutiny from the resources of local and national government if they were to be fulfilled. Thus L'Arche became accustomed to working in partnership with other professional agencies, agencies with skills and expertise in the care of physical and mental health, and in the provision of appropriate support, food and accommodation for those with special needs.

By contrast, the Roslin Community never sought partnership with professional agencies. Instead, they relied entirely on the personal resources of the Community's members, and on the spiritual disciplines on which their communal life was founded. This may have limited the extent to which their small Community was able to integrate people with disabilities fully into the Community's life.

Before long, governments came to regard L'Arche as an outstanding 'service provider' for people with disabilities, and L'Arche became adept at working in harmony with government policymakers, securing the funds which enabled the core members and the assistants to build the life they shared. An expanding enterprise, with so many communities in so many different countries, required a complex network of communication and a connected decision-making structure. Under the watchful eye, guiding hand and steady influence of Jean Vanier, these resources came into being. Leaders and assistants did their utmost to integrate their individual L'Arche communities with the overall endeavour without imperilling the intimate character of each L'Arche house, flat or work service.

In what contrast stood the tiny Community of the Transfiguration. Earlier stages of this narrative have revealed Roland's ambivalence towards large organisational structures. But the ethos of L'Arche, orientating its energies as it did towards the poor, did succeed in pervading the breadth and depth of its networks. In addition, the relationship between Roland and Jean Vanier was one of great shared respect, verging on mutual reverence. As a consequence, however inclined Roland might usually feel to satirise a large organisation, the Church itself more than any other, he made great efforts to understand L'Arche's extended framework and to recognise its positive value.

In January 1997, Jean Vanier and a number of leaders of L'Arche accepted an invitation to visit Roslin, where Roland was to address them and lead a day of contemplation and retreat. He began by saying, 'I want to give a tribute to L'Arche; to say what it has done for us, and the dynamism afforded by our contact with it. It's kept us dynamically on the move, in our hearts, in our minds, and in what we apply ourselves to. And I think I am speaking for our whole Community – that is, all three of us!'

Roland admitted that he became lost in the intricacies of L'Arche's organisation and was unable to follow the leadership into its upper levels of authority – 'into its Himalayas', as he said. He spoke of himself as operating away down in the foothills. But he went on to talk in high praise of a then recently published book by Jean Vanier, *The Heart of L'Arche*. Roland said, 'I would like to see it included as the prelude and appendix to the Catechism of the Catholic Church.' He also recalled a Good Friday television presentation of a Communion service in the early 1990s, a Mass celebrated in a L'Arche community. In the service, broadcast live, a young boy in the pew, a core member of L'Arche, responded to the breaking of the bread with profoundly moving inarticulate sounds. Roland discerned in those cries from the boy's heart the action of the Holy Spirit, responding to the presence of the broken body of Christ in the broken bread of the sacrament. Roland gave honour to L'Arche for confirming the truth proclaimed by St Paul in his First Letter to the Corinthians (1 Cor. 1:27–8): 'it was to shame the wise that God chose what is foolish by human reckoning, and to shame what is strong that he chose what is weak by human reckoning; those whom the world thinks common and contemptible are the ones God has chosen'.

This perspective in L'Arche was exactly matched in Roslin.

The remarkable affinity explains Jean Vanier's love for Roslin, this tiny religious community: 'For me,' he said, 'it was like a light shining in the darkness. And I believe that there is a kind of mystery – that the little has to remain little. Then it is and remains a sign; not a solution. So, I just felt a very deep communion with them.'[6]

Jean Vanier celebrated the small size of the Roslin Community. And he recognised that the expansion of L'Arche, extending its size and its reach, further demonstrating its effectiveness in caring for disabled people, brought dangers for its own defining characteristics.

'So, there is the sign,' he said, looking at Roslin. 'And the sign always has to be small, temporary ... I mean, with L'Arche what will happen I don't know. It can be a sign. Or it may move away from being a sign to being a solution.'[7]

Between Roslin and L'Arche Edinburgh, the closest of ties were sustained. John contributed to L'Arche's programme of mutual listening, known as 'accompaniment'. In Roslin and at the L'Arche house in Leith, he supported assistants and core members, spending time with them and listening to them. 'I do what L'Arche call "spiritual accompaniment," said John. 'I think the Spirit is about everything, so it's not just some special little "holy" bit of life we talk about when they come. It's the whole of life; whatever they want to talk about. And always they want to spend time alone, quietly, in the stillness of our wooden chapel.'

13

At Last, a Roman Catholic Joins

On a number of occasions, Roland led retreats and days of reflection based on three blessings which he had received. Each of these three blessings had its own importance for Roland and marked a crucial moment in his life. In relating their significance, he would describe where he was when the blessing was bestowed, and he would give details of the person through whom the blessing was conveyed. In each case, the blessing was imparted in an encounter with a person highly regarded within their own Church, but who represented for Roland an aspect of the universal Church. John Halsey, who more than once heard Roland speak of these three blessings, commented that 'the three men were spiritual giants, pioneers, innovators in different ways'.

The third and final blessing in the series was communicated by Greek Orthodox hermit Father Amphilochius of Patmos, whom, as we have seen, Roland visited in 1963 not long after he moved to Roslin. Father Amphilochius, who lived from 1889 to 1970, is regarded as a saint in the Orthodox world, a holy man in the Orthodox tradition. During the years of the Fascist occupation of the Greek islands, he organised secret schools to keep the Greek language and the Orthodox faith alive. He also founded a convent in the 1930s which still flourishes well into the twenty-first century. The Orthodox nun at the Patmos convent, who translated for Roland in his conversation, predicted that the words of the hermit Amphilochius would stay with Roland for the rest of his life. At a chosen moment, Father Amphilochius disclosed his insight about John the Disciple: 'Saint John was near enough to his Lord to hear his heart beat.'

Then Roland spoke to him briefly about his hope of founding

a religious community. Father Amphilochius asked Roland some searching questions. 'Would you still go on if no-one joined you? And would you still go on if everyone left you? For, if you have not considered these questions, do not even begin.'

When it was time to go, Roland knelt for a blessing. But Amphilochius said, 'We don't do it like that here,' that is, in the Orthodox Church. He told him to get up. He embraced him, and gave him a blessing with tears streaming down his face.

Amphilochius's words about Saint John would remain a guiding image for the Community as year after year they meditated on the life of Jesus and sought to attain the life of a disciple.

The previous blessing, the second of the three, Roland received from Father René Voillaume on a visit to London in 1959. In his last years in Cambridge, Roland spent his long vacations in Europe, 'looking round Christian groups and communities to see if I could pick up the authentic sound and voice and vibrancy of Christian commitment'.[1] He found it most strongly in the French fraternities of the Little Brothers of Jesus. Roland over many years developed a profound respect for the rigorous disciplines of the Little Brothers, and an equal affection for the almost Franciscan poverty of their way of life. Their example inspired much of his thinking as he formulated his plans for training ordinands, the Sheffield Twelve, and as the vision of a religious community began to develop in his mind.

Once Roland was installed in Sheffield, members of the Sheffield Twelve frequently visited the house of the Little Brothers in Leeds. Roland learned from the Brothers in Leeds that the founder of their fraternity, Father René Voillaume, was to be visiting the Little Sisters in London. Voillaume was a French Roman Catholic priest, who in 1933 had founded the congregation of the Little Brothers of Jesus. The Little Sisters of Jesus were founded in parallel in 1939 by a Frenchwoman, Madeleine Hutin, who took the religious name Little Sister Magdeleine of Jesus. The spiritual foundation of each of these fraternities was the writings and example of Charles de Foucauld. Voillaume's book *Seeds of the Desert*, the life story of Charles de Foucauld, was on the 'essential reading' list for the Sheffield Twelve.

Roland had great admiration for Voillaume, sensing that Voillaume and the fraternity expressed truths which lie at the very heart of the Christian life. He very much wanted to meet him. So, he arranged to call on the Little Sisters when Voillaume was visiting. The Little Sisters lived in Lambeth, in a flat above a greengrocer's shop. With the customary humility of their tradition, they had a discreet sign on the door, the motto of the order, 'Jesus Caritas', translated into English, 'Jesus Love'. As a consequence, they received letters from Littlewoods Pools and others addressed to 'J. Love, Esq.' Roland and Father Voillaume spoke together. Before Roland left, he asked Father Voillaume to give him a blessing. Roland knelt; Father Voillaume asked for the Lord's blessing on him. To Roland, this blessing was a sign of the indissoluble bond with the Little Brothers and Sisters of Jesus which was later to be confirmed in the ethos and character of the Roslin Community.

The very first of the three blessings to which Roland attached such significance was conferred on him many years earlier. We have already witnessed it in our review of Roland's days as a student at Kelham College. Abbé Paul Couturier, the almost lone Roman Catholic apostle of ecumenism, had spent some days at Kelham; and Principal Herbert Kelly assigned young Roland as his guide for the visit. At the farewell, Roland accompanied Abbé Couturier to the railway station. Roland asked Couturier to give him a blessing. 'I will give you a blessing on this condition: will you promise to do all in your power, in your ministry, to work and pray for the unity of all God's people?' There, on the station platform, Roland received the Lord's blessing from Abbé Couturier. That moment confirmed Roland's life-long commitment to ecumenism.

If Roland was to found a Community, it would be ecumenical. Fortified by the three blessings, Roland inspired the other members of the Community with this vision: together they could be pioneers of a movement which recognised an essential unity among all Christians, irrespective of the different denominations from which they might come. This commitment to the unity of the Church was spelled out in the Community's Rule:

Our form of life is inspired not by any particular church tradition, but by the Gospel and the Lord of the Gospel and the
tradition of the universal church.[2]

From the very beginning, therefore, the religious community
in Roslin was conceived as an ecumenical enterprise. Certainly
Roland was an Anglican priest, whose personal history was shaped
and trained in the Anglican Church. The two younger priests who
joined him in founding the Community were also brought up and
trained as Anglicans, and so were all of the four other members
who in due course, one by one, joined the Community: Bishop
Neil, Patty Burgess, 'John Mac' and Jonathan Jamal. Nevertheless
the Fraternity, and later the Community, was always described
and known as 'Ecumenical'. We have already noted that the Fraternity demonstrated its ecumenical intentions by inviting as its
earliest 'Guardians' senior figures from the Scottish Episcopal
Church and the Church of Scotland, with the Roman Catholic
Abbot of Nunraw as a valued counsellor.

The international dimension of their ecumenism was strength-
ened by the Community's continuing links with Taizé, for which
Roland himself had such affection and admiration. From Sheffield
each year, the members of the Twelve had spent time at Taizé.
The Community at Roslin and the Taizé Community also shared
the same feast day, the Feast of the Transfiguration, 6 August.

But although the Roslin Community established strong and
cordial relationships with many individuals and groups in other
denominations, to their great regret they remained entirely Anglican in their membership. In 1978, in a review of their community
life so far, they recognised that the ecumenical dimension of their
achievements was very limited. Employing a phrase from Winston
Churchill's wartime strategy of attacking the enemy Axis through
its weakest point, namely Italy, the Community recorded that so
far they had been working only on the 'soft underbelly' of ecumenism. Their ecumenical contacts had been with the Scottish
Episcopal Church, with Anglicans, and with the Presbyterians
of the Church of Scotland, with Baptists, and with Independent
Evangelical and Charismatic churches. All of these were mani-

festations of the Reformed Church. This was, in a sense, the easy part. Yet, of all the Christians in Scotland who took their active faith seriously, one in two was a Roman Catholic. In order to live out the ecumenical dimension of the Community's Rule, they really wanted to make profound links with the Roman Catholic Church. They wondered hopefully, 'Could a Roman Catholic come into membership of the Community?'

They decided to pray that the Lord would bring them a Roman Catholic member. Having clarified this objective in 1978, their aim was fulfilled three years later. No-one, however, foresaw the means by which this would be attained. For, in 1981, Roland was himself received into the Roman Catholic Church.

This outcome took many of Roland's Anglican and Presbyterian friends by surprise – and, as a result, he was often invited to explain how it had come about. Roland used to narrate how three things happened whose cause he could not explain. The first concerned his diary. Annually, he bought a Roman Catholic diary. In the front is a place to write your name and that of a contact. That section reads: 'I am a Catholic. In the event of an accident, please call a Priest.'

'I always used to cross out "Catholic",' said Roland, 'and I'd cross out "Priest". Instead I would write, "I am a Christian. In the event of an accident, please call another Christian".'

But in 1979, he said, when he bought his new diary and tried to make those amendments, his pen would not write. He thought at first that it was just the pen malfunctioning. But, the following year, he got his new Catholic diary and found he could no longer cross that sentence out. He wanted it to remain as it was. He then thought, 'That's strange. I must, somewhere in myself, want to die as a Catholic: and, if I want to die as one, does it mean I ought to be living as one?'[3]

He described two other changes in his behaviour for which he could give no rational explanation. Roland frequently travelled to Lindisfarne to stay at Marygate House, the guest house which was an informal place of retreat. He took the train as far as Berwick-upon-Tweed. For 25 years, it had been his custom then to go and pray in the Anglican parish church before getting the bus to Holy Island. Yet, he said, on this particular occasion he pressed a button on a mechanical map of the town, and a light came up saying 'The Catholic Church'. He said that he then found himself going to pray in a small Catholic church, Our Lady and St Cuthbert, in Ravensdowne, a back street of the town.

Similarly, whenever he went to York, he always used to go and pray in the Minster. He would attend Evensong and then go and have tea with the Holy Paraklete Sisters in the Minster Court. On this particular occasion, however, he said that he found himself going to pray in the little Catholic Church, St Wilfred's, at the west end of the Minster.

In all Roland's accounts of this period of his life, he consistently presents himself as taking these steps without knowing why, and discovering their significance only later. He first discussed these 'irrational' impulses with the Community in their chapter meetings. As a result of their discussions together, the Community advised Roland to talk with their Visitor, Father Jock Dalrymple. He was the obvious person to consult, being not only the Community's Visitor but also a Roman Catholic priest.

According to Roland, when he explained to Father Jock that he felt he was being drawn towards the Roman Catholic Church, Father Jock said, 'Roland, nobody can help you with this – not me, nor anyone – everyone is in their own box. Only God can help you with this. You will have to speak to God about it – with big, Jewish prayers.' Roland saw in this a reference to the Hasidic tradition of the petitioner looking God straight in the eye and being very firm and direct with him.

'Ask God either to make it stronger or to take it away,' said Father Jock. 'Pray for two years. If the feeling gets stronger, then you know you have to do something about it. If it doesn't get stronger, you know it has been only a flash in the pan.'

In the account recorded by Jonathan Jamal,[4] Roland followed Father Jock's advice and prayed about it for two years. His sense of being drawn towards the Roman Catholic Church grew stronger. He discussed each step with the Community in chapter, and then with Father Jock. The Community encouraged Roland to take the matter further. As a matter of courtesy, Roland went first to see the then Bishop of Edinburgh and Primus of the Scottish Episcopal Church, Bishop Alastair Haggart, and explained his situation. Bishop Alastair said, 'Well, Roland, if you will mess around with this Ecumenical stuff, you can expect such things to happen.' And he gave him leave to go and see Cardinal Gray.

As he went up to the entrance of Cardinal Gray's house, Roland prayed, 'Lord, if this man talks to me about your Church, I shall know this is not from you. But if he talks about you and your Son, then I shall know it is of you.' The Sister opened the door to him and invited him in.

Cardinal Gray came forward with his dog Rusty under his arm, and took Roland into his sitting-room. The cardinal said to Roland, 'Can you tell me what makes you think you are being called to do this? To do something which may seem strange to yourself, strange to your Church, strange to your own Community, and may I say strange to us as well?'

Roland told the story of the three preceding years. The cardinal paused and reflected, then said to Roland, 'This is not primarily about you, nor about your Church. It is about your Community. I would like you to go back to your Community and ask them *one question*. In their vocation to witness to the unity of the Church, are they prepared to undergo the pain of Christ at the Church's disunity – the sixth wound we inflict on the body of Christ – which your Community will experience at the Eucharist, like a sword piercing the heart of your Community's life? They must understand this as not just their own pain, but as the pain of Christ. This is a pain which I never feel, nor your own Church, as we all celebrate with our own. But your Community will experience this at each Eucharist.'

'If they say "Yes",' the cardinal advised, 'then come. But if they say "No", then stay where you are. I will quite understand.'

Having made this direct request to Roland, that he should go back and talk with the Community about whether they could take on such a task, the cardinal reflected on the issue facing the Church. 'The way forward to full unity', he said, 'will come only when the Church understands this: that the Eucharist is not only a joyful celebration of all that Christ has done and given us, but also displays the cost, the pain, that sixth wound, of which in practice we are not aware, celebrating separately in our own denominations. Yes, ecumenical conferences and dialogues are necessary and important; so are joint services for "unity", and exchanges of pulpits and so on. But these do not reach the heart of the matter, the pain of Christ, in the way that your Community will.'

The cardinal then said, 'Come to my chapel, and I will give you my blessing!' The cardinal blessed him; and, as Roland got up, he saw that there were tears in the Cardinal's eyes.

Roland returned to Roslin and met with the other members of the Community. Many years later, John Halsey recalled that when Roland came back that day, and set out before them what the cardinal had said, it was obvious that the cardinal had a much deeper grasp of the meaning of Roland's move, for the whole Church, than any of the Community – including Roland himself. 'We were able to see Roland's move in a new dimension,' said John. 'We simply had no option but to go with the now-obvious flow of our Rule, in combination with what had been going on in Roland. To do otherwise would be back-tracking.'

Roland went back to see Bishop Alastair. He was sitting behind his desk. Bishop Alastair said, 'I can see from the look on your face you have come not to ask advice, but to tell me a decision. What is it?'

Roland told Bishop Alastair he had decided to make the move. The bishop made him promise that he would keep links ecumenically with the Episcopal Church, and occasionally lead retreats or quiet days, and give spiritual direction to Episcopal clergy when requested. Roland was more than ready to continue doing all he could for the Scottish Episcopal Church. Bishop Alastair gave him another blessing.

This step towards the future involved a high degree of risk, both to Roland's standing as a priest and to the existence of the Community. For it was by no means certain, were Roland to resign from his Anglican priesthood, that he would be ordained a Roman Catholic priest. Nor was it certain, were he to be accepted for training for the Catholic priesthood, that Roland would be allowed to continue in the Community. Indeed, Bishop Alastair

Haggart thought that Roland's step would mean the end of the Community.

Roland was received into full communion with the Roman Catholic Church on the first Sunday of Advent 1981 by Father Jock Dalrymple in his parish church of St Ninian and St Triduana in Restalrig in Edinburgh. Roland was already 64; and in the event, because he had been a teacher of New Testament in Cambridge and of theology in Edinburgh, he was not required to spend time in a Roman Catholic seminary. Instead, Cardinal Gray sent him to Cumbrae for three months with the Bible and the Documents of Vatican II.

'So, what did you make of the Documents?' asked the cardinal when Roland returned.

'I think they're full of unexploded bombs,' Roland replied, 'which have never been discovered, and which will go off at some point.'

At the beginning of September 1983, 22 months after being received into the Roman Catholic Church, Roland was admitted to ministries. One week he became an Acolyte, and the following week a Reader or Lector in a service at the diocesan seminary at Drygrange near Melrose. Then he went through the rite of candidacy at the cardinal's house. And, on 29 September, he was back at Drygrange to be ordained to the diaconate. Exactly two years after being received into the Catholic Church he was ordained to the Catholic priesthood by Cardinal Gray himself in his private chapel on the first Sunday of Advent, 27 November 1983.

Frequent celebration of the Eucharist was the Community's pattern. After November 1983, the Anglican Eucharist and the Catholic Mass were celebrated alternately in the Community's chapel at Roslin. The historical division of the Church, embodied in Roman Catholic discipline, was constantly present, causing pain on both sides of the divide. When John Halsey celebrated the Eucharist, Roland refrained from receiving the bread and wine; when Roland celebrated the Mass, John and Patty refrained from receiving, out of respect for the Community's Rule which states, 'Let the commitment of obedience be set within the framework of each brother and sister's churchly discipline.'[5]

This new demonstration of division made its impact in other areas of the Community's life. Roslin had greatly enriched the contemplative life and the worship of the Community of Celebration in the Episcopal Cathedral of the Isles. One of the American members of Celebration, who saw in Roland a love for everyone and a love for all God's creatures, including her dog named Amos, recalled how shocked she was when Roland no longer shared in receiving the Eucharist with Episcopalians as once he did.

'I remember that, when he became a Roman Catholic,' she said, 'he now only *held* the plate and the cup. I felt an agony about that. I was in tears. The Eucharist was the heart of our life. It was such a separation. I thought it must break God's heart that we could be so separate. I happened to be at the point in the queue for the bread and the wine where I could see all this happen.

'I was encountering someone who was absolutely delighted with life, no matter what its difficulties might be. And the lovely way he treated my dog ... And now he was so separate.'[6]

Any non-Christian whose interest in reading the narrative has been sustained to this point is likely to be utterly baffled at one Church's unwillingness to share the bread and wine of Communion with another. The main reason for Rome, like the Orthodox Churches, not allowing other Churches to share in the reception of Communion is that Rome understands the sharing of Communion not as a path to unity but as a sign of unity achieved. Roland used to explain the difference in terms of contrasting perceptions of the sacrament. 'The Reformed Churches', he said, 'see the Eucharist as a sacrament only of Christ. The Catholic Church certainly sees it as a sacrament of Christ, but sees it also as a sacrament of the Church.'

A non-Christian observer may well be equally astonished at the intensity of emotion generated by this impasse. Even some other Christians, who belong to traditions which place their primary reliance on Scripture or on the presence of the Holy Spirit, may find incomprehensible the pain experienced by the Communities of the Transfiguration and Celebration when they accepted that they could no longer share the hospitality of the Communion table. But, while absolute division at the sacramental table was undoubtedly a consequence of Roland's step of being received into the Roman Catholic Church, it was also, amazingly, a reason for him to take the step.

Why, then, did Roland become a Roman Catholic? The above account, which accords with the memory of others to whom Roland explained his mysterious journey, suggests that his reasons were twofold. First, it was to embody the Community's hope of including in their membership at least one Roman Catholic, in fulfilment of their ecumenical aspirations. Second, Roland's membership of the Roman Catholic Church became the means by which the Community exposed itself inescapably to the painful reality of the division between the Churches. At the Eucharist, the moment at which many Christians find themselves most closely united with God and with each other, the Community now faced division.

Reflecting on it many years later, John Halsey said, 'I don't think anyone chooses to experience pain for its own sake. So, what has it been for, this pain at the Eucharist? Perhaps in some minute way we were able, through Roland's entry into the Roman Catholic Church and our consequent division, to help the whole Church to move towards that unity for which Christ prayed and died.'

In *Mole Under the Fence*, Roland ponders a possible further element of his own motivation towards being received into the Roman Catholic Church:

> You can say there's a psychology to it. For example, it is quite clear to me that an old man, especially a celibate old man with no sons or daughters, needs Mother ... And, quite frankly, I have found to my delight that Rome is truly Mother Church in a way that I don't think other forms of British Christianity have been.[7]

Other factors may also have played a part. In his young days, Roland was given a welcome by the monks of Quarr Abbey on the Isle of Wight. His first experience of Quarr – arriving slightly late when High Mass was in progress, with the incense wafting high up into the roof of the vast Abbey Church – created an indelible memory. His immediate impression, as a 12-year-old, was that what was being done there was nearer to heaven than anything else on earth. He recalled, also, that the abbot had prophesied that Roland would die in Quarr. Perhaps the movement towards the Roman Catholic Church had its first impulse in those early days.

In the 1970s, Roland spoke to a former student about his sense of the future. While he gave no hint of departing from his affiliation to the Scottish Episcopal Church, Roland mused that perhaps only the Roman Catholic Church had the structure and the substance to carry the Gospel through the turmoil he foresaw in the coming century.

Roland's precise motivation remains unfathomable. At a loss, perhaps, to provide a rational explanation for his move, but recognising that it was the outcome of something deep within him, he sometimes said, 'It was my guts.'[8] But his change of allegiance was embraced by the entire Community. In the minutes of their chapter meeting, they pasted the following resolution:

The Community which since its inception in 1965 has always envisaged the possibility of Roman Catholic members, makes the following resolution on the occasion of the reception of Brother Roland into full communion of the Roman Catholic Church while maintaining his life profession within the Community.

The Community resolves (1) to enter into the realism and pain and absurdity of Christian disunity in its hardest, seemingly intractable area by our own obedient acceptance of the Eucharistic and ecclesial discipline of the Churches to which we belong. (2) to manifest a unity by God's grace, which will overcome and transfigure in Christ the division of his people by our prayer and life together in the common harness of the monastic life. (3) to travel forward into the perplexity, pain and joy of total ecumenism after our experience over the past 16 years of non-RC ecumenism.

This resolution, we believe, stems from our contemplative and monastic vocation, and the growth of the use of solitude.

It is not envisaged as a private venture of one member of the Community. Advent 1981.

The admission of Roland into the Roman Catholic Church substantially increased the interaction between the Community and the Archdiocese of St Andrews and Edinburgh. At a later stage of the minute book, we find pasted a certificate signed by Cardinal Gray's successor, the then Archbishop Keith Patrick O'Brien. It includes these words:

I wish to certify that the Ecumenical Community of the Transfiguration is a charitable institution recognised as such by the Roman Catholic Church in this Archdiocese. Along with Church Leaders of other denominations, I recognise the Community of the Transfiguration as a bone fide Religious Community being ecumenical in nature. The Community renders a very wonderful witness in the Church and in the world of today. I myself am very happy to be one of the 'Protectors' of this Community – with Father Patrick Fallon [who succeeded Father Jock as Visitor] being my immediate liaison with the members of the Community.

Not long after Roland became the Community's first Roman Catholic member, it seemed possible that a second Roman Catholic member might be added. On 2 July 1983, Father Jock Dalrymple, the outstandingly gifted parish priest who was also, currently, the Community's Visitor, wrote a letter to Roland.[9] He initially hesitated to send it, but a fortnight later sent it in a shortened form:

Dear Roland,
I have been thinking – praying for three years now, of offering myself to the Community of the Transfiguration as a member. I have hardly the courage to say this face to face with you, so I am taking the cowardly way out and writing it. ...
(1) Does your experience tell you I am in any way suitable for your life?

(2) Is it proper to give God (and yourselves) the fag end of my life – as if I wasn't generous enough to do this in my twenties, so do it now after my 'career'? I am 55+ damaged heart.

(3) I do not know if I would stick even a fortnight because of all my weaknesses and lack of 'contemplative courage'. I am no romantic, and see your place as a damp dump (if you will forgive me). I am, also, not sure I could stick a quiet life of prayer after 30 years of activity among people.

(4) And, of course, my bishop might not let me go, even after a struggle. I am under obedience to him.

I have spoken to no one about this, not even my spiritual director. (I am scared in that direction too.) I thought it best to open my heart to you first. Because if you say 'no' now, I need go no further. No hurry for an answer. No one here knows of these intentions of mine. Can you keep them confidential? Subject of course to your community having to know? But if possible, not as yet, even to them.

Yours, Jock

The whole Community held Father Jock in the highest regard. Father Jock was recognised as a man of prayer, and he was much in demand as a leader of retreats and quiet days. He lived with a definite discipline: his bed was the floor; he rose very early; his food was simple. The parish house at St Ninian's in Restalrig was known as a place of open hospitality, similar in character to the Roslin Community. Father Jock welcomed the poor at the table, wayfarers could find a bed and a breakfast, and there was always conversation and a meal.

Roland had become a close friend. But it had never crossed the mind of anyone in the Transfiguration Community that Father Jock might have been imagining himself as a possible member. In his reply to Jock's letter, on 21 July, Roland said,

My dear Jock,
It's so hard to say, 'God's will be done' when you have such high interest in what it may be! But your letter came allowing

me to entertain as a possibility what would be such a lifting of our hearts. But I must be mute. We can but put before you the horrors and ineptitudes of our life – but one thing we say now – there is no question of 'fag end!' – rather the unlooked for possibility of perhaps our absurd place being part of a larger altar on which the sacrifice has already been offered over so many years ...

Many prayers from my heart, yours ever,

Roland

Father Jock's journals carry only fleeting references to Roslin in the following seven months, during which he continued working in the busy life of the parish. In January 1984, he spent two weeks giving a series of lectures in Galilee. The plan was made for him to spend a week at Roslin, on personal retreat, at the end of February.

The week before he was due to visit, the Community in Roslin found themselves in crisis. Down-and-outs from the city had started to come to receive the hospitality of the house, and they had a different way of life from the travellers, the wayfarers. The two groups did not get on. The wayfarers themselves said the Community was taking on too much. In the annual chapter minutes of 1983, it had been reported 'that over the previous year there had been an average number of three and a half guests per night'.[10] Jonathan recalled, 'Some of the city down-and-outs had lice, and one morning one of the wayfarers saw the lice. At once we had to deal with it. We spent two days burning the mattresses out in the garden, and the bedding too. And there was disinfectant. And we told the wayfarers and city men to bath and disinfect themselves. Roland got lice too. He said, "If these are the fruits of the Spirit, I don't think too much of them."'[11]

They wondered if they should cancel Father Jock's visit. But they steadied themselves sufficiently to allow the visit to proceed as planned.

Daily entries in Father Jock's journal for that week show that he found the living conditions very cold and damp. However, in the times of solitude in the well-ordered pattern of the Community's daily life, he discovered a renewed interest in *lectio divina*, the Benedictine method of meditative prayer, as he read the Gospel of Luke. But it is also clear from his journal that he found that Roland talked a lot. 'Evening in front of community fire: lots of Roland ...'; 'I had two and a half hours with Roland freewheeling in the morning.'[12]

After supper on his final evening, Father Jock spoke with John Halsey. He told John of his anxiety, fearing that the combination of his and Roland's different personalities living in community at such close quarters might be a difficulty. John revealed to him that it had not been easy for the Community when both Roland and Bishop Neil Russell were part of it, and that those difficulties might be repeated if Father Jock joined. 'But,' said John, 'we grow through pain.'

Roland, while full of hope that Father Jock might indeed become a member of the Community, was sure that it could happen only if Father Jock had a clear sense that God was calling him to do so. The week at Roslin brought clarity to Father Jock. Roslin was not for him. In August 1985, almost a year and half later, reviewing these events in his journal, Father Jock recorded,

> At the end of February 1984 I made a retreat at Roslin in cold weather in one of the huts. Out of it came a renewed discovery of Lectio Divina through reading nothing but St Luke's Gospel, and secondly the realisation that I could not live at Roslin because of Roland's temperament. Both were positive answers to prayer.

The sorrow that the Community felt at not receiving Father Jock into their midst was tempered by the affectionate way he continued to conduct his role of Visitor to the Community. A much greater sorrow visited them when, just a week after that last reflective entry in his journal, news came of Father Jock's death at the age of only 57.

The Roman Catholic Cistercian monks of Nunraw had made Roland welcome from his earliest days in Roslin in 1963, when he was priest-in-charge of Rosslyn Chapel. They remained valued companions of the Community of the Transfiguration throughout their monastic journey.

'The beauty of Roland,' said the Abbot of Nunraw, Father Mark Caira, reflecting on Roland becoming a Roman Catholic, 'the beauty of Roland was that you could not see any difference between who he was before as an Anglican, and who he was later as a Catholic. Does that mean he was a crypto-Catholic before? No, I don't think so. Just that he was fully immersed in the long tradition of the Church.'[13]

14

Other Communities

The monastery at Nunraw provided support and a perspective for the Community of the Transfiguration from the beginning. Soon after Roland had 'returned empty to Scotland' in 1962 and was installed as priest-in-charge of Rosslyn Chapel, he found his way to the Cistercian monastery 20 miles away, out on the edge of the Lammermuir Hills. There, very quickly, Roland and Abbot Dom Columban Mulcahy established a friendship and discovered that they shared an ecumenical aspiration. When the new Community was coming into being, Dom Columban, from his order's centuries-long experience of community living, was a source of wisdom and encouragement. In the three-day retreat which he led for the three Anglican priests immediately before they made their profession in August 1965, he gave them three simple themes which became an abiding memory in their Community life. 'God loves you.' 'You can love God.' 'You can love one another.' And, as the foundations of the Community were being set in order, the members were aware that they were in the prayers of the monastery, their near neighbours.

In their turn, Roland and the Community provided a certain companionship to the monastery. The monastery, established in 1946 in a large country house with its extensive outhouses and surrounding farmland, undertook the development of a substantial new complex of buildings, a monastery for over 50 monks. When the monastery was under construction, the monks transformed the old house into the guest house for wayfarers and other visitors. Reflecting on that era many years later, some of the older monks remembered Dom Columban's wistful comparison of Nunraw and Roslin. 'I remember us out in the garden at the guest house,' recalled one of the monks, Father Hugh, 'and Columban saying, "I wish I wasn't setting up this great monastery. We could have had something like they had in Roslin – we could have used the old farm buildings as 'Nunraw Barns', like the Roslin huts." I think he felt a little yearning for their simplicity.'[1]

The communities of Nunraw and Roslin were very different in history and size, but they were companions. After Roland entered the Roman Catholic Church, he came a number of times to spend two nights at Nunraw. In the evening, he would give a lecture in the monastery library, which one of the monks would record. From his visits, Nunraw accumulated quite a library of Roland's recorded talks, a tangible testament to the close ties between the two religious communities.

There were links between Roslin and many other religious communities. When Roland in his Cambridge years was searching for 'the authentic sound and voice and vibrancy of Christian commitment',[2] he formed a very high opinion of the experimental ground-breaking Scottish initiative, the Iona Community. The Iona Community was founded in 1938 by a Church of Scotland minister, George MacLeod. MacLeod was a magnetic figure. In the First World War, he was awarded the Military Cross and the French Croix de Guerre for bravery. Appalled by the carnage of the war, and horrified by the poverty he saw in Britain's cities in the post-war years, he gradually moved towards socialist and pacifist views. He became the minister of Govan Old Parish Church, in a very poor industrial parish in Glasgow. Govan was a Clydeside ship-building community where unemployment was rife. MacLeod conceived a plan to invite unemployed shipyard workers to join with young ministers and to use their skills to rebuild the ruined medieval abbey on the island of Iona. His enthusiasm and vision attracted many men to the Christian ministry and to a commitment to working in the hard-pressed industrial areas of the country.

On Iona, ordinands and young ministers worked alongside tradesmen and labourers as they set about the task of rebuilding. MacLeod recognised this as a direct way of addressing the gulf between a largely professional-class Church and the working or workless classes who were alienated from the Church. As the rebuilding of the abbey proceeded, the shared endeavour drew people closer together. After a short time, it became obvious that a common bond was developing among those who were working together on Iona. Gradually, with the co-ordinating vision of MacLeod, the Iona Community grew and developed. This Community was composed largely of ordained Church of Scotland ministers, with a number of other men in social and caring professions and some who worked in industry. Annually, some of them would take periods of leave from their professional work, in order to spend time on Iona. There they would work alongside the tradesmen and labourers rebuilding the abbey and its domestic buildings; they would engage in Biblical study and discussion, and spend time in prayer. MacLeod had an ecumenical vision, and the Iona Community's membership was opened to welcome people of denominations other than the Church of Scotland. Drawing on the traditions of Saint Columba, who had first established a religious community on Iona, MacLeod led a revival of Scottish interest in Celtic spirituality, which had been displaced by Roman influences since the Synod of Whitby in 663/664.

The various communal bonds among the members and associates of the Iona Community were characterised by an orientation towards areas of urban poverty and deprivation, and by their adherence to a number of articulated disciplines which they maintained in solidarity with each other. Throughout the year, the members and associates met locally in groups across Scotland to strengthen their common vision and to encourage each other to sustain their agreed disciplines. A prayer discipline committed them to a daily time of Bible reading and prayer. In their financial discipline, they pledged to place a percentage of their weekly earnings into a common pool to cover the expenses of the Community, and to make money available, if required, to members in need. Some of the ministers worked in industry, and many committed themselves to working in the areas where low-paid industrial workers lived. In the early days of the Iona Community, there was an unspoken but definite inclination towards the ministers remaining unmarried, so that it would be simpler for them to fulfil the austere demands of the Community's chosen path.

When not wearing the clerical collar, Iona Community ministers sometimes wore a dark blue shirt symbolising their commitment to blue-collar workers.

In the years following the Second World War, the Church of Scotland generated an enthusiasm for establishing church congregations in the areas of new housing which national and local government were constructing in and around the large towns and Scotland's four cities, Glasgow, Edinburgh, Dundee and Aberdeen. In what was called the Church Extension movement, ministers were appointed to supervise the planning of new congregations and the construction of new church buildings in the new housing areas of the cities and large towns. The Iona Community had by that time developed a most effective training and support system for ministers in such areas. The Iona ethos was offering ministers and lay leaders the possibility of a shared approach and a network of supportive thinking. In many of the new Church Extension churches, the minister was a member of the Iona Community.

Although they recognised that there were points of difference between them, Roland Walls and George MacLeod had a long and productive association. When Roland became Dean of Corpus Christi College in 1952, he started to bring groups from Cambridge to Iona. A little later, when Roland was assembling the first group of ordinands to join him in Sheffield in 1958, he was glad to have contact with MacLeod; and, on MacLeod's recommendation, Kenneth Hughes from the Church of Scotland was one of the first tranche of the Sheffield Twelve. In addition, MacLeod was instrumental in finding Roland a housekeeper. 'Unless I can find a housekeeper,' Roland said to MacLeod, 'I shall have to marry.' Macleod arranged for Roland to meet in a Glasgow cafe with a Miss Black from Lismore. They sat next to a jukebox, and neither could hear a word the other spoke, but they agreed to join forces.

Roland ensured that the Sheffield Twelve experienced the atmosphere of the island of Iona itself: the final week of their Sheffield year was spent on the island. When they travelled north, they spent a night in Glasgow. They stayed in Community House in Clyde Street, where the Iona Community interacted with the city-centre life of the homeless and the addicted. Once they reached Iona, the

Sheffield Twelve went to daily worship in the restored medieval abbey, and took part in the programme of work and Bible study and shared meals with the young ministers and the tradesmen and labourers working on the abbey renovation. On their last day on Iona, always 6 August, the Feast of the Transfiguration, the Sheffield Twelve had an early-morning communion service in the tiny St Oran's Chapel. Then they would catch the ferry to the Isle of Mull, then the bus, then the ferry to Oban and the London train.

When Roland moved to Scotland and to Roslin, and when the Community of the Transfiguration was founded in 1965, the Iona Community was an important influence in Scottish Church life out of proportion to its relatively small size. Roland was sometimes invited to lead a retreat on Iona, or a Day of Reflection, as also was Bishop Neil Russell – and this consolidated the relationship between the two Communities. For a time, consideration was given to Roslin establishing a small retreat centre for themselves on Iona. Roland and George MacLeod were both figures of stature, and their inter-relations were not always smooth. They disagreed particularly in respect of the place of women in communal structures. One year, Roland was invited to lead reflections at the annual meeting of the Iona Community, the high point of the Iona Community year. Only men could be members of the Community. Women were not admitted to membership of the Iona Community until after George MacLeod stepped down as leader in 1967.

At the time of the annual meeting in question, wives could accompany husbands to the island but could not attend or participate in the discussions or meetings. Roland questioned this and insisted on meeting the wives so that they could talk about their situation. Roland saw it as a foolishness of the institutional Church that it would not find an equal place for women.

'Beware, Roland,' the principal of Westcott House, Kenneth Carey, had said to his friend in their Cambridge days, 'beware the valetudinarianism of the Iona Community.' Carey was cautioning Roland concerning what Carey considered a tendency of the Iona Community, namely to discern all the faults of the Church but few of its own.

That the disagreement between Roland and George could be robust is borne out by the memory of someone who as a young girl was a babysitter for the MacLeod children in their days as a family on Iona. She recalls seeing George's wife Lorna, Lady MacLeod, chasing Roland from the house, and all down the garden path and out of the gate, after Roland and George had been arguing.

The insights and activities of the Iona Community, however, were in so many ways in harmony with the expressed and implicit aims of the Roslin Community that it was natural for the two Communities to remain closely linked. The Transfiguration's chapter minutes for 1977 record that the members of the Community of the Transfiguration, as an expression of their close ties, had spent Christmas on Iona. They had hoped for a substantial discussion of ways to strengthen their links. But Iona was thronged with visitors, many from America, seeking to taste Christmas against the background of a historic place of prayer. There was no opportunity for the discussion they sought. The Roslin Community saw 'that the most profitable way forward was to link with local groups of the Iona Community, and especially those in the Edinburgh area'.[3]

The Iona Community, with the focus in their early decades on church ministry in housing schemes and other working-class areas, often combined their emphasis on St Columba and on Celtic spirituality with playing a public role in the championing of political causes. Although on many such issues Roslin would have an outlook similar to that of the Iona Community, a public political role was outside the contemplative character which shaped the life of the Roslin Community. They were guided, too, by the direction in their Rule that they were to guard their anonymity.

Yet one issue particularly united them. George MacLeod was a major figure in the public debate about nuclear disarmament. In powerful speeches to the Church of Scotland's General Assembly, he was an influential voice in persuading the Church of Scotland to condemn Britain's reliance on nuclear deterrence. With the Feast of the Transfiguration being celebrated on 6 August, the anniversary of the destruction of Hiroshima in the explosion of the first atomic bomb, the Roslin Community too were outspoken in their opposition to Britain's policy on nuclear weapons. Indeed, one of Roland's few published written works was a theological leaflet, *The Final Choice*, with a dramatic black cover, condemning the reliance on such weapons of terror.

Thus, although there were no formal links between the two Communities, there was a constant and mutual acknowledgement of their kinship.

We have already caught sight of the companionship enjoyed by the Roslin Community with the Little Brothers and Little Sisters of Jesus, with the L'Arche Communities of Inverness, Edinburgh and world-wide, with the Community of Celebration and the Worker Church Group. Roslin also had substantial ties with the Sisters of the Love of God at Fairacres in Oxford. Each of the Roslin Community members would go on retreat to Fairacres. From 1965 to 1990, Fairacres provided Roslin with spiritual guidance through the Sisters who acted as Warden for the Roslin Community, successively Mother Mary Clare, Sister Jane, Mother Anne and Sister Helen Columba.

In addition, Roslin was latterly listed as 'Franciscan Hermits of the Transfiguration', pointing to their close links to a great range of Franciscan communities, both men and women – especially the Poor Clares, Anglican and Roman Catholic, in Britain and abroad, especially in Germany. Continuously, day after day in the wooden chapel at 23 Manse Road, Roslin, prayers were said for an enormous number of these other communities to whom the Roslin Community had ties as close as any family. There were men's communities; women's; mixed; Anglican; Roman Catholic; and Buddhist communities.

Sister Eleanor Rogers, one of the Daughters of Charity of St Vincent de Paul, worked for many years at St Joseph's Hospital, Rosewell, near to Roslin. There would be up to 200 residents there, people with learning disability. And often people who were staying with the Community at Roslin would go as volunteers. Before St Joseph's closed, Sister Eleanor went to look after St Mary's Hospital in Lanark, but she kept in touch with Roslin and with Roland. She invited Roland over to stay at the hospital, and he went for three days.

'Roland was a wonderful influence,' she said, 'and said such wise things. I remember him once saying, "When I come into prayer in the morning, I say, 'Good Morning, Jesus'. And then I just sit. I don't do anything else. Sometimes if a friend is coming to see you, you don't read a book to them – like reading the Psalms! You just sit with them!" He was a joyful person, full of joy. Lots of laughter. Always smiling. I would say he was lost in God.'

Regrettably, in this book there is neither time nor space to do justice to the affirmation which the small Roslin Community drew from the bonds of association and affection they shared with their brothers and sisters in all these other religious communities. But the annual chapter minutes record year by year individual members coming from a wide range of communities all over the world to spend days with the Community – the men at Roslin, the women at Loanhead. 'Another remarkable event was the visit of the Venerable Ananda Maitreya with his disciple. It was a great privilege and a memorable occasion to have with us this 90-year-old Buddhist abbot from Sri Lanka, whose holiness communicated itself so vividly by his (few) words, his silence and his presence.'[4]

Sometimes Roslin would receive a visit from a group of people hoping to establish a form of Community life based around their shared Christian faith. In 1979, such a group of young Christians formed themselves into a Community in the south side of Glasgow, in Pollokshields at the corner of Albert Drive. They lived as individual families, but their houses were in close proximity to each other. They worked in a variety of occupations: some worked in social care, others in health; others again were employed in education; and some expressed their gifts in the creative arts and in the media. They had common disciplines and met for communal prayer and worship. Based at that corner of Albert Drive, their Community in due time became known affectionately as 'Bert'.

One of the founding members, Ian Milligan, had been a 16-year-old church member when in 1970 he first encountered Roland at the Scottish Christian Youth Assembly. Ian had been part of a small 'house church' from his mid-teens, and was listening for voices that would give signals towards a genuinely Christian way of living. At that Youth Assembly, he was excited to hear evangelist Jim Punton talk of 'cell churches', small communities of believers who shared faith and life together. At that same assembly, Roland was speaking about 'Ecstasy in Worship', but Ian found nothing in that talk for him. At the age he was then, he later recognised, he was looking to advance into action, not to retreat into prayer.

But, when Ian and his friends formed their Christian community, 'Bert', in January 1979, they heard very admiring views of Roland and the Roslin Community within Church circles from Jim Punton and Ron Ferguson. A key word for the members of Bert was 'community'. As their life together began to explore the meaning of that word, the members of Bert found Roland and the Roslin Community a valuable point of contact. Two or three of them used to go through from Glasgow to Roslin several times a year. 'We went just for a chat,' said Ian. 'Roland seemed one of the few people who understood and appreciated what we were about. Of course we saw him, John, Patty and Neil as much more dedicated and wiser than we were. And of course Roland was just so much fun to be with! He was irreverent, yet crackling with spirituality and insight.'[5]

Ian recalled that, on his first visit, he sensed that the Roslin Community was really very poor. 'I saw how scabby and cold the house was, and how little money they had.' Ian was aware that John worked in the garage to keep the Community, and reckoned that Roland and Neil might have pensions. And he knew that they welcomed lots of poor wayfaring strangers. Nevertheless, he was quite shocked at the poverty of their setting. And he was very cold, sitting in the unheated kitchen eating bread and cheese for lunch.

The next time Ian went, he was accompanied by two other members of Bert, namely Rachel Smillie and Ricky Ross. Among Bert's communal disciplines was a commitment to giving an agreed proportion of their common purse to charitable causes.

'We decided to bring some lunch to add to the feast,' said Ian. 'That was OK. But it was bitter winter, and I had asked Bert if we could take some money for them, so that they could put on the heating a bit more. I tried to give Roland £25.

'He just laughed, and with a sweep of the arm said, "No, no, give it to the poor!"

'I was a bit crushed – I thought they *were* "the poor"! But of course I was learning some lessons as well.'

Members of the Bert Community continued their regular visits to Roslin, and they regarded their visits as valuable and support-ive. Roslin's words, however, were always realistic: no empty praise. Ian Milligan recalled, 'I suppose we must have been going for almost ten years, and I was fishing for some kind of compli-ment about our staying power. Roland just said, "Once you've been going for ten years, then you've made a start."'

Roland's next words had their effect also. 'You've got to live as if you're going to live your whole life there.'

'It was a hard message but a good one,' reflected Ian. 'Without being dogmatic, I think Bert has had a sense of commitment to the area, and most of us have stayed in the area since we joined. We know that some people will leave and move on, but we do have a sense that you've got to stick if you can. Roland and Roslin encouraged that.'

Yet Bert's encounters with Roslin, while challenging, brought a profound sense of companionship. Ian recalled that, on one visit, Roland made his usual friendly enquiry, 'How are you getting along, then?'

'I replied, or it might have been Ricky, "Just trundling along. Not much to write home about." Roland chuckled, and said, "I like that: 'Not much to write home about.' Just like us!"'

The members of Bert lived with their own families in their separate family homes. Yet they were genuinely an intentional community, in that they lived in close proximity to each other and met together regularly for prayer and worship and communal planning. Over a period of more than 30 years from their foun-dation, Bert secured stability for their own families and imparted a sense of permanence in an area of the city which was very much in transition. Bert were still encouraged by the example of the Community of the Transfiguration. 'One of the things we learned from Roland', said Ian, 'was that God could do something really good through a small, fragile group. Roland did want the Roslin

Community to grow, and he was disappointed by the lack of new recruits, yet he still kept the faith. We were just inspired by his faith in this. I suppose this begins to be a way into something that is crucial for me – the confident belief that God works at the bottom, from the poorest. Life is not about having power or money, but about persisting, holding to the radical Gospel.'[6]

Another Community greatly influenced by Roslin was the Northumbria Community. It has grown into a dispersed Community with many hundreds of people connected world-wide, drawing inspiration from the saints of the north-east of England. This Community arose in an unplanned spontaneous way around a small group of people whose interest had been excited as they studied the early saints of Celtic Ireland and their impact on the spirituality of north-east England. The preliminary steps towards a Community were taken by Anglicans John and Linda Skinner and Roman Catholic Andy Raine, who created worship and prayer materials for the daily use of their own group, and which they also used in leading worship on Holy Island on Easter Sundays from the early 1980s.

John Skinner first met Roland in 1979 when Roland was speaking about contemplative prayer at Lincoln Theological College, where John was an ordinand. John Skinner was very taken by what Roland said, having been intrigued by his tramp-like appearance which so much belied his academic status as a Cambridge don. The image of Roland stayed with him. After John Skinner left Lincoln, he went to a curacy in Newton Aycliffe, County Durham. After two or three years, John left the parish for Northumberland to explore his vocation to a New Monasticism which was to attract wide interest in later years. John and his wife Linda went to stay at the Franciscan Friary at Alnmouth. Brother Ramon was there, who as Raymond Lloyd had spent over a year at Roslin and from there had gone on to Glasshampton. John Skinner discovered that Roland was not very far away, at Roslin. So, he went to see Roland there. Brother Ramon had been encouraging John Skinner to continue to explore the New Monasticism, a disciplined devout Christian life 'outside the cloister'. John Skinner felt he had found this pattern expressed in the Community at Roslin. Roland agreed that John could come regularly to see him, and Roland thus became John Skinner's mentor and spiritual guide. And so, in a sense, Roland became a mentor and spiritual adviser to the whole Northumbria Community as it developed.

In the mid-1980s, the Nether Springs Trust was formed, which enabled John Skinner to exercise a ministry of spiritual direction within a contemplative calling. A few years later, a group led by Roy Searle, a Baptist minister, called Northumbria Ministries, met the Nether Springs group, and they found that they could share their work and their journey. They spent a lot of time thinking about what a monastic, contemplative life could look like outside the cloister. Was it possible for people to develop a new monasticism without the unvarying, traditional form of celibacy and poverty? People found that the Northumbria Community offered them, in their family settings, an accessible pattern of commitment to prayer, to simplicity of life, and to study of the scriptures. In local groupings, they encouraged each other in their committed disciplines. 'Availability' and 'vulnerability' were seen as the defining characteristics of the Northumbria Community and all its subsequent Companions.

Other innovations in the Northumbria Community were influenced by Roslin's experience. When they first developed a Mother House at Hetton Hall near Wooler, they had a chapel but also cells around the grounds, places for private prayer, not unlike the arrangement at Roslin. They also brought Charles de Foucauld's Prayer of Abandonment into their daily meditations and gave a central place to Psalm 27 in their Daily Office.

The influence of Roslin continued not only through Roland but also through John Halsey, who for many years was the spiritual adviser to another of the leaders, Trevor Miller – a relationship that continues to this book's time of writing. John Skinner moved away to live in Turkey, in Seljuk (modern Ephesus), near the tomb which is the burial place of St John the Evangelist, near to the place where St John lived after taking Mary, the Lord's mother, in order to look after her.

According to the tradition important to the Northumbria Community, the Celtic Northumbrian saints – Aidan, Cuthbert and

Hilda, who were central to life in that part of England – were in their day very much influenced by St John the Apostle. They saw St John as their spiritual Father, and they would make pilgrimages to the Apostle's tomb. 'Part of our Celtic vision in understanding and developing the Community here in North Northumberland,' said Trevor Miller, 'was to walk again the sacred paths from Ireland to Northumbria to Turkey, once walked by the early Celtic missionaries. And so Seljuk in Turkey became a holy place of pilgrimage for us. Roland and John Halsey did not always find this an easy thing to understand!'

The Northumbria Community never advertised themselves widely, and in this they were consciously following the Community of the Transfiguration. 'It was from the Roslin Rule,' said Trevor Miller, 'that we learned about quiet anonymity, not seeking publicity. So, we have never really advertised ourselves. And initially, we even agonised over whether or not to have a website. But in the end we decided that on balance there was a possibility of it doing more good than not having one. We do write booklets and produce resources, along with a quarterly newsletter for our own Community Companions and friends. As part of that, we put together a set of prayers and daily readings for our Community Companions. Somehow HarperCollins got hold of it and contacted us to ask if we would let them publish it. We agreed, and they published it as *Celtic Daily Prayer*, and it became a very popular book.'[7]

Roland Walls found the concept of a geographically dispersed community very difficult to grasp. He said to Trevor Miller, in his own mischievous way, 'I don't understand your "dispersed community". Because true community can only be where you are sitting round a table, eating together, and looking at each other eye to eye.'

Trevor recalled, 'I tried to explain the concept of the dispersed community, but he didn't see it the same way. But he had that way of saying, "It's nonsense", but yet giving you encouragement all the same.'

Trevor Miller continued, 'The embracing of poverty was big in the life of the Community in Roslin. I always was renewed, always greatly challenged, by the deeply authentic way they kept their life simple. If you were there at lunchtime, you would have a stool at the table, and there would be an onion, garlic, and home-made bread, with Stilton cheese and perhaps an apple. And at one o'clock the news on the radio – everyone quiet to listen. But just the headlines, usually. "Have we heard enough?" Roland would say as he turned off the radio.'

The significance of Roslin for the Northumbria Community is encapsulated in this account of a conversation between Trevor Miller and Roland Walls.

'I remember being at Roslin one day, it must have been in about the year 2000,' recalled Trevor Miller. 'I was coming from the chapel, and Roland was entering the Enclosure. He looked very down. Very depressed almost, as I had never seen him before.

'"How are you then, Roland?" I asked him.

'"Ah," he said, "I'm looking at everything here, and thinking, 'We've been here all this time, and what is there to show for it? Nothing!'"

'I said to him, "Roland, if it had not been for you, if it had not been for the Community here, there would have been no North-umbria Community."

'I said that we as a Community continually gave thanks to God for Roland and John and Patty and the Community, for they had modelled a life that was foundational for our own ethos and Rule. "We owe our existence to you."

'He stopped and said, "Isn't that extraordinary!"

'You don't often get the opportunity to encourage someone like Roland. I am so glad that I had that moment to speak to him.'[8]

From among the many religious communities with whom the Roslin Community formed links, I will mention only one more. During a pilgrimage to the Holy Land in 1985 Roland visited the monastery of Deir Hanna, near Nazareth. When Roland heard of its history, and of the tenacity of the monk who had been instrumental in its foundation, it presented itself to him as in many ways similar to the experience of the Community of the Transfiguration. In the annual chapter minutes for 1995, it is recorded, 'Solitude has been very much part of our life, and the Franciscan emphasis on poverty was there from the first. Our vocation has been sustained by solitaries, and by others including Father Ya'akov Willebrands, whose eremitic [hermit] group in Deir Hanna is in style and rule almost identical with ours.'[9]

Father Ya'akov Willebrands was a Cistercian monk from the Netherlands, who overcame many obstacles on the way to fulfilling his vision of founding the monastery near Nazareth. He was born in 1918, became a Cistercian monk in 1941 and was ordained a priest in 1943. One day after the war, he was living in the monastery when his uncle came to give a talk to the 80 monks, relating his war-time experiences. This uncle was a parish priest who had spoken out against the deportation of Jews from the Netherlands. This led to his arrest and his own deportation to the prison camp of Dachau. He had sustained a severe leg injury, so he was kept as an experimental patient: a succession of serums were injected into him to see their effects. He survived, and was freed when the camp was liberated at the end of the war. Having seen the sufferings which the Jewish people had undergone, the uncle now took a great interest in the emergence of the new state of Israel. He longed to go to Israel to witness the beginning of the new world opening up there for the oppressed Jews. However, his age and frail health rendered that impossible. Father Jacob (as he was called then) wondered if perhaps he could go in his uncle's stead.

In his own religious life as a Cistercian, he found the idea developing that he should found a religious community in Israel. He asked his superior if some of the 80 monks in their monastery might go and begin a community out there. But the prospect was too difficult and remote, the organisational problems too complex.

But the vision remained, and eventually sympathetic superiors were persuaded. In attending a 1959 conference on Liturgy in Missions, Willebrands asserted his conviction that his Order's missions exhibited 'too much weight of European power, too big buildings, and too much stress on Cistercian uniformity'.[10] His hope of moving to Israel was reinforced.

In 1961, he went to live near Nazareth in an empty house made available to him by the local bishop, who hoped to see a religious community established in the area. Father Jacob was keenly aware that he was now living in the area where Jesus had lived his 'hidden' years. He learned Hebrew and Arabic.

While remaining under the authority of Rome, he left the Benedictine Order and became, instead, a monk in the Melkite Greek Catholic Church, becoming known as Father Ya'akov. The first two candidates for joining the community were Mr Theo Koperdraat and a Syrian of Jewish origin, Sylvain. The aims of the community would be prayer, a certain seclusion, and a simple life. They decided to make Hebrew their first language. Any Arab-speaker who came as an enquirer was given leave to do their part of the liturgy in Arabic. When a majority of Arabs were present, they did everything in Arabic.

He tried and tried to buy somewhere to begin the community. Six times, his offers were refused. Finally in 1967, after several years of asking, an Arab family sold them part of a mountainside. That year, on 17 July, three weeks after the Six-Day War, they went to the mountain. There they built some modest premises to live in. They then discovered that there was a cave nearby, on the land of another Palestinian family. After more than three years of requests, they purchased the land and the cave. With three further years of hard labour, the cave became the community's chapel.

Several candidates for membership of the community entered and then left. Life was not easy there. There was no running water, no electricity, no heating in the winter. But they became established. People from all over the country, Jews and Palestinians, frequently visited the chapel. There were excellent relations with the Muslims of Deir Hanna. Individual Israelis liked to spend days of recollection at the monastery; they experienced it as a place of peace.

When Roland went to visit the monastery, he and Father Willebrands exchanged greetings from one Community to another. Roland told him a little about Roslin, and Father Ya'akov reflected on his own experience of the life of a small religious community. 'Do not keep in your Community anyone whom God does not intend to be there. Do not keep them because they are nice, or because they are useful, but only because God intends them to be there. It is better to go on with very few than have many who should not be there at all.'

After the monastery of Deir Hanna had been established for 25 years Mr Arikraz, mayor of the 30 surrounding settlements, made an important public statement. He said, 'You are a very positive influence in the area. You have good relations with everyone, and you should be accepted.'

In 2002, they celebrated 25 years on the mountain, by which time Father Willebrands was the archimandrite of four monks. 'We count our presence a daily miracle,' he said. 'We continue as "watchmen for the morning".'[11]

As with so many of the religious communities with whom Roslin felt such close ties, the monastery at Deir Hanna lived with a sense of their own fragility and transience, regarding themselves as dependent on a power beyond themselves. As the Community of the Transfiguration acknowledged each year as the opening sentence of their annual chapter minutes, written in John Halsey's crisp, clear hand, 'Chapter believes it to be in the Lord's will for the Community to continue.'

15

The Franciscan Influence:
Bringing it All Together

To people unfamiliar with the religious life, there may seem little difference between one monk and another, one nun and another. Variations between this religious order and that religious order may seem unimportant and without significance. Yet the distinctions are deeply marked, and each discipline makes separate demands and offers different returns. It is not unlike the differing means of propulsion on an ocean voyage: one vessel is propeller-driven, the next a hovercraft, another a hydrofoil, while yet another is driven by wind in its sails. It took many years for the Roslin Community to determine its true home in the family of religious orders.

A Franciscan friar walking through a city centre today stands out from the crowd. With his long brown habit and a cord tied round his waist, with his shoulder cape and hood, and his open-toed leather sandals, he is instantly recognised as somebody different. When Francis Bernadone, later known as St Francis of Assisi, chose that style of clothing, he was deliberately choosing garments that would enable him to blend in with the ordinary population, for in Francis's day these clothes were standard wear for the poor. As a rich young man, Francis had taken pride in looking spectacular. After his conversion, he abandoned his finery, and instead wanted to look just like all the other poor men of his time and his city. It is an irony that today the attire of a follower of St Francis marks him out as conspicuously different from everyone else, especially the poor.

Roland Walls displayed a readiness, like Francis, to be identified with the poor by the way he dressed. Even when he was on the staff of a Cambridge college, he was known for the scruffiness of his clothing. He raised College eyebrows by occasionally making the floor of his college room available as a bed for the homeless.

Repeatedly through the following years, people remarked on his appearance.

'I first met Roland in 1976 on Iona. It was a week on the topic of "Prayer and Politics", and it was led by Roland. My young brother Ben Jamal said of Roland, "He looked a right tramp".[1]

'Roland had a sophistication, but he didn't use it. He could look as if he'd just climbed out of a rubbish bin,' said Jodi Page Clark, who knew Roland through the Community of Celebration on Cumbrae.[2]

'I first met with Roland in 1979,' said Simon Hughes, 'when he came to speak at the Portobello Baptist Youth Fellowship. I saw him come into the hall, and he was wearing a workman's jacket, I think it was bright orange. "Here's a dosser," I thought to myself.'[3]

'Roland preached at the consecration of two friends as bishops in St Paul's Cathedral in September 1980. When he arrived at the cathedral, the man on the door tried to turn away this apparent tramp, saying that an "important service" was about to begin. He was disconcerted when the "dosser" explained that he was the preacher.'[4]

Such testimonies to Roland's dishevelled appearance demonstrate that he chose to identify himself with the poor through how he presented himself. It seems that something of the Franciscan outlook was present in him from early in his life.

The Community of the Transfiguration displayed many similarities to the Franciscan way of life: the simplicity of the house, its furnishings and its diet; open-door hospitality and a welcome for the homeless wayfarer. Roslin was also notable for lightness of heart, and for the laughter which constantly accompanied discussion. Furthermore, the world of nature was an unfailing source of pleasure as they watched the changing seasons, the trees and the grass and the meadow flowers of the Enclosure, and the birds which came flocking to their bird-table. And, at the heart of it, there was a sense of gratitude for their constant experience of Jesus Christ revealed in the life of the poor. But they never characterised themselves as Franciscan.

Among many fruitful contacts with other communities, however, was their friendship with a small Anglican Franciscan friary in the east end of Glasgow. One of those Franciscan brothers, Brother Juniper, was preparing to join the Roman Catholic Franciscan Order, and in 1988 he came to stay at Roslin for some months before being received into his new home. Juniper had first visited Roslin as an Anglican Franciscan in 1977, and was immediately aware then of these Franciscan characteristics. By 1988, he sensed that the Franciscan themes were still very much present. 'There was a strong sense of their contemplative life,' said Juniper. 'And as a Community they were a real fraternity, they shared everything. They had no telephone and no television. They had an open door and a common table at which you might meet a cardinal, a bishop, a professor and a wayfarer. Their life was quite stark, and there was a lack of heating. In January it was freezing cold.'

The Franciscan character of the Community was still unstated but was about to be articulated. We can discern the development as we observe the Community grappling with the Community Charge – the notorious 'poll tax'. The poll tax was introduced into Scotland on 1 April 1989. The chapter minutes for that year record that all the Community members went to a protest meeting in Edinburgh, and to several local meetings in Roslin and Loanhead, 'at which a good deal of fury was vented'. After some discussion, the Community decided to take advantage of a provision for 'religious communities' to be exempted from the tax. They reasoned that 'no privilege is involved, and the responsible use of our money requires that it is used for the poor, rather than the Exchequer'.

In the chapter minutes for 1991, however, we find that discussion has taken place and that the Community have made a different decision: the Community will now pay the poll tax after all. The following entry appears: 'Efforts to clarify our position with the Poll Tax people issued in a firm commitment, surprising to us in its reversal of previous intentions. Now, guided we believe by the spirit of St Francis, we have decided that the Community *cannot* and *will not* claim any status or privilege, social or economic, which removes us from the "common life" of the poor. We thank God for the clarification this has brought.'

They attribute this change of direction to the spirit of St Francis. What can have happened, to bring St Francis thus into focus?

Just after Easter in 1990, the Community had received a visitor. Brother Johannes Küpper of the Order of the Friars Minor, the Franciscans, was on a sabbatical from his friary in Cologne. Wearing his brown habit girdled with the Franciscan cord, he arrived unannounced in Roslin, having heard of the Community when he was visiting a small Franciscan friary in Newcastle. Roslin and Johannes now found in each other the perfect partner. Not yet 30 years of age, Johannes was an effervescent guest. He introduced a note of excitement and adventure into the Community. He embraced Lady Poverty with an enthusiasm reminiscent of St Francis himself. On leaving Roslin at the end of his first visit, he would be heading for the main road south, where he would hitch a lift. To help him with the expenses of his journey, the Community gave him £20. 'This!' Johannes said in the tones of a prosecutor, holding the note up between finger and thumb, 'This has been the cause of all the problems of the Franciscan Order!' And, to the consternation of the brothers gathered to bid him farewell, he tore the note into small pieces and laid the fragments on the table.

The advent of such an unorthodox visitor was in itself a delight to the Roslin Community. But, in addition, Johannes's arrival gave rise to an important discussion. Roland was counting the cost of celibacy. He spoke of how, as a celibate man, what he missed in his old age was not the companionship of a wife in his bed; what he regretted was not having a son. He had come to terms with the sex issue, but the loss of fatherhood was a painful reality. He told the Community of his prayer: 'I know it's a dotty prayer, Lord, but you made Abraham a father in his old age. Could you possibly do the same for me?'

Celibacy had never been a major problem for the Community. 'I had several friendships with women before I joined the Community,' said John, 'but nothing came of them.' John recalled that, in the early days, the Community members took their vows for three years at a time. 'I suppose that made a difference: it was for a period of time, not at that stage for ever.' He remembered, too, how hectically busy life was for the small Community. Celibacy seemed to secure their availability for all the interests and responsibilities which were coming their way.

Nevertheless, at this later stage of his life, Roland felt the absence of a son. But, in Johannes with his fearless Franciscan zeal, Roland found that spiritual son. To a friend he said, 'I adopted Johannes as my son because he is crazy!'

Many years later, Johannes looked back to that first visit.

'When I arrived at the Community, it was love at first sight. What attracted me? The open hospitality. When we arrived, we were welcomed wholeheartedly and I found a community which was beguiling in its simplicity. The accommodation reminded me of the first Brothers of St Francis in its total lack of luxury. The door was never shut, always left open. Anyone, from the brother or sister on the streets to the university professor, had access to the community. Everyone was invited to take a seat at the kitchen table. It was this that reminded me of my vision of the Franciscan life. Francis was available to all and made no distinction between rich and poor.

'To this day, the symbolic image of the way of life in Roslin is for me the picture on the wall of their kitchen: Jesus eating a meal with others in an inn. Such an open hospitality was not to be seen in most of the Franciscan communities where I had lived – the brothers from the street are not normally admitted to the monastery, but have to eat their meal outside.

'This kitchen table at Roslin remains in my mind as a symbol of Franciscan hospitality which I aspire to wherever I happen to be.

'And then I saw the huts, the little garden huts of the brothers, just big enough to hold a bed and a desk. The garden was a bit wild. Then there were two huts joined together which served as a chapel. The first thing I said to the brothers was, "This is Assisi! This is Portiuncula!"

'In June of that year, I was on a retreat with Father Roland. I stayed in one of the huts myself. There I gained a full under-

standing of the secret of simplicity. The total focus on the Holy
Scriptures without any distraction brought me very close to Jesus.
The bustle of life distracts, but total concentration leads to God.
Later on, I read the words of Mother Rose, founder of the Wald-
breitbacher Franciscan Sisters, "It is only through poverty that
you will receive everything." How true that is.'[5]

The following year, 1991, Roland was invited by the Archdiocese
of St Andrews and Edinburgh to go to Cologne to pursue some
scholarly research into the life and work of John Duns Scotus,
who is buried there. The Vatican were preparing to declare Duns
Scotus 'blessed' (to 'beatify' him), a step on the road towards him
being declared 'a saint'. Roland's work, together with that of
others, would endorse the case for his 'beatification'.

Duns Scotus, who lived from around 1265 to 1308, was ordained to the priesthood as a Franciscan Brother. His name points
to him having come from Scotland, from Duns in Berwickshire.
He was educated at Oxford University and went to teach in the
University of Paris. He was known as 'the Subtle Doctor' on account of the nuances and delicate distinctions of his thinking.
Thousands attended his lectures. He addressed major mathemat-
ical and philosophical issues. The central thesis of all his work,
however, was that the Love of God is the source and destiny of all
that is; and he introduced with intricate arguments the significance
of the Immaculate Conception of the Virgin Mary. His opponents
ridiculed those who followed Duns Scotus's lines of thought, and
called them 'Dunses' – a name which has come down through
the centuries as 'dunce', an insult to a person's intelligence. In
1307, Duns Scotus was called to Cologne for reasons no longer
known; and there a year later he died. On his tomb, in Latin,
an inscription reads, 'Scotland bore me, England sustained me,
France taught me, Cologne holds me.'

In Scotland, Roland worked on the cause of Duns Scotus with
his friend Professor James Torrance, a frequent visitor to the
Community, and they co-operated in writing a booklet about
Duns Scotus.[6] In Germany, Roland translated into English some
of the material written by Father Herbert Schneider, at that time

the Definitor-General of the Franciscan Order in Rome. The work in support of the cause was successful, and the Community's chapter minutes record that 'March 20th saw the beatification celebrations of Duns Scotus in Rome. The Community attended simultaneous celebrations in Edinburgh, the fruit of much work by Roland and others ... A great and mysterious privilege for the Community, through Br Roland, to have been caught up in the rediscovery of Duns Scotus – like that man finding a treasure in a field.'[7]

The time spent in scholarly research in Cologne, the city of Brother Johannes's friary, led to Roland and Johannes planning to make a pilgrimage to Assisi. For Roland, a pilgrimage to Assisi was the fulfilment of a long-held hope. He kept a brief record of their progress day by day. Consciously styling his writing in the manner of St Francis's own spiritual writings, *Fioretti* (*The Little Flowers of St Francis*), Roland called these notebook entries *Fioretti – Little Flowers*. Here is how the first notebook began (Johannes being referred to as 'Brother John'):

> After our good Lord had put it into the hearts of Brother John and Brother Roland to make the pilgrimage to Assisi and visit the places where blessed Francis had left his name, they agreed to meet in a crowded place near Cologne. Brother John let his brother know where he was in the crowd by playing his recorder. 'Bless the Lord my soul, and praise his holy name' is what he played, for it had been sung at his final Profession, and Brother Roland knew it well. It was thus that they found each other in the vast crowd and embraced with the kiss of peace.

Johannes proposed that the two of them should walk and hitch-hike to Assisi. But, in consideration of Roland's age, the superior of the friary overruled the plan, and they travelled to Assisi by train.

As they traced the footsteps of St Francis, visiting places where significant events of Francis's life had occurred, Roland and Johannes spent a lot of time in quiet prayer and contemplation. From another of the *Little Flowers*:

How the brothers were by God's guidance brought to La Verna, and how they made cells for themselves on the top of the holy mountain.

The brothers, remembering the occasion when S. Francis spent the night in prayer out of earshot and eyesight from S. Leo his companion, resolved to do the same during the day. They made for themselves between the rocks, cells at a distance from one another. They set up Tau crosses,[8] and brought only the Holy Gospels with them. Hours were spent like this, for the brothers at La Verna had given them three days' hospitality. Each, after a long time, would call to the other, and if the other replied they would set off for food or Divine Office to the monastery. If either brother did not reply, the brothers remained in prayer and solitude until both agreed to depart.

So profoundly did Roland enter into thought about St Francis, and so memorable were his encounters with the landmarks of the saint's life, that on his return to Roslin he influenced the Community to engage more fully with St Francis's spiritual insights. Roland knew that it was not likely that he himself would return to Assisi or to the famous sites in Umbria where St Francis is especially remembered. So, in order to enable himself and others to draw more deeply on the Franciscan tradition, he established Franciscan pilgrimage places in the countryside around Roslin. Hill-tops, river-banks, clusters of trees, outcrops of rock – each represented a different and specific Umbrian scene. There were nine different localities, and all were within walking distance of the house in Roslin.

Roland employed the medium of the *Little Flowers* in keeping a simple record of the occasions when he and Johannes undertook Franciscan pilgrimages around Roslin, and on Cumbrae at Snoopy House, known now as 'Skylight Hermitage'. In three small, cheap red notebooks, he composed accounts of their journeys, their thoughts and their times of prayer, all in the style of the writings of St Francis.

Roland was always aware of the responsibility that he carried for the very existence of the Community. To an enquirer who was considering becoming a member of the Community he once said, gesturing with a wave of his arm to the House, to the Enclosure, the Chapel and the huts, 'You see, this is all my fantasy.' He sensed the significant role he had played in establishing the way of life, and also shaping the future, of all the members of the Community. The responsibility weighed on him.

The final entry in the third volume of the *Little Flowers*, written at Roslin and dated 1995, reflects his awareness of the responsibility through a particularly Franciscan theme.

How Br Roland was comforted by a small bird (ein Spatz!)

One afternoon it was very hot, so Br Roland sat outside his hut. He was reading about St Francis and how Br Elias changed all that St Francis wanted for his Order. Br Roland began to think of his little family of brothers – so weak, so small. How will they be in the future? Just as he began to think of these things, a small sparrow (Francis used to say the sparrows were really Grey Brothers) came and sat on Roland's shoulder. He was quite happy, and remained there, next to Br Roland's ear, for one minute. Then he flew to a nearby bush.

Br Roland knew the bird had been sent by the prayers of St Francis to help him not to worry about his brothers. God himself will look after them. Amen

It was in 1995 that the Community moved towards formalising their place in the Franciscan family. The chapter wrote a letter to the two bishops, the Warden and the Visitor, asking them to authorise the required steps.

'From the beginning in 1965 we followed Dom Columban's advice not to be impatient about the question of our particular vocation, which would ultimately be given to us ... From 1990 onwards, Br Roland's association with the OFM [Franciscans] Cologne Province, and before that his ministry from 1983 to the Poor Clares of Liberton, and gradually with other Poor Clares houses in Britain and Germany, brought us in close contact with the Franciscan family. (The OFM [Franciscan] small friary in Newcastle was initiated after planning with us in Roslin.)

'In the light of all this experience, and in consideration of the inevitable tiny size of our houses (now and in any foreseeable future), we have come to clarify our identity. We have a mutual joy that we have been led at last, over many years, to recognition of our special vocation.'

A visit from a senior Franciscan, Father Herbert Schneider, assured them that in the developed pattern of their religious community they were already following the Third Order Rule of St Francis. Under the guidance of their new Visitor, Father Ninian Arbuckle, another Franciscan, all necessary steps were taken to secure their place as Franciscans.

In the following year, Brother Johannes was admitted as a member of the Roslin Community, a Little Brother of the Common Life. Though he would continue to be based in Germany, he would be consulted on major decisions affecting the Community in Roslin.

Many years later, Johannes affirmed, 'I owe the vision which I received for my Franciscan life to the association I had in Roslin with John, Patty and Roland. May God grant that I will express it in new ways through my life.'⁹

Being now incorporated within the Franciscan family, the Community were given access to a special trust fund which enabled John Halsey to make what was, for him, an unprecedented pilgrimage to Assisi just after Easter in 1997. John's diary of the visit begins: 'April 1st. Tuesday in Easter Week. What better day than April Fools' Day for a little brother of St Francis, "le jongleur de Dieu" ["God's wandering minstrel"], to set out for Assisi.'

On his first day in Assisi, he went to visit Portiuncula, the little church which Francis had found in ruins, and which he thought God had called him to rebuild.

The Portiuncula which St Francis had first rebuilt, and which had been so long in my thoughts, had originally been a modest little chapel hidden away in the woods; surrounded by woodland shelters and home-made shacks, it had been the base for the brothers living in the freedom and joy of the Gospel simplicity, and in a total poverty that they had made their one desire.

And now it was encased in the grandeur of a basilica, with all the attendant symbols of power and wealth, and at the centre of a town with traffic roaring through, and giant coaches bringing crowds from all over the world.

There was a vast piazza. Ranged along one side were stalls forming a permanent market, and at the east end the towering facade of the basilica. With a great mixture of emotion, I entered the building which so dwarfed the little Portiuncula chapel, nestling in the distant east end. I made my way there and found a corner to be still and try to absorb it all.

John's diary reflects on the contrast between the historical life of Francis and his brothers, and the vast religious and commercial industry which has accumulated around the famous sites. And he muses that a pilgrimage to holy places is essentially about the lifelong pilgrimage of the heart.

John visited some of the locations which Roland, in designing the Franciscan pilgrimages around Roslin, had superimposed on the local Midlothian landscape. He found that there were so many highlights in the ten days 'that the word highlight rather loses its meaning'. One of the last entries in his diary demonstrates the cumulative effect of years of contemplative prayer, and perhaps indicates something of the inner structure of John's character:

On my last day, I was diverted away from a visit to the Basilica of St Francis by a poster which seemed to suggest some sort of Franciscan Encounter, and directing me through a doorway in the wall leading to the Basilica and bordering the piazza. What could this be? The directions led to a cloister adjoining the basilica. Turning left on entering the cloister was a display of material – pictures, symbols and writings devoted to Father Maximilian Kolbe and his descent into the hell of Auschwitz.[10] I can say only that it was a searing experience, in which nothing was spared. On turning right at the entrance, there was a complementary display devoted to the life of St Francis, and leading to the marks of crucifixion, the stigmata, which he experienced. The focus, as it were linking the two halves of the display and situated in the open air in a corner of the central area of the cloister, is a figure in metal of Il Poverillo [the little poor man] superbly expressing radiant praise – out of rags and poverty – of the Creator, symbolised by a tree with all kinds of flowers, fruit and birds. The whole was magnificently designed to express, for me, the contemporary Franciscan path – which is the path for us all – through suffering crucifixion and hell to Resurrection and God's future.

For me it was significant that this exhibition adjoins the great Upper Church, thronged by crowds drawn to the beauty and triumphalism of the Giottos and the wealth of art treasures – the splendour of the past. The exhibition is perhaps an attempt to redeem it, and to provide a glimpse of the significance of St Francis for us today, and a glimpse also of what is coming towards us.

The Franciscan inclinations of the Community had been evident for many years. But their vocation as Franciscans was now fully acknowledged. One signal of their association with the Order of Friars Minor, the Franciscans, was their wearing of a particular cross, the 'Tau' cross shaped like a capital 'T'. It is widely accepted that St Francis was present at the Fourth Lateran Council in Rome in 1216, and that there he heard Pope Innocent III promote the 'T' cross as a symbol of the Lord's crucifixion and as a sign of the Lord's followers. From then on, the Tau cross became Francis's own coat of arms.

Thomas of Celano (1200–55), a Franciscan friar who composed admiring biographies of St Francis, wrote, 'Francis preferred the Tau above all other symbols: he utilised it as his only signature for his letters, and he painted the image of it on the walls of all the places in which he stayed.'

Due, no doubt, in large part to Francis's own affection for the Tau cross, it has been an accepted Franciscan symbol for centuries. It remains so today.

At the head of Roland Walls's grave, in the steeply sloping churchyard below Rosslyn Chapel, the headstone with its simple inscription is of course in the form of a Tau cross.

16

The Influence of the Community on Individuals

Scattered throughout this narrative have been examples of the transforming effect which the various members of the Community and the atmosphere of Roslin had on individual visitors.

From the day Patty Burgess first emerged as a deaconess in Loanhead in 1972, she showed a capacity for welcoming the unexpected. A team of young teenagers from the Loanhead street corners came to visit her, intrigued by the woman who had moved into her little flat without furniture or carpets.

'The thing was,' said Patty, 'they came from all over. It was quite extraordinary. They came from Gilmerton, Roslin and Penicuik. And, before they came, I had no idea at all what to do. So I sat on the ground, in the corner over there, and I darned my stockings, as I did in those days.

'I thought to myself, "Well, I'll have to be doing something when they come."

'That was crazy of course.

'"Why are you doing that?"

'There was one who had a sense of humour. He was older, and the kids were likely to follow him. And now he runs the butcher's shop just next door. So, when I came back in 1983, he was in Campbell's the butcher's.

'And he said, "Are you going to run the club again? Are you going to do it again?"

'And I said, "No. I'm old, and wiser. But *you* could do it perfectly well."

'"Oh, but I've got my family," he said.

'But he could. And that is what is needed in Loanhead. It needs a lot of silly places like this, that allowed kids just to come. Of course they did knock the place about a bit. One kid put his foot through the wall, I remember.

'"Must you?" I said.

'And I think that this, the immediate reaction of not shouting and screaming, was what made him think he was into something that was different.'

Anthony Kramers, for 12 years the leader of L'Arche Edinburgh, recognised that Roslin offered acceptance and understanding for an unusually wide range of people. 'The Roslin Community are a witness to the value of accompaniment. They are comfortable with the odd, the unresolved and even the psychotic – the crazy bits of each of us. They were comfortable with people in any condition.'

One of Roland's students, who maintained a friendship with the Community from its beginning, remembered how the atmosphere of Roslin could restore him when he suffered a psychotic episode. 'Roslin was always a haven for me. Roland took me in during times of breakdown, at those times when it was quite difficult to distinguish between reality and extra-reality.'

Another of Roland's students recalled that Roland rescued him when he suffered a breakdown in health when on holiday in the Greek islands.

'There were discussions about whether I should be allowed to go to Greece,' the student recalled many years later. 'To my horror, the view was "No". Roland probably – plus my mother – thought I should not have gone. But I did go. And I ended up in hospital.

'I was away on the island of Naxos. I had a term off, and my health collapsed at the end of it. I'd been there for three months. I remember Roland marching into the flat in Naxos. He was always full of laughter and glee, very much supplied with resources, a powerful challenger. Roland's humour was a key element of his contribution. I remember he came out and managed things, when I was feeling very low. Roland had made friends with my mother, and came and made friends with me. Almost like a senior nurse, or a medic. But I was very, very unwell when he arrived. There was a stunning sunset, and I remember refusing to look at it.'

The student proceeded to describe one of the steps Roland took to help him towards coming to his senses.

'What are those insects that crawl around damp areas – it begins with a "c"? They have crustacean outsides? Cockroaches? They were everywhere in the Naxos flat, in the kitchen. On this occasion there were two. One Roland called "Eustace". The other he called "Cyril". Roland could mock the unpleasant. By laughter he showed how you could surmount your hostility, your anxiety. He was "elastic". Giving those things names made them into good company.'

The readiness of Roslin to be comfortable with 'the odd, the unresolved and even the psychotic' is reflected in the Acknowledgements at the beginning of a study of St Paul[1] by the New Testament scholar Douglas Templeton. There he pays tribute to Roland Walls: 'I thank Father R. C. Walls, who knows nonsense when he sees it and likes some of it.'

A long-standing friend of the Community recalled in detail the effect which the Community – first Roland, but then the whole Community – had on her life.

The Community at Roslin have made a deep impression on me for most of my adult life. I was 25 when I met Roland in Orkney. He'd been invited by John Roebuck, the Episcopal priest, to speak in each of the different churches in Kirkwall during Holy Week.

I was in Orkney staying with my sister and her husband, who was assistant minister at St Magnus Cathedral. I thought I was about to get married, but suddenly there was a phone message that seemed to shatter that, and I was really upset. So, I decided to leave and go back to Glasgow, but my brother-in-law took me for a walk, and I only met Roland because I missed the ferry (as my brother-in-law intended).

So that evening – I didn't want to go to church – but went along with the others to the Salvation Army Hall. Roland was just extraordinary. He was beaming ... glowing ... and the things he said, and what he looked like ... I'd never heard any-one speak like that.

I stayed on, and a group of us followed Roland round the different churches. On Maundy Thursday, we were in the Episcopal church for a very simple, beautiful Eucharist. I was Church of Scotland, and that Eucharist felt like a very quiet but big moment.

After the service, John Roebuck stopped us at the door and said, 'Sybil's making bread in the kitchen' (Sybil was his wife). So, we went through, and Roland was there in the kitchen. We said, 'Tell us about Roslin, about your Community'. He started to speak. I remember him saying that in our lifetime the insti-tutions of the Church may well break down and maybe even disappear, but wherever two or three gather together in the Lord's name the Church will continue. He spoke about the real-ity of evil – and I'd never heard anyone speak about such things before. He had a joyful authority about him, so authentic, kind of earthy. He could relate to us, and made theology real.

What happened that evening doesn't fit into words, but I remember the feeling of peace and joy – that the Christian story was really true; that someone could live like they were living and could get up and speak like that and make us laugh and then say important things so that you remember them. I have a sense that Roland could have lived in any age; a man outside of time somehow.

We all felt that evening was special. Perhaps I was a bit vulner-able ... open to being deeply affected. But a door opened, and I was suddenly introduced to something so important. Good Fri-day was wild and quite cold. Roland had been tramping around in the mud. We were in the little St Rognvald Chapel within the cathedral for the service that evening. Roland, in his muddy boots, knelt for ages. The minister was keen to get started, but Roland remained there praying.

On Easter Saturday, I went for a long walk by myself on the beach and decided to end my relationship (we'd known each other for seven years) and have one final meeting to say good-bye.

On Sunday evening, we wondered if there would be a repeat of what had happened in the rectory kitchen on Thursday. So, we all gathered together again in another place. But Roland was very quiet; he hardly spoke, preferring to commune with the dog – a beautiful golden retriever. Later he remarked lightly, 'You can't just turn on the Holy Spirit like a tap.'

I went back to Glasgow, met my boyfriend for that 'final meeting', and we walked down to the Broomielaw. Before I had time to tell him anything, he asked me to marry him – and I said 'Yes'!

In 1982, I met Roland again. We'd moved to the Borders, and I read in the local paper that he was speaking on 'Simplicity' in Penicuik. So, I went. Afterwards, I gave him a lift back to Roslin – and that was how I went to the Community for the first time. Patty took me out to see the Chapel. That was the start of it ...

Then our son (aged about 4) was ill and developed double vision. I was told that he'd likely always had a squint and that I just hadn't noticed it. I knew this wasn't true, so – it was Maundy Thursday – I went to Roland. He was at Mass somewhere, but Patty and John were so kind. They encouraged me to stay until he got home. I could hardly speak, but Roland just sat beside me and said he would come down to see our son. He came on Easter Tuesday and played with the boys. He blessed our son and gave me a little icon from Greece of Mary 'Our Lady of Tenderness'. He said, 'Mary will help you to be a mother'. My husband came home as Roland was leaving. He was doing building work, and they employed him to renew the tin roof of the main Community building. The V-shaped roof caused lots of problems, as the valley gutter leaked and the books in the library were going mouldy. My husband used a new product called Plygene to line the gutter. Roland was intrigued and thought it would be good to have their clothes made out of it, as they would be waterproof and durable.

After Roland had visited and blessed our son, we both coped much better. I hung the little icon there by the stove. It's become really important to me. But I suppose, with the steam from cooking, little by little she began to fade; the features flaked off. I liked having her there, though, and it didn't seem to matter that she faded and faded. Look ... now there's nothing left of her ... only the space where she has been. She's completely disappeared. But then, in Roslin, they were given a stained-glass image of Mary for the chapel. Roland showed it to me and said, 'See ... Mary is clear glass ... it's beautiful, Mary became nothing ... Mary made room for God.' For someone like me – not academic, needing images and symbols, Roland made sense of things. He could relate to anyone.

I started to go the local Catholic church; it was Easter 1981, and I'd just had our second son. I was late, and I couldn't get into the Church of Scotland; the door was locked or jammed. It happened three times, and so I went to the Catholic church. The Eucharist recalled the Eucharist with Roland in Orkney – I kept going, but I wasn't Catholic, so I couldn't receive the Eucharist, and I got stuck on that 'fence' for about 16 years. I didn't want to cause any division within my family – none of them are Catholic. Yet, in the Eucharist I saw things holding together; holding me together – even though I couldn't receive. But, by then, the Community were living in that broken place, and they weren't able to share the Eucharist together. Roland refused to plaster over the cracks and pretend that the Church isn't broken. I feel so grateful for what they lived – and I think that, by becoming Catholic, Roland opened up the Community to Catholics.

Kay Ramsay, such a close friend of the Community at Roslin, finally nudged me off that 'fence' that I was tangled up on. She said to me, 'I think you should ask your priest if you can receive Communion at Easter.' Kay said this would be a way of finding out if I really wanted to become Catholic.

So, I asked the parish priest, who asked me, 'When would you like to do it?'

'On Maundy Thursday', I said.

So, on Maundy Thursday, after the Washing of the Feet, I did receive the Eucharist. And I did know after that.

The humility of the Community is what makes it different

from anywhere else I know. Thinking now of John Halsey; such a humble presence; humility, simplicity and complete openness. That door into the kitchen … open to anyone that pitches up. There's room for all the craziness and the bits that don't make sense. They never put you in a box … no 'clubbiness'.

They lived in the most basic way that anyone's living in Scotland today. The huts … close to the earth and the weather; few possessions or comforts. They have the essentials sorted out, and it's been the same for all these years. They live an authentic life – everything is stripped away except what's real.

Look for instance at the kitchen. All the old cutlery and crockery … only what's useful, essential. The laundry on the pulley; the paintings and things on the wall – all stand for something – reminders of what's important – relationships, memories, people and animals; the long story that that we're all part of – the place where we're all welcome and accepted.

* * *

Another person for whom the Community at Roslin was a pivotal influence was William Henderson, who became a theatrical director in Melbourne, Australia.

I've known Roland since I was a child. He came on holiday with us every year. My father was a Scot, my mother from Australia. They were in Cambridge where my father, an economist trained under John Maynard Keynes, was on the staff of Corpus Christi College. Roland was on the staff there too, the College chaplain. One year, Roland was on holiday on his own in Galloway. My father told him to look out for a house for us. Roland phoned to say he'd found something that was very nice. 'Buy it, then,' said Mr Henderson. And that was it. Roland was such a trusted friend.

Roland himself, on one walking holiday in Galloway, met up with a gentleman who was also out walking. They walked and talked together, and Roland said how much he hoped he might find a little Galloway cottage to stay in. 'I think perhaps I have one that would suit you,' said the gentleman, who turned out to be the local landowner, William Stewart, Earl of Galloway. So, Roland had the use of a small country cottage there for many years.

The first time I went to Roslin as an adult was in 1991. I was in a poor way. I had just lost the love of my life. I was teaching drama, not very well, and I was left with a huge sense of failure. I went to Roslin. There was this dark house, with its strange ways, and all the times of prayer. And on a walk I picked a flower – the rarest in the forest, which you're not supposed to pick – and everything was going wrong. I just couldn't take it. It was all too foreign for words. I decided it was time for me to go. So, I got everything together and made ready to leave.

The Russians have a custom. Whenever they are about to go off on a journey, they sit down quietly for a short time and think. That's seemed to me a good thing to do. So, I went into the big sitting-room and sat down quietly for a little before departing. As I sat there, Roland came into the room and sat down. 'Well then, Will,' he said, 'what's been happening to you?' And, in response to his gentle question, I was able to unload the matters that were weighing on my life.

He'd been observing me closely and kindly. He knew before I did that I wasn't going to stay. But I spoke and he listened. And sometimes we laughed. Laughter was one of Roland's gifts. Through his laughter he let me see, with a huge sense of relief, that you could be in the most dreadful situation but still keep going. Laughter is so powerful. He said, 'You can bring down the House of Commons with a laugh. And the only thing a dictator cannot stand is being laughed at, being mocked.'

There was always laughter. People saw the laughter, but Roland was not only genial; they also met a highly cerebral and rigorous intellect. Roland had a deeply refined instinct for the pain of the others – the pain invisible. I remember thinking, when I came later to the Community, 'This little Community is larger than the institution of the Church.' Roland once said, 'The Vatican is a sweet little old lady, surrounded by men in black with Kalashnikovs.'

The Community demonstrated that you can be disorganised and still be holy. You can have the cat on the altar. You can stop the service if the drunk man comes in and interrupts.

* * *

If you spend a little time walking among the trees of the Enclosure, you are sure to see the three sculptures. One is a piece of driftwood from the seashore of the Firth of Forth. A tree-root with sharp and pointed limbs sticking out, it looks a little like a person running. 'This is the Devil,' said Roland, 'and he's running away!' Among the trees is a three-quarter-size statue of a seated figure, smiling and making a generous gesture with his hand: this is St Francis, a gift from a friend. On a tree-stump rests another gift, another stone sculpture. It is of two men in a close embrace. Their arms are round each other; each rests his head on the other's left shoulder. The men seem identical. But one of them has the nail-marks, the stigmata, through the centre of his hands. Here now is the testimony of the sculptor.

I've been thinking about all this, and about what I would say. The Community is almost in its endgame now. With just the two of them now, John in Roslin and Patty in Loanhead. But I feel that it reverberates and continues, and that it will go on doing that. For, once you've had that contact with the Community, you are different – many people find that their life is changed. They carry on the idea of community they have encountered there.

Just the way you greet someone, once you've seen them doing it. The way you respond to someone, even someone you might expect to be quite antagonistic to.

The effect they have is like ripples going on and on.

It's in their actions, the way you see them respond to people. Making them welcome at the kitchen table. Take the way that Roland spoke to the Jehovah's Witnesses, for instance. I would only have a brief word with them at the door and see them on their way. There they're welcomed in and share the meal. Roland wasn't threatened by them in the way I'd have felt threatened.

A little thing like that has a big impact on me. It's nothing for them, but it's a big thing for me – it has ongoing ramifications. It has its effect. You change the way you see things. I feel privileged that I had that time staying with them many years ago. It was an answer to prayer. Maybe, of course, everything is an answer to prayer. That would mean that prayer is part of your being.

I'd come from the Plymouth Brethren. They were very strict, very theologically based, and with a very black-and-white agenda. I was about 14 when I first met them. And in time I would be set up to be married to a Church person. And in time I would probably have become an elder.

But I worked in the garage industry as a spray painter, and there weren't a lot of Christians in that kind of work. Most of the men in the Church were professional men, or in the university. The women were teachers or librarians, and were mostly women without a career who looked after the family at home. But, in my job, I remember thinking it would be great to have a companion at work who would not give me a hard time. I used to pray that God would put me to work beside another Christian. I went to work in the garage in Loanhead, where John Halsey worked. I remember thinking that God had a sense of humour putting me beside John. Here was me, an unbending Plymouth Brethren, meeting a softy – a liberal, woolly Christian with no principles – that's what I thought John was when I met him. I remember many conversations with him which showed the contrast between us.

I was invited out to Roslin, and I met Roland and Patty. They had a cutting from a newspaper on the wall of the kitchen; it was of a picture of the Last Supper with these big, strong-featured men. They made such a big thing of this little paper cutting. So, I copied the picture off that little cutting from the paper, and I painted them a version of it – that's what I do: I'm a painter. And it's up on their wall in the kitchen still. The Last Supper. And I introduced Roland and John to the Colourists. They could never have afforded a painting by one of the Colourists. But they could have a copy, so I painted one and gave it to them. It's somewhere in the house yet.

I worked with John from 1977 to 1980, three years. And I've kept up with them since. They saw me through difficult times. In the 1980s, I was coming to terms with being gay. I know if it hadn't been for the Community I'd not have been alive. I'd have died by my own hand.

And I know that there's a large number of people I've listened to, and sympathised with, and laughed with, who might have been gone, too. They'd have died. Taken their lives. And the world would have been the poorer. Because when someone takes their own life they take the decision out of the Creator's hand. It's a very big choice to make.

So, I think of myself as owing them, the Community, everything. They don't see it that way, as me owing them something. For they don't see themselves as giving. But they are a beacon, a light.

They've been that for so many people.

I'm just a tiny little raindrop among all the people they have influenced.

Their influence is incalculable.

My contribution to the world is because of them.

The Community and its way of living has formed me.

My outlook has been shaped by them.

I think of them very often. Even now, I can hear Roland's voice. I sometimes ask myself, and wonder, 'What would Roland think of this?' When you've known the man, you know what he might say. You know that at some things he might laugh, and say, 'It's quite preposterous! Ridiculous!'

The impact of his life, the Community's life, has been immense. As an artist, I reflect on things I've done. I have done things. But, even if that's all I've done, it has been because they made it possible for me to live. And if the Community had only met the needs of one person, and changed that one person's life, then it would have served a great purpose. And when you think of its value to the rest of us – its influence is incalculable.

It's like a gong has been hit, and the sound goes out and out and out. And it makes other gongs ring, and the other gongs go on sounding and starting yet other gongs to sound.

There are people I've helped, for instance. They say, 'Why do you do such a thing?' And truly I take it from the Community. Their philosophy is about being together, giving help when you can give help. The value the Community gives you is the value to appreciate each other. I've been in the camp of need. And I've been in the camp of being able to give.

So, how did the Community save me, then?

Homosexuality has to be established in the history of our society. So that people can know what it was like to be homosexual those years ago. My partner and I have been together for over 30 years. In this current generation, there's no awkwardness about it. People have known him and me all their lives. They know who we are. And young ones in their teens who know us can express their emotions freely. They can hug us and give us a kiss on the cheek when they see us. Maybe our society will come to terms with it. More and more people know someone who's gay – and have someone in their family that's gay. That is all making a difference. But it matters very much when leaders make hostile statements, Church leaders and politicians, Cardinal O'Brien saying homosexuality is a disordered state of being.

Roland saved me from taking myself to the Forth Road Bridge and jumping off.

I had tried, the night before, to kill myself on a motorbike. I went over the road known as 'the Wisp'. It's a dangerous road. I knew I was going to end my torment. I decided that I would drive straight at the very first vehicle I saw. I saw this van coming towards me, and I drove straight at it. Somehow he swerved away at the last moment, and the bike and I crashed into the side of the van. I and the bike were bounced on to the roadside. I was on the ground, with the bike on top of me, the engine still running. The van had stopped about 100 yards down the road.

Instantly, I knew what the driver was doing. 'You bastard!' he shouted as he ran up the road. 'I'll kill you!' I picked up the bike and drove off, unharmed. I never looked back, and drove at high speed all the way home. I went through any number of red lights on the way and never stopped until I was home. And I went to bed, still with my crash helmet on, and cried myself to sleep.

I woke up. I'd puked inside my crash helmet. I'd pee-ed myself as well.

I got into the shower. 'This can't go on.'

'I'll go and tell the Community. If they say nothing of any use to me, I'll go to the Forth Road Bridge and jump off. There's no way back up when you've jumped off that.'

The Community were at their evening prayers. When it was finished, I was in tears. Everybody left the chapel except for Roland.

'Come on,' he said. 'What's the matter?'

'I think I'm homosexual.'

'Yes. Well?'

'I don't think I want to be.'

'God's given you it. You can't choose.'

To hear this very holy man say that, it was a real validation. I felt he had plucked me from the jaws of death. He didn't know my plan. He didn't know that, if he'd said what the cardinal said, I could not have borne it any more.

Though I could not believe I was hearing the words.

I thought, 'He hasn't heard me correctly.'

But he had. So, I stayed for a month. The Community let me be. Never said anything. I'd lost weight. Why eat if you're going to die? I'd drunk tea and water, so I had survived this long. They just let me be. I remember that life just carried on round about me. No questions. They let me come round until I was ready to express what I wanted to do next.

And this acceptance of me being gay released all kinds of things within me. I had lost my Mum when I was young, and had never been able to grieve for her. But now, suddenly, it became possible. And one stormy day I went down to the beach at Bilsdean near Cockburnspath and found a piece of sand-stone. And there on the beach, in the wind, with the breakers crashing on to the sand, I carved it, sobbing and sobbing in grief for my Mum. And it became an image of the two Adams. The Second Adam, with his pierced hands, in an embrace with the first Adam who had brought doom on himself and on us all.

And I took it to Roslin, and it's there now in the Enclosure.

17

In Roslin and Loanhead

This book has sought to present a history of the Community of the Transfiguration. It has drawn on a variety of sources to illuminate different facets of the Community's life and activity. But how did the Community appear to ordinary residents of Roslin and Loanhead? Did local people understand its sense of purpose, or fathom its hopes? Here are some voices which shed light on those questions.

Tony Macgregor has lived next door to Patty in Loanhead for 17 years. Tony is a musician, and for seven years he worked with the Cleansing Department as a binman in Edinburgh. What has he made of his neighbour, Patty Burgess?

* * *

Tony Macgregor

When Amanda and myself first moved into this house, we were poking around the garden trying to make sense of our non-senses when a wild, beaming face appeared at the fence with an extended hand clutching a tuft of long grass in a great clod of earth. This was Patty. She explained that a custom of the Maasai people was to exchange clumps of earth as a kind of peace offering – so, we handed her a great clod of ours and knew we had a very interesting neighbour. We then discovered that this woman in her 80s, bursting with vim and vigour, slept in a shed in the *garden*. We have been in awe ever since.

She once told us about the time some boys jumped on to the shed roof in the night. When we asked her what she did, she said, 'I just started to pray very loudly, in a very low voice, and they quickly scarpered.' I can only imagine the story they told their friends.

A lot of different people come to see Patty. But I don't think it is widely known that there is a Community over in Roslin, and that this is an annexe of it. People come; they arrive over the years. We've been here since 1996, and never a day has gone by without someone coming to see Patty. From all over the globe. They have known Roland, Patty and John. But it's not advertised.

Years ago, all the children used to come here to Patty's house. They came often. One of those children was my wife's cousin. It was all the 'tearaways'. They'd gather in the vennel, the little passageway through the buildings to the back. It was right next to the café, so they'd come out and gather there and do all their wild-child stuff, shouting and writing on the walls. This would have been the early 1970s. They started asking Patty who she was and what she did, so she invited them in. A lot of the marks and burn-marks on her chairs are from that time. I'm not sure that the neighbours liked it so much. One of the children had written on the wall, 'Burgess is a Pro'. It didn't bother Patty at all, but one of the neighbours was absolutely horrified. After quite some time, the neighbour realised Patty wasn't going to remove it, so quietly did so herself.

My wife's cousin came round to see us a few years ago.

He said, 'We used to come and visit an old woman up that stair.'

'That'll be Patty,' I said.

'Auld Burgess is still alive?' he shouted. 'You're kidding me!'

Of course, he's been a tearaway all his life – he's in his 50s now! She used to have them all in her house. And they just hung about there and had a laugh. Patty would get on well with them, talking to them and trying to give them advice.

There are a lot of local people come to see Patty. There's all sorts of people. In one of her hospital spells, I remember, a lady was in praying with her at her bedside. There's a whole cupboard of people from all round the place.

I suppose part of it is her personality that keeps people in touch with her. She's very calming and she's very funny. I'm not part of any religious organisation. She's just a very funny person, with a quick mind.

One of my very first interactions with her was – I was trying to fit some panelling at my front door. It wasn't going well, and my language would be terrible, shouting and cursing. Patty passed quietly by and up into her house. Later that afternoon, I found a little bag on the door-handle with a note: 'Some hotcross buns for some hot cross neighbours'. And if ever she puts a note through the door, she uses an old junk envelope, and she always edits the printing on the envelope in some amusing way.

I remember one time when Roland had become less able to look after things, and John was in hospital. Patty hadn't been too well either, so we had a system where I would look in on her at night and see that she was OK. This day, Patty had been out and hadn't come back. I looked for her in all the obvious places, but no Patty. The door was open as always, the light was on and the heat was on, but she wasn't there. I couldn't get in touch with Roslin: no-one answered the phone. So, I called the police, imagining my 90-year-old friend in a bush somewhere.

Next thing, half of the Lothian and Borders police force arrive with their cadaver dogs to carry out a search, poking all over the place shouting 'Mrs Burgess!' into the bushes. They asked where else she might be, so we gave them the Roslin address. They went to the house at Roslin to check the premises. Of course, finding the door unlocked, they let themselves in. There she was, sleeping somewhere, to keep Roland from having to be in the house on his own. And, with their torches and their cadaver dogs, the police woke them up. Roland's memory was not good by then, but the next morning he could certainly remember that.

I feel that Patty is a kindred spirit. I have a want to defend that sort of independent character. Too many people get to a certain age and find themselves swept into care homes – and anyone who knows Patty knows she needs her own space and her own pace. I feel it's my job to help make sure she has that.

It's our good fortune to have got to know Patty and John, and it's a regret that we didn't really get to know Roland. We've met a lot of people over the years who have been touched in some way by them – and they truly have helped people. In such a misled, morally confused society, finding Patty and John gives us hope that all is not lost.

* * *

As this book is being written, Patty approaches her 97th birthday. In recent years, she has appreciated some domestic help in the house. Lorraine Dalgety, who was a nurse before she left work to have and raise a family, has been taking cleaning jobs to help with her family life. Patty knew Lorraine from going to St Margaret's Church, Loanhead. How does Lorraine view Patty and the Community?

Lorraine Dalgety

All my life, I've lived in Loanhead. And I've been aware of Patty all my life. She was always popping into the church, St Margaret's. I used to see her going to Mass on Sundays and other days.

When I was younger, I always thought she was a bit eccentric. Because she's got a very basic lifestyle. She's not bothered about what she wears. When you're young, you think you should wear things that are smart. She has a long blue anorak. I remember thinking it looked very old and strange. But it was because of Patty that another friend and I went to some L'Arche meetings in Edinburgh when they were starting up L'Arche there.

In more recent years, I would bump into her in the street. She was just part of things. She did stand out, of course. Probably what made me think about it was that on a Sunday you'd always put on your Sunday best. But Patty didn't. As a child, you noticed that. Everybody made an effort to look their best going to the church. But not Patty.

I know her differently now. But, when you don't know someone, you go on appearances. Even my kids, who are from 16 up to 20, probably can't comprehend someone having such a simple lifestyle as Patty. When I bring her long blue anorak back to wash it, the kids can't understand how she can wear such a thing.

I know now that she's part of a Community. I really didn't know that before. Not really. But Father White was our parish priest when Roland became a Catholic, and I learned more then. Because she was associated with the church, I just thought she was a Catholic. Only recently, I discovered she was from the Scottish Episcopal Church.

My Mum died six-and-a-half years ago. She was only 59. Patty was very supportive to me then. Everybody's sympathetic, but then they go back to their normal lives. But Patty kept her concern. 'Come down to the house,' she'd say. And I did. And I'd known her formally before. But after that it was different. I'd talk to her about life in general. The fact that she just took the time to talk about things, not just about my mother. It was funny how she knew I had kids and was always asking about them.

I knew that she had her own family, and that she had left them to come here. She talked about it being what she needed to do. And, because I thought her eccentric, it fitted with how she was. Because when somebody's unconventional, you don't expect them to do what other people do.

I think she's one of life's saints.

She's so kind to people. Not judgemental. So unconventional. As I say, I thought she was Catholic. But she lives such a genuinely Christian life. She doesn't let herself get caught up in all the trappings that other people get caught up in: where they live, what their occupation is, what kind of car they drive – the things they use to judge people in society. These things mean nothing to Patty at all.

The things that matter to Patty are, first and foremost, her family – even though she left them! And then she treats people equally. I know when I started going to Patty's, I would see people who had known her longer and I would say had known her better than me; you can tell what depth of bond they have. But Patty treated us all the same.

I've never been in the house in Roslin. A lot of people had more to do with Roslin than here.

And then there's the hut. When I first started meeting Patty, she showed me the hut. She said I could go and use the chapel. I couldn't believe that she slept in it. I remember she asked me to come and help her out with the cleaning. She wanted to pay me for it. I felt she had such a basic life that she couldn't afford it. So, I spoke to my priest about it. My priest said that if it makes her happy I should take it – and I could do whatever I wanted with the money after that, give it to something if I wanted. And so, every week she gives me the money.

When I started, she told me she'd never cared about it, tidying everything. So, I didn't move everything about. There's a lot of boxes and piles of papers that I leave where they are. But I just go and do basic things, and that keeps things ticking over. She's so grateful for every little thing you do for her.

Sometimes when people grow old, they feel they have a right to everything they want. Not Patty. She's always grateful for everything. And when you spend time chatting intimately – things you wouldn't talk about with everybody – you can speak about everything. Patty would respect confidentialities.

And you see, when I lost my Mum. You learn ways to cope without these people. For me, carrying on and living a fulfilling life is a testament to my Mum. My Mum would never want me to sit in a room and mope. So, you must get on.

Just Patty's acknowledgement of my sorrow when everyone else had gone back to their own life – Patty was very aware of me needing to have someone. Patty is very intuitive: without being told, she knew.

I've seen a couple of people from the church seeing her, too. And there's lots of people come and go to her. I have never said to people how she's been so helpful to me. So, there's probably lots of others that she's the same for.

* * *

Along in Roslin, Rosslyn Chapel stands surrounded by the fields of Slatebarns Farm, the farmhouse less than 100 metres from the Chapel. Farmer Robin Crawford has lived there all his life, and his wife Moira grew up on a farm outside Aberdeen. They have been closely involved in the life of the village.

Robin and Moira Crawford

Robin

My family's been on this farm since 1886. Our grandchildren are the sixth generation on this land.

We used to have cows, and we delivered milk. Then in the 1980s we started a caravan site. And it was that *Da Vinci* that stopped it – with all the traffic coming to see Rosslyn Chapel, our customers and their caravans couldn't get in and out. It's made a terrible change in our lives, that *Da Vinci Code*. When Tom Hanks came to do the filming, he was very nice, we liked him a lot. But that Dan Brown. Moira got after him and told him the troubles he'd brought on us.

Moira

I gave him quite a telling-off. Then I asked him for his autograph – I only had a wee scrap of paper in my bag. Here it is. I don't think many people will have his signature like that: 'With my apologies, Dan Brown'.

And our daughter set up a wee stall and a notice: 'da Vinci horse manure: 50p per bag'. It was all over the papers!

Robin

Roland and my father were great pals. We had cows in the field at the back of Rosslyn Chapel; Gardner's Brae, the field's called. Very steep. You could never plough it. My father would go and check the beasts in the evening, and he'd meet Roland out for a walk, with his pipe. And they'd chat and put the world to rights. Roland was Canon Walls in those days – lived in the parsonage at the top of the Vennel. When he first arrived, Alfie Young had a sweetie shop. Alfie said to him, 'Have you come here to dee [die] and all?' He was a great lad, Roland. I used to chaff him, and on his birthday I'd take him a bottle of whisky. 'No. No. Give it to the poor,' he'd say. But I'd make him take it.

When my Dad died in 1994 – he was born 1910 – I asked Roland if he'd take his service. 'Bob would turn in his grave,' he said, 'if he thought a fully paid-up Catholic priest was taking his service!'

But he came, in his robe, and he knelt on the floor beside the fire. And, with all the other old ones there, he said a lovely simple service. He said, 'If ever I had a problem, there were three people in Roslin I could go and talk to. Now there's only two.' I don't know who the other two were.

You could always have a laugh with him. Not long before he died, someone dropped off a load of logs outside the house. I said to him, 'Nobody ever gives me a load of logs.' He said, 'When we came to Roslin, a rumour went round that we were very poor, and we never denied it!' Geordie Peston the undertaker, when Roland became a Catholic, said to him, 'When I'm taking your funeral, Roland, I'll stop the cortège at the top of the main street, and I'll get you led down the street with the flute band playing *The Sash*!'

'Ah, but Geordie,' he said, 'maybe you'll go first!'

And I remember Neil, Bishop Neil. One Christmas, I remember him coming down to the farm for some milk. There was two or three inches of snow on the ground, and he came in his shorts and sandals with no socks. He was just back from Africa.

We always called their place the Tin Hut. In the wartime, it was the fire station. But, when Roland was there, there was some weird and wonderful guys came and stayed. I remember one of them came to thin the turnips. His mind was miles away – couldn't do it.

I don't really know what they did, no. You presumed that he was the preacher, and that was his house. And we knew that John worked. But, because they were always there, you never asked. They took in waifs and strays. They always bought a lot of milk – not just two pints. There was one lad stayed there a while. I think he was titled. An earl or something. You could tell he'd a problem. He'd walk up the middle of the road, up the white line. And, when he wanted to turn off, he'd put out his arm to signal – like he was a car – and then he'd turn and go down that way. Everyone knew him.

Roland was a known character. Everyone in the village knew him. He wasn't involved in gala days, the miners' gala – that was the high spot of the year when I was at school. But he'd speak to folk, speak to kids, dogs, everyone. He always had the time of day for you. John's a quiet man, and doesn't always chat. Roland would want a chat.

But what were they doing, at the Tin Hut? They were like a recluse. It was a bit of a mystery what they were doing. But I think they were like the Good Samaritan, giving these lads a chance. They kept themselves to themselves. I remember once going through looking for them, and there were three or four of them sitting in the Chapel, so I just left them to themselves. When Roland was quite poorly, I went to see him in the house. He was in the wee front room, in his bed. The cat was sitting on the mantelpiece.

When he died, I was asked to take a cord at the burial, for lowering the coffin into the grave. And they were waiting for someone to take another cord. 'Where's Pete? Where's Pete?' Peter Burgess it was, Patty's son. And he came forward at the last minute.

I believe they had another place up in the Pentlands, a recluse did they call it? No, a retreat. Up by Flotterstone. And another at the Cleugh, where that old fellow lived that was a Communist spy.

Moira

I don't really know what they did. I was too busy, I suppose, to ask. I grew up on a farm outside Aberdeen, so I've always worked hard. But I remember how Robin's dad liked talking with Roland, a humorous, lovely guy.

The day they buried Roland, the birds were singing the whole time. I'm a country person. I love my birds. I thought, 'What a send-off! I hope the birds are singing when I'm going down here.'

* * *

Another person who knew the Community from its earliest days – when it was the Fraternity of the Transfiguration – was Charlie Middleton. What did he make of the Community? Did he have a clear understanding of their purpose and their hopes?

Charlie and Heather Middleton

Charlie Middleton

I came from Loanhead. My Dad built a house in Roslin, and we moved when I was 10. I was the youngest, and my three older brothers were away from the house by then. Moving was awful – it was like moving to Australia.

I'd guess that I first met Roland and John through mischief. We got a room from them in the Tin Hut, where we played cards, and got a row from Roland for swearing. When Roland was at Rosslyn Chapel, we used to get to pump the organ – we weren't religious – half a dozen of us. We weren't dressed up for it, though sometimes they gave us a white thing to wear. There was no electricity in the Chapel, so we had to pump the air to the organ.

Robert Haslam and my Dad used to run the youth club in their back room. Robert got a place in Loanhead – it was a row of houses all joined together – a sort of community hall. John did badminton in a church hall in Manse Road – the BB hall, the Boys' Brigade.

I still don't know what their 'Community' is. And I didn't know what it was then. (Though Roland and John married Heather and me in our garden at Rosebank.) When we were young, we never called them 'the Monks'. You were scared for the Church of Scotland minister – he was unapproachable, you would say. But John and Roland never preached religion to you, so you believed what they said. Roland was a great man. They were different. They never needed to explain anything to us. There was six or ten of us. We'd sit about, make a cup of tea, play dominoes, and smoke. And Roland would come in to the room and say, 'There's an awful lot of effing going on in here. I don't want my neighbours upset hearing that word.' But he wouldn't say effing, he'd use the whole word.

Especially as we grew older, we saw there was people coming, people who had had a hard time in life. Some of them stayed a long time. One guy I remember, he used to work in the hotel. He'd collect up the empty glasses. He never got any money for it, he was just a young lad, and he got a couple of pints for his work. Well, this time he got some money, and went to Oban. And he was found dead in his room. The others that stayed a while, you got used to seeing them in the village. I would be between 10 and 14.

Heather and me are foster carers – ten years we've been doing it now. And, if you think about it, what I did, going round to Roland and John's, it could be a bit daunting. You'd not get doing it nowadays. But our parents were perfectly happy with it.

But I remember there was about six of us, we found some bits of brass on the railway – I'd be about 12. We thought it was gold! But we got caught by the policeman, and we were charged – charged with stealing tons of the stuff. It seems that, when they were building the bings, these brass plates were protecting some concrete slabs. And some guys had unscrewed them and stolen loads and loads of them. But they caught us with wee bits and charged us with stealing the whole lot. Robert Haslam came and stood up for us at the court. That was the only time I ever saw him with the dog-collar, the clerical collar; he did it for the court. We were all just admonished.

I remember that they had a hut up in the Pentlands. You'd ask, 'Where's John?' 'He's up in the hut in the Pentlands for a week – he's not speaking to anyone.' It did strike us as strange.

I don't think they had any religious effect on us. But they had a good friendship with all ages. I'm not the greatest religious person. They didn't inspire me to go to church. But, as Heather says, there, they've obviously meant something important to me, for I've always kept in touch with them.

I'm remembering now one Christmas Eve when we were young. They got us to pare the candles, so they'd go in the holders.

'What'll we do with the parings, Roland?'

'Just stick them on the fire.'

Well. We put them all on at once. And we had to call the fire brigade. Nearly burned the place down.

I think everybody in the village knew them, and knew of them. They've done a lot for people. They were just part of the village. Not that they ran coffee mornings or anything like that. But they were always going about saying hello to people. Not preaching, or being in people's faces if you know what I mean. I've met Patty two or three times over the years.

I had a milk round, and the laddies on the van would say, 'How many pints for the Monks?'

On a Sunday, I remember Canon Walls would walk down to Rosslyn Chapel. And there was the service at Christmas, when it was year about: one year in Rosslyn Chapel, the next year in the Church of Scotland, year about.

One of our wee foster girls used to tend Roland's grave, putting flowers on it. And, before his stone was put up, she used wee stones pressed into the ground to write his name.

18

The Music Lasts

In the safe-keeping of a drawer in the library of the house lies a large, hard-backed notebook. On its orange cardboard front cover are written the words:

House of the Transfiguration
Roslin
CHAPTER BOOK
1969–

This is the 'log-book' of the Community, containing the minutes of the annual meetings of the members, 'the Annual Chapter' as it was known. It is bulging with added pages. In each year, there are at least three reports inscribed on the pages or typed out and pasted into the book. One report is from the Roslin house by John Halsey; one from the house master – for many years in the handwriting of Brother Jonathan Jamal; and a third from the Loanhead house by Sister Patty Burgess.

The successive reports paint a picture of the Community's life. John's yearly report is called 'Review of the Year'. In part, this provides a panorama of the journeys made by Roland, leading retreats and days of reflection in religious communities and churches the length and breadth of Britain. Then in 1987 it is agreed that Roland, for the sake of his health and in recognition of his advancing years, 'will cut down on more distant assignments'. John's reports also record the many individuals who come to stay at the house to test if the life of the Community might be for them. Of these, one or two stay only days, others stay for weeks, some for periods of over a year. Despite hopes that each might one day proceed to full professed membership of the Community, they all move on to some other future.

John's reports analyse the sense of direction which progressively develops within the Community, alert to new intimations of their bonds with the world's poor and with the individuals and communities who have chosen or stumbled upon a path similar to that followed at Roslin. John constantly articulates the Community's search for the will of God as they respond to the visitors who continue to visit the house.

Jonathan as the house master, charged with looking after guests, presents the Annual Chapter meeting with the statistics of the visitors in the preceding year. We have already seen that, in 1985, at the time of the infestation of lice, the wayfarers themselves were saying that the house was trying to do too much, with an average of more than three people staying each night. The Community thereafter reduced its capacity, and chose to accommodate a smaller number of people, focusing on offering a longer-term stay for men who might benefit from it. In 1990, for example, Jonathan reports, 'In the past year we had 63 people staying: 13 Guests, 36 wayfarers, 14 Retreatants. One of these guests was a long-term resident who stayed here for a year, and has since moved on. Since then we have had, on and off during this year, one wayfarer who has been trying to come off the roads after over 40 years on the roads.'

In the same report, Jonathan indicates some of the issues with which the Community are still confronted through their commitment to offering hospitality to whoever comes. 'We need to be vigilant in reference to those who seem to use this house for fraudulent purposes, defrauding the D.S.S. [Department of Social Security] and conning the Community out of money.

'Apart from one minor incident, we have been free of drink disturbances reasonably this year, with the increase in our number of wayfarers.'[1]

The following year, Jonathan reports that there has been some unease at incidents of night-time prowling by guests. There is discussion of whether a bolt should be fitted to the inside of the Enclosure gate.

The yearly Loanhead house report from Sister Patty relates how she engages with churches and the community through prayer groups and a Justice and Peace group which meets in her flat above the shops. In 1984 and 1985 during the miners' strike, Patty spent a lot of time in the company of the miners' wives, meeting them at Mass in St Margaret's and in the Miners' Welfare buildings. Her report for 1985 records that, when the strike was over, the miners' wives presented her with a miniature miners' lamp in appreciation of her support.

Her small chapel dedicated to St Brendan, in a wooden hut in the garden, is the focus for much of her own time, and it draws other women to its silence. In her 1988 report, Patty says, 'Technically I am still on my own here – although the fact that 640 people of all shapes and sizes have come through the door over the past year might seem to contradict what I've just said. Only 42 have stayed overnight; some have come for quiet, some to pray. Most have come to talk – one of these on a regular monthly basis. One was someone who had lost her way and was here for a week.'

By 1988, it was already clear that there might be no permanent additions to the membership of the Community. However, Jonathan, that year, formally requested Final Profession in the Community. This motivated the Community to reflect 'on the responsibility undertaken by a community as small and fragile as ours, and the meaning of such a profession in the possible event of Jonathan being left on his own'.[2] They were greatly concerned that, if all three senior members of the Community were to pass away, their own unique status as a solitary ecumenical religious community might leave Jonathan marooned and without support.

In consultation with their friends at the monastery of Sancta Maria at Nunraw, the Community were advised to renew their profession under the Cistercian rite. They therefore proposed to adopt the Cistercian rite, and to adopt the Rule of St Benedict in addition to their own Roslin Rule. This step effectively aligned them with the whole Benedictine tradition. In the event of Jonathan being left as the only member of the Community of the Transfiguration, he would now have supportive links and the opportunity to explore a range of other communities – both

Anglican and Roman Catholic – within which he could fulfil the commitments of his profession.

John's review of that year concluded with the recognition of the continuing fragility of the Community: 'This year we are older, weaker; there is less optimism around, with a future as uncomfortably unmanageable and unpredictable as ever before. But this should make it easier for us to hear more clearly what Jean Vanier said to us at the beginning of 1990: that the wonderful gift of our Community is in its littleness and weakness.'[3]

Into the orbit of the Community, the year 1990 brought Brother Johannes Küpper of the Order of the Friars Minor, the Franciscans. Like a new planet entering their solar system, he altered the course of their lives. As Roland, through Johannes and through his study of Duns Scotus, associated more closely with the Franciscans, the Community all became increasingly aware of the kinship between themselves and St Francis. John Halsey's review of the year in 1991 reported that the Community had adopted a new name.

'The decision to call ourselves "Little Brothers and Sisters of the Common Life" results from an interweaving of various strands of events and encounters on which we have reflected. These reach back deep into our origins in the Church's tradition – our connections with both the Cistercians and the Franciscans (Roman Catholic as well as Anglican); the Sisters of the Love of God; and the Poor Clares; to the Little Brothers of Jesus and Charles de Foucauld; de Foucauld himself driven by a Franciscan impulse from a Cistercian vocation; reaching back to the mediaeval lay communities of the common life, somewhat analogous in their day to today's "base communities". The strands reach back to St Francis and the "fratres minores", to St Clare, and back to St Benedict; they interweave with the Desert Fathers. With the word "common" we are led back to the fellowship of the first Christians whose common life was open to all those whom the Spirit called to join them. And so here, surely, the life of the Community will be found, in a growing awareness and commitment to the glory to be discovered hidden in the common life of the poor all around us.'[4]

In 1993, the Community decided that John should retire from his work in the garage. He was now 60 years old and suffering from rheumatoid arthritis. With John now home in the house and able to assume duties there, Jonathan was relieved of some of the responsibilities he carried and was able to look for work outside the house. Jonathan secured a training opportunity in care work in a Church of Scotland home for the elderly in Loanhead. At the end of the six-month course, the care home were so pleased with Jonathan's work that they asked him to take full-time employment with them. This unsettled Jonathan, who could not see how to combine his religious life in Roslin with full-time employment in Loanhead. So, in 1995, Jonathan made a very difficult decision, and after 14 years in the Community he left in order to begin his new working life. He moved into digs in Dalkeith and continued his care work with the elderly.

The Community now numbered only three.

Who can tell why, over the years, the Community of the Transfiguration did not grow larger? John Halsey, reflecting in conversation with the monks at Nunraw in 2013, wondered if perhaps people could not manage with the level of strictness which the founding members adopted as their pattern of life.

Father Mark recalled, 'Brother John said he didn't think that people would take the level of austerity that they accepted at the beginning. And I remember Roland once saying that they should perhaps have gone back on some of their commitments.'

'But I remember Roland not wanting to take holidays,' added Father Aelred. 'He said, "The poor can't take holidays", and so, even when he was not well, and medical advice was that he should go away for a rest, he didn't want to.'

The strictness of their regime was never a subject for debate among them.

Perhaps it was not everyone who could live in close association with so commanding a figure as Roland. In the 1960s, Bishop Neil, who had always worked on his own as a parish priest and then as a bishop, made a conscious decision to join the close fellowship of a religious community. To make such a complete change of milieu might never have been a trouble-free process for him. But he seemed to encounter a difficulty in balancing his role alongside so dominant a personality as Roland. A similar apprehension may have clarified for Father Jock Dalrymple that Roslin was not, after all, for him.

Whatever the reasons may have been, the Community's membership throughout the years never rose above five in number. It always seemed very small; its premises never appeared crowded. Things moved slowly, and the atmosphere conveyed no aura of establishment, no permanence of institutional power. Hence no visitor felt intimidated or overwhelmed. It was, as they described it themselves, 'the experiment, under the aegis of Nunraw, of a family-size form of the religious life'.[5]

With Jonathan's departure, the Community now rearranged their organisational allegiance. No longer was there the need for the link with the Benedictines, which would have been the safeguard for Jonathan were all the senior members of the Community to pass away. They wrote to the two bishops and to their Warden and their Visitor asking for their agreement to a new arrangement.

'Yes,' said Father Donald in discussion at Nunraw, 'they had a big issue about whether they were Cistercians or not. They had to decide whether they were Cistercians or Franciscans. But in the end they chose the Franciscan, and there was a point where they changed from having the belt round their waist like the Cistercians, to having the all-purpose cord of St Francis.'

They now called themselves the Franciscan Hermits of the Transfiguration. Their life would now be guided by a Franciscan Rule[6] in addition to their own.

The brothers and sister now comprise two hermitages:
The Hermitage of S. Damiano (Roslin) – two hermit brothers.
The Hermitage of S. Clare (Loanhead) – one hermit sister.[7]

The solitary element of their life – the time spent in solitude and personal prayer in their own individual huts – had gradually grown more significant as they grew older. Some of the men and women who relied on contact with the Community were made anxious by the implications of solitude and withdrawal inherent in the words 'hermit' and 'hermitage'. They feared that their access to the members of the Community might be restricted. However, the Community concluded their chapter entry with this affirmation: 'We are open and available to the needs of those whom God sends to us.' And so they sought to remain. Inevitably, however, the advancing years took their toll on the strength of the individuals. In 1998, the Community recognised that they could no longer sustain the same levels of engagement with visitors. They set a pattern which kept Saturdays free of visitors altogether. They committed themselves to going on retreat for ten days before Christmas, Easter and the Feast of the Transfiguration. And they secured for Brother Roland three one-month-long retreats on Iona, in February, June and October, without any visitors at all.

After a retreat on Cumbrae in August 2000, Roland acknowledged that he must reorder the use of his time. He would now continue his engagement with the Holocaust not by gathering more fact and figures, nor by reading or talking, but only by prayer. Neither had he any longer the resources within himself to continue his former work of listening to people and being a spiritual companion to them. Accordingly, he would now devote his time to solitude, simplicity and avoidance of complexity.

By this series of decisions, the Community recognised that, while their vocation remained unchanged, the reach of their life was diminishing. One or two concessions were made in respect of living arrangements for Roland. In the wintertime, he would live in the house, where there was a small bedroom for him. For the first time, a telephone was installed in the house in case of emergency.

This time of adjustment in the life of the Community coincided with serious illness befalling both their Warden, Sister Helen Columba from Fairacres, and their Visitor, Sister Margaret Connor. In their quest for a new Warden, they approached a Church of Scotland deaconess, Kay Ramsay.

'I was horrified,' recalled Kay.

'"Spiritual responsibility for this community? What precisely do you want me to do?"

'"Oh. Nothing," they said, and explained that their last Warden had never been able to visit them as she was a sister in an enclosed order, but had certainly spent much time in prayer for them and had written many letters.

'"So," I said, "if I were to go on doing just as I do just now, loving you and praying for you and coming to see you as often as I can, would that be all right?"

'"That would be just fine," they said.'

Sister Margaret intimated to the Community that on account of her illness they should no longer view her as their Visitor. The Visitor was the channel of communication between the Community and the Churches, and in this new and delicate era of the Community's life the role was as important as ever. The Community asked Archbishop O'Brien if he could help them by suggesting a suitable person to carry out the Visitor's duties. Receiving their request with great sympathy and understanding, the archbishop suggested the name of a distinguished Jesuit, Father Gero McLoughlin SJ, a suggestion endorsed by the Scottish Episcopal Bishop Brian Smith.

'I distinctly remember my first meeting with them,' said Gero, 'which was through in the far room, yes, "the mouldy room" as you say. There seemed a great deal of reserve on the part of Roland. Perhaps he expected a Jesuit would be authoritarian, mixed with perhaps a fear that an Ignatian source might threaten their Franciscan identity. If I had expected to meet an eccentric, slightly dotty person, I immediately discovered that here was a truly saintly, learned and shrewd man. And I grew to love them all, deeply. I was able to convey to them that, for all their eccentricity (in the very best sense of that word), I respected what they were about, and I respected their origins. They lived good lives and excluded no-one. Remarkable. Yes; remarkable.'[8]

Gero conveyed to them that he took them seriously. He arranged that there would be an Annual Visitation, a practice from his Jesuit origins. In the Annual Visitation, Gero took the opportunity to have an individual, serious conversation with each of the three members of the Community. He would ask if they had freedom to fulfil their own vocation and gifts, and he would enquire about the quality of the relationships within the Community. Then they would celebrate the Eucharist. Then there would be a meal, followed by a Community discussion.

Gero would follow that visit with a summary of what he had found – a 'Memoriale'. He would send it to them at Roslin, and copies to the two bishops: Bishop Brian Smith of the Episcopal Church, and the cardinal archbishop.

'In the course of my first Visitation, I looked at their accounts,' said Gero. 'I was stunned, stunned, at how modest their style of life was. They were depriving themselves. Their simplicity of life meant actual deprivation for themselves. And the remarkable thing was that in no way did that conflict with their open, generous attitude to other people.'

Each year, the Community gave their surplus funds to charities, annually several thousand pounds. One year it was £10,000.

As a Jesuit, coming from the Society of Jesus who live as a Community, Gero had a standpoint from which to view another form of Community. He remarked, 'There was no doubt that in that community there was so much inspiration, so much holiness, in a completely unconscious way.'

What did Gero mean by 'holiness'?

'I always had that sense that in all their varied activities, beyond all the actual things they did, they had their eye fixed on God. That what they were doing was not consolidating the relationship between themselves and God, but a profound, generous and self-forgetful living out of the relationship between God and themselves. A complete lack of self-centredness.

'As I have often said to people: these were people who very clearly were not living from the outside, in, but from the inside, out.'

In each Memoriale, Gero reviewed the major events of the preceding year and painted the landscape that lay ahead. His enjoyment of the company of the Community, and his esteem for the effects their way of life had on others, shone through the restrained dignity of his writing. He observed and affirmed the power of their simple way of life.

In a reminiscence, he said: 'I used to have hilarious moments when I was with them – huge laughter at their foibles. One of the best laughs I had was when they told me the story of how they had generously taken in a young man who had no home. They housed him in "the Snug", beyond the kitchen. Naively they took little note of his wanderings, or of how nattily he was always dressed when going out. They were puzzled when one of them was sweeping out the Snug and heard a funny "clink" from something under the floor. Then there was a visit from the Lothian and Borders constabulary, who asked about their new tenant. On raising the floorboards in the Snug, the police found a cavity stuffed with alcohol, bottles and bottles, stolen from a local supermarket and being reset from the house.

'It was so characteristic of their goodness and unworldliness.'9

Gero in his role as Visitor became a vital resource for the Community. His sense of history enabled him to discern the inexorable effect of the years on the health and strength of the Community's members. He was alert to the way in which John Halsey was almost imperceptibly increasing the time he devoted to accompanying Roland as Roland's own capacities diminished. Gero observed the toll which this responsibility took of John's own energies – and, in successive Memoriales, delivered following each Annual Visitation, he paid tribute to him. In later conversation, Gero remarked, 'My personal view (which I don't think I have ever expressed to John) is that John is a very holy person. In fact, I think he's a saint ... He is immensely self-sacrificing in practical matters.'

The Community continued, however, to be the people to whom many people brought their anxieties, their joys and their unbearable burdens. A nurse working in a most demanding psychiatric unit came each month to sit in silence for several hours in the chapel. Bruno, still mourning his young son, came each Christmas to pray, bringing memorial flowers. People anxious for sick relatives came and wept in the chapel. Men and women wrestling with their faith and their doubts came, knowing that their despair was understood.

And then an entry in the chapter minutes:

'The disappearance of Alan Templeton who visited Roland at Gilmore Place [St Joseph's House, the care home run by the Little

Sisters of the Poor, where Roland had been spending two weeks in respite care] shortly before he was last seen on 26 November 2006 cast a shadow over the year, as it still does while we continue to hold Alan and the family in our prayer.'[10]

Alan's parents Douglas and Elizabeth Templeton were constant and long-standing friends of the Community, and they and the rest of their family were sustained through years of hope and fear by knowing that a small photograph of Alan was visible in a front corner of the Community Chapel, among the icons. The photograph remained there in the Chapel, even after Alan's bones were found, more than five years after his disappearance in Edinburgh at the foot of Salisbury Crags.

Friends and companions of Roslin came to realise that the Community had reached a new stage. As Roland withdrew more and more into himself, approaching his 90th birthday, John became his carer, his companion and his remembrancer.

'Do you remember, Roland? Do you remember how it was at Kelham, when you first arrived? And your first lecture from Father Kelly? How he took you all from the classroom across to where they kept the pigs?'

'Oh, yes,' said Roland nodding, smiling, 'I believe I do remember.'

And so John would rehearse the events of Roland's life for him. He would lead him through encounters and turning points, stories which John had often heard and which he knew as well as if he had been there himself. With an unequalled patience, John enabled Roland to be at the heart of communal memories and shared laughter long, long after he might otherwise have withdrawn totally into himself. But Roland was frail, and there was always an anxiety that he might fall in the night. John was on watch all the time.

Brother Johannes kept in close touch from Germany. 'It was particularly moving,' said Johannes, 'to see the brotherly way that John looked after Roland when he needed care. Over the years, he increasingly withdrew and became totally devoted to Roland. That was the living Gospel which bore witness to me and others.' Good friends of the Community came to look after Roland so that John might have a day away; and once he was away for a whole week.

Marguerite Kramers from L'Arche Edinburgh recalled that era of the Community. 'John was caught up in that closeness of life with Roland,' she remembered, 'but he prioritised his connection with L'Arche. He'd get people in to be with Roland to free him to come to a L'Arche meeting.

'I think of that time when John was supporting Roland so beautifully out there, where their day was even more simple than it had been when they had the simple daily life of the Community. Built around the central vision of that simple life, some things came into a new focus. The cat. The blackbird. John was discovering what L'Arche people come through when supporting people to live in their own surroundings. That connection between L'Arche and Roslin was very strong; the connections and parallels are very concrete.'

Then, unsought and quite unexpectedly, Rosemary Lee arrived at Roslin. Having at one time hoped to join the Community, she then spent 20 years with the Sisters of the Love of God at Fair-acres in Oxford. Released from her vows in 2002, she lived in the south of England for five years, looking for what to do. She found employment in nursing homes and a hospital. During those five years, she occasionally visited the Community. She would stay with Patty in Loanhead for a week, and walk over to Roslin along the old railway to see John and Roland.

In May 2007, from her flat and job in Salisbury, she came on a visit to stay with Patty. 'I walked over to Roslin,' she said, 'and sat in the garden with John. He knew that I always hoped to come back to the north-east of England. And he said, "If it would suit you for your own purposes to come back north to Scotland, and if you would like to stay here, it would be a help to both of us, Roland and me."

'I thought for a day or two. And I said, "Yes".'

The chapter book that summer records, 'The arrival of Rose-mary on August 10th has already made an enormous difference to life at Roslin. She has come as a companion/help on a voluntary basis; the arrangement is provisional and to be kept under review, and it needs to be emphasised that there is no plan for her to join the Community. The Community are extremely grateful for her generosity which has made this possible.'[11]

Gero McLoughlin's Memoriale for 2009 signals a forthcoming change.

'All that you shared with me, of your joys and your tribulations, made the visitation a renewed experience of the goodness of God embodied in your life.

'It is because of such an awareness of God's goodness that we were able to acknowledge serenely that the life of the Community is ending; that, in the very near future, its shared residential character will cease.'

Gero guides the Community members to be at ease in the necessary relaxation of their discipline of praying the Office. He cautions them to be very careful about the expectations of friends of the Community who (even unconsciously) would like the Community to remain as it has always been for them.

John was aware that Roland was in need of full-time care, and he spent much time asking Roland most gently if he was ready to make the move from Roslin to St Joseph's House. It seemed that Roland did understand that it was necessary – and, in February 2010, he moved to St Joseph's. There he was received as an honoured guest. Now that he had withdrawn from beloved Roslin, it was of immense significance that Roland was embraced in the community of the Little Sisters. He had never before been resident in a Roman Catholic community; and they cherished him as a priest. The ethos of prayer, the daily Mass, his room being near the chapel where he could sometimes sit quietly when no service was taking place, all helped to soothe the experience of loss. Aided by these gifts of the Christian community, even as his strengths diminished, his own qualities of simplicity, kindness and warmth continued to shine. John visited him several times a week. He would read to him from the Bible, and would say prayers with him. He would also read to him from *Mole Under the Fence* – yet again enabling Roland to cross the barrier of forgetfulness and to revisit his own life. John read from that book and from *Little Flowers*, Roland's own account of the pilgrimage he made with

Brother Johannes to Assisi. Punctuating the reading with an occasional enquiry, 'Do you remember, Roland?' he would see Roland nodding and smiling in assent.

Back in Roslin and Loanhead, John and Patty continued in regular contact, with a chapter meeting for business each Friday morning, and a celebration of the Eucharist at 12 noon. Often, some close friends of the Community would come for this and share a simple quiet lunch after it. Patty, a year older than Roland, looked after herself in the flat in Loanhead. But, in her own frailty, she had a number of falls and several times had to be in hospital, and was then enabled to recuperate in the home of her eldest daughter.

Roland received visits from many people who valued him highly. Father Mark Caira, the Abbot of Nunraw, recalled, 'Some of us visited Roland when he was being finally cared for at St Joseph's. We would sing a hymn with him. They say that, when holy people die, their whole attention is on God. Even when their close friends come to visit them, there is not the same sense of close relationship as there was before. Roland was still friendly but did not give the same attention. It was obvious that the visit had to be short.'

On 7 April 2011, John Halsey and Jonathan Jamal, together with some of the Little Sisters, were at Roland's bedside when his life drew peacefully to its close.

Kay Ramsay wrote of it: 'He moved at a measured pace into that other country which had always been his home, and where he was awaited with so much joy, being himself the herald of joy.'

In his final Memoriale in 2011 – the Community by then having only two members and being therefore no longer, canonically, 'a community' – Gero affirmed the significance of the Community and its two members:

'Two characteristics of the Community continue to be important. Firstly through more than 40 years, the Community's members served for hundreds (at least) of burdened and even fragile people as "a very present help in time of trouble" (Psalm 46.1). Secondly the Community served as a focus for a wide-ranging network of relationships and as a point of connection between large numbers of highly committed people. In these ways the Community has touched the lives of innumerable people unknown to you.'

John Halsey and Patty Burgess continue to be the living presence of a Community which has been so significant and influential. However, they have both indicated the general pattern of their respective funerals and are already familiar with the place, near to Roland, where they will be buried.

What then will become of the two hermitages – the flat in Loanhead with its hut chapel of St Brendan in the garden, and the Tin Tabernacle with the Enclosure and the wooden chapel and the five cell huts?

Father Simon Hughes, the young priest in Falkirk who once thought he might join the Community, said, 'I wanted Roslin to be where I lived. As I do still, now. In fact, I'm sure I've thought that Roslin is such an important place that maybe one day I should go there and keep it going.'

Franciscan Brother Juniper said, 'I stayed at Roslin from Advent 1988 to Easter 1989. Even then, it was a very Franciscan house. I have wondered if one day it might be possible for me to go with two or three brothers and make Roslin a small friary, connected with St Theresa's here in Edinburgh.'

Roland himself wondered what would happen to the hermitage at Roslin when the Community came to an end. 'I wonder if perhaps some big church could find room for this little chapel. This wooden chapel could sit somewhere at the back of the church, under its great roof, as a place of prayer for people. Just as St Francis's little church sits within the big basilica at Portiuncula below Assisi.'

But, to John Halsey, the matter was simpler. '"Dust thou art, and unto dust shalt thou return" (Genesis 2:7). It's how it is,' he said.

Father Aelred at Nunraw, on the other hand, looked further ahead. 'A great influence on them, I remember, was Charles de Foucauld,' he said. 'A lot of inspiration came from there. De Foucauld couldn't keep novices. His standards were too strict for them. They just couldn't do it. I think perhaps the same was true of Roslin. People who came over the years – and they did come – just couldn't live with that level of austerity.

'But, after those years, long after Charles de Foucauld died, his influence brought into being the Little Brothers and the Little Sisters of Jesus. If Roslin now fades away, if it reaches the end of its life, is it not possible that the same may happen? It is not beyond possibility that the powerful experience that people had of the Community at Roslin might give rise to something similar springing up after they themselves have gone.'

But Father Gero McLoughlin, the spiritual Visitor who saw to the heart of the Community, and who recognised the unique qualities of its ministry, and whose sense of history could contemplate with equanimity the Community's end, enabled the Community to make its own plans.

'I think that the provision they have made', he said, 'is very much in keeping with the life that they have lived. It is in the constitution that, on the death of the last member of the Community, the trustees will sell the flat in Loanhead and the house and Enclosure garden in Roslin, and will distribute what remains of their assets among the poor.'

This book closes with words of T. S. Eliot. With these words, Father Gero concluded his homily in the little chapel on the Feast of the Transfiguration, 6 August 2010, looking to Roland, Patty and John, and thinking of the years of the Community's life:

... or music heard so deeply
That it is not heard at all, but you are the music
While the music lasts.[12]

Appendix 1

In thy light shall we see light

The Rule of
the Franciscan Hermits
of the Transfiguration

Preface

This Rule can be undertaken only in faith. It must never become the means of our self-justification either corporate or individual. It is an aid to faith in God our Father and service to our neighbour. It must never take the place of either lest we receive the grace of God in vain.

To God alone be glory. Amen

1. Aim and Purpose of the Community

Brothers and Sisters:
Your vocation is none other than the call of God, who wills you to live to the praise of his glory – the light of that glory he has revealed in the face of Jesus Christ.

God in his mercy has called us sinners to witness to the fellowship of the mystery of Christ. See your calling as a token of the calling of everyone.

Your function within the Church and to the world is to be a sign:

First: to be a sign of Christ in his detachment from all to belong to all – a sign of Christ's poverty by which he made all men rich, a sign of Christ's chastity that he might become the Brother of all and the Father of the poor, a sign of Christ's obedience that he might give to everyone his true freedom.

Secondly: to be a sign of our baptismal promises whereby we have renounced the vain pomp and glory of the world, and all the sinful desires of the flesh so that we will not follow or be led by them, and have promised to keep God's holy will and Commandments.

Thirdly: a sign to all people of the life to come, in which our life does not consist in the abundance of things which a man possesses, in which we neither marry nor are given in marriage, in which no-one who has loved their life will keep it.

Your calling is to a life of prayer in the world, to be at the same time united with Christ and with the world which he came to save.

Be content to live an anonymous, unspectacular, misunderstood life. Choose where possible those places and jobs where people are oppressed or deprived. Let Christ transfigure the darkness in ourselves and in the world. Let his presence and promise shine like a lamp in a dark place until the Day dawns and the Daystar arises in our hearts.

The Community is bound to poverty of means. Let there be no large expenditure on buildings or equipment, no projects or responsibility for organisations either of Church or society. Let there be great care to maintain simplicity of presence amid the human. Love what is obscure and little, for there you will find Christ. Make yourself available to all people by simplicity of life-style, dress and conversation.

'Open yourself to all that is human and be present to the time in which you live.'[1] Respect the primacy of humanity over religious observances and institutions. 'The Sabbath was made for man and not man for the Sabbath.' It is this humanity which Christ embraces, wears and represents. To seek it, bear with it, love it and pray for it can never remove us from Christ, for he is present in it.

'Love your neighbour whatever may be his or her political or religious views.'[2]

Let your form of life and engagements be open to all whom God shall call to it, since it is inspired by the Gospel and the Lord of the Gospel and the tradition of the Universal Church (not by any particular church tradition). Let the commitment of obedience be set within the framework of each brother and sister's churchly discipline. The Office and Liturgy should express this ecumenical dimension of your vocation.

In your earnest attention to the mission and unity of the Church, you should allow the 'dynamic of the provisional' to exert itself in prayer and life. Structure and order need to be inspired by Spirit and life as we move forward towards our goal in Christ. But let nothing be done which has not the consensus of the Church.

You must guard your special calling from the corruption due either to self indulgence, which could so easily attend your life in the world, or to mistaken demands of 'efficiency' and advertisement. But do not regard your form of life as something valuable in itself. It is wholly for others. Do not complain when demands of men and women upset your tidy programmes and timetables, but do not use this availability as a pretext for laxity or disorder.

You are committed to a life of prayer. Therefore take every opportunity during the day for communion with God. Look for occasions of solitude, prayer and meditation, and let no one hinder another in this by unnecessary noise and distraction.

II. The Company

Let the brothers and sisters be careful to help and encourage those who wish to live in the mood and discipline of this rule in a way which is appropriate to the status and function they have in society.

III. The Engagements

A. Poverty

'Poverty is not to be without money, but to have to go without the things we would like.'[3] The brothers and sisters will have to guard against the temptations to forego the infinitely small but real hardships this entails. Only desire to share in a small way the lot of the deprived majority of the world, to share the voluntary poverty of Christ and his saints, will keep this engagement alive in the Community. Poverty includes a detachment from our desire to live here rather than there; to be assigned to this room rather than that; it has to do with where we die as well as where we live. It embraces poverty of spirit of those who are the first to be called blessed.

Let the annual review of the Community possessions be thorough, lest we become anxious about our life, what we shall eat or what we shall wear. We must live in the faith that our Heavenly Father knows we have need of all these things. We must be free to seek the Kingdom of Heaven first in all things, and avoid giving offence to any person in this matter.

'The spirit of poverty is to live in the gladness of today.'[4]

B. Chastity

To undertake an engagement of chastity is permissible only for the sake of a greater love than that which we renounce. This way of life is so repugnant to our natural self that it can only be sustained by an ardent love of Christ and a daily generosity to our neighbours. It requires an openness and simplicity of heart and much patience with ourselves. There are some who have made themselves eunuchs for the Kingdom of Heaven's sake. To be able to receive it will require the grace of God.

'There is no love of our neighbour without the Cross.'[5]

C. Obedience

Life in a small family of God's servants may imperil a brother or sister's diligence in this undertaking of obedience. Let the Community make no major decision without consulting the appropriate authority. Let none on their own account forego the keeping of the rule of the Community. Let each seek permission for the private use of the common goods as need arises. Let the decisions of the Community be administered by the brother or sister in charge. Have continually in mind the voluntary obedience of Christ to the will of the Father and the involuntary obedience of the poor and the oppressed. Like Christ, you have not come to do your own will, but you seek to do the will of him who sends you.

IV. Life in the Community

A. Love

Jesus said, 'I give you a new commandment: Love one another as I have loved you. By this will everyone know that you are my disciples if you have love for one another.' He prayed to the Father 'that the love with which you loved me may be in them'. Your life together is of no value whatever if this love is not given room to grow until it becomes your very life. Therefore be on your guard in your conversations and in your thoughts against the temptation to criticise, to pass judgement on, or to analyse the motives of others. If you give room to these things, you will banish the Love of God. 'Judge not and you will not be judged.'

The tongue is a pest that will not keep still, full of deadly poison. Let the Gospel rule be observed among you: 'If your brother does something wrong, go and have it out with him alone. If he refuses to listen, tell it to the Community.' Otherwise imitate the Abba Macarius who hid faults he saw as though he had not seen them, and those of which he heard as if he had not heard them.

B. Prayer

The ordering of your life must have in view the end and purpose of your special calling – the contemplation of the glory of Christ as we allow the transfiguring of ourselves and this world in the light of his glory. Let there be in each house of the Community a chapel set apart for corporate and private prayer, and let each brother and sister be ready to spend their time in generous intercession and communion with the Lord.

The Divine Office is the Prayer of Christ continued in his Church which is his Body. Let the Offices of Morning, mid-day and evening be performed joyfully, simply and with loving attention. Be careful to show the joy of heaven come down to earth by your singing. As often as circumstances permit, let the brothers and sisters say the Office of Compline before retiring. Always make your Offices available to guests and let them sit among you as brothers and sisters in Christ.

The hour of adoration may never be omitted except for grave reason. Like Peter, James and John, we are called up to the mountain of the Transfiguration and into the Garden of Gethsemane to watch and pray with Christ in his glory and his passion. We shall do well to remember that the hour is not for our comfort, though often it will be. We spend it as companions of Christ, as he intercedes for the world he died for.

C. Solitude and Retreat

Let the brother or sister in charge make arrangements for each to spend at least 24 hours a month in a place of retreat apart from the group. Such time in the desert is given to us to renew our attachment to God alone. Let your monthly retreat be seen in the light of the history of the people of God – their law was given in Sinai; prophecy was initiated by Elijah; their first love was renewed by a return to the wilderness; the invitation to the coming kingdom was given in the desert by John the Baptist; Christ was tempted in the desert; the revival of faith and hope has come from the founders of the religious life in the deserts of Egypt, Europe and Russia.

Let your solitude be a sign of the primacy of God and his coming Kingdom.

Each year, let each brother and sister make the long retreat of eight days.

In this matter of prayer and solitude, let the Community respect the special leadings and vocations of individuals and let a brother or sister take counsel from a wise director.

D. The Use of Time

See that the day is used as by those who serve God and his people. Fill the spaces between work, Offices and meals with meditation, prayer, acts of charity, reading. We may not waste God's time or hinder others from using it. There is no excuse for disturbing others by lack of punctuality. Avoid useless and prolonged conversations during working hours. Let all things be done to the glory of God. 'Throughout your day let work and rest be quickened by the Word of God.'[6]

E. The Community House

Let each be assigned a task in the ordering of the house. Tidiness and good order in all things help to maintain the peace and availability that should prevail. Each house must be ready to receive guests as Christ himself. Do not embarrass the guests by private conversations, neither let the guest disrupt the work and prayer of the brothers and sisters unless his need demands it.

V. Conclusion

This rule does not exempt us from evermore 'seeking to discover God's design, the Love of Christ and the Light of the Holy Spirit. Its purpose is to free us from useless shackles so that we may better bear the responsibilities of our calling and make better use of its boldness. Like every Christian, we must accept the tensions between the total freedom given by the Holy Spirit and the impossibilities in which we find ourselves due to the false nature of ourselves and our neighbours.'[7]

Remember always that God has called us to show by our life together the joy, the simplicity, the compassion of the Holy Gospel. Let these three qualities be jealously guarded. Let us take care to live in God's Today, so that we may in some small way help the human race to prepare for Tomorrow. Let our life therefore be provisional and a sign of our faith in God's future. May our prayer and hope be fixed on that day of the Lord when his Kingdom comes and his will be done.

MARANATHA

Appendix 2

The Sheffield Twelve

The individual participants in the Sheffield experiment – at least those who could be contacted – were invited to send a simple autobiographical note for inclusion in this Appendix. Other entries have been submitted by friends and relatives.

1958/59

Bruce Anderson (1934–91)

Bruce, vicar of the parish of St Ann, Lydgate in Oldham, died suddenly when he was on a summer holiday in 1991. He was only 57.

As a young man, Bruce went exploring in the Middle East. On one occasion, his party was waylaid by bandits armed with rifles. Bruce and his companions laughed and waved their arms. 'No, no,' they said, 'you don't mean that!' And the bandits, smiling, put down their weapons. This story epitomises the charm and the unflappability which characterised Bruce's personality. It was a personality of deep inner resources, which would serve him well in a demanding ministry of 31 years.

The Revd Chris Ford worked as a curate with Bruce for three years. He described Bruce as a multi-dimensional man, full of depth and full of surprises. His easy-going style belied an attention to detail and a very real concern for the minutiae of the parish. What saved him from intensity was his modesty about his own importance. Bruce's style was to point his parishioners towards the things that matter in a parochial situation – loving God and loving one another and throwing the perplexities and frustrations up to God. But Bruce's spirituality was far from escapist pietism.

He had firm opinions on race, poverty and social justice. He was passionately concerned with a fair use of God's gifts in creation; a concern which was expressed in an interest in ecology and also in his paintings and sculpture.

Bruce, who positively loved his Lancashire parish, taught people to love who they were and where they were. His stillness and sense of peace sprang from holy contentment and a constant intercession of thanksgiving. And there was nothing for which Bruce gave more thanks than for his family – Rosemary, Richard, Katy and Sarah.

John Glasbrook

During the first six months in Sheffield, I worked in the heavy machine shop at Jessups, the steelworks owned by BSA, as the proverbial dogsbody. Ken [Hughes] and I were looked after by Mrs Butterworth and her daughter Sheila in Handsworth.

During the second six months, we flirted with radical Christianity and pipe-smoking, with Roland as role model at 393 Fulwood Road. As a finale, we spent time on a fog-bound island. It was Iona.

I continued my training for the Anglican ministry at Westcott House, where Ken Carey and John Habgood endeavoured to put those from Sheffield – Walls or Wickham folk – back on the straight and narrow.

I was made deacon at Stretford, Manchester, where I became a life-long Manchester United fan. The parish had an enormous church youth club, which I persuaded the PCC, with great difficulty, to make an open club. A band lived next door, which graced us with their presence every week.

This may explain why, when recovering from a diabolical bout of chickenpox, I considered that my future was not to lie in the ministry of the Church.

Insider/Outsider ... Inclusive/Exclusive ... Saved/Damned ... Spiritual/Material ... Other-worldly/This-worldly ... Heaven/Earth ... Sacred/Secular ... and so on.

And so, and so, and so ... I withdrew into God's secular earth and have been happy ever since.

John Hammersley (1934–2004)

John was born in Middlesbrough. After reading Classics at Keble College, Oxford, he trained for the ministry at Westcott House. Oddly, for one so moderate and tolerant, whose subsequent ministry was so distinguished, John was asked to leave Westcott House shortly before his ordination, on the grounds that he was 'upsetting the others'. Fortunately, Leslie Hunter, Bishop of Sheffield, came to the rescue and decided to ordain him without any further ado. He was ordained in Sheffield at St Swithun's, where he served from 1960 to 1967. At this time, he began to work in religious broadcasting through BBC Radio Sheffield. It came naturally to him, and his frequent broadcasts were widely appreciated.

In 1967, he began a long association with Parish and People. He succeeded Canon Eric James as its executive secretary, and worked closely with the late Canon Peter Croft to address developments in team ministry, synodical government and church unity. In 1970, he worked with several others to merge renewal movements of the mainstream churches into ONE for Christian Renewal. Parish and People continued as a sub-group and developed a deanery resource unit.

Around this time, John moved to Lincoln, where he continued to develop his ideas for team ministry as priest-in-charge of St Mary-le-Wigford with St Benedict. In 1978, he moved to Tettenhall Regis, where he became a team vicar and in 1981 a prebendary of Lichfield. In 1985, a working party was set up by the General Synod to look at team and group ministries. John, a member of it, wrote a popular guide, *Working Together in Teams and Groups* (1989). In 1987, John joined the Northumbrian Industrial Mission's chaplaincy at the MetroCentre in Gateshead. John was often seen on Tyne-Tees Television and heard on radio.

John moved to Slough in 1994 to be a team vicar in Langley Marish, and director of the Thamesway Programme. He retired to Sheffield in 2000.

John maintained a life-long interest in the liturgical movement. He produced his own 'Psalms of Life' for use in worship and conferences and in private or group prayers. Many of his psalms he skilfully gathered together in *Every Step of the Way* (2003).

Kenneth Grant Hughes

Kenneth was born in Glasgow in 1937 and educated at Jordanhill College School from 1942 to 1955. He entered the University of Glasgow in 1955 and graduated MA in 1958. The Student Christian Movement, strong in the 1950s at Glasgow, provided numerous ecumenical opportunities. One of six who made up the first Sheffield 'Twelve' intake, he worked as a rotary hearth operator in the heat-treatment and wire-drawing section of Arthur Lee & Son, Crown Works, Bessemer Road, Attercliffe. He went on to St Mary's College, University of St Andrews, 1959–62, graduating BD with a special interest in ecclesiastical history. In retrospect, he regrets the inordinate amount of time spent on Greek and, particularly, Hebrew for examination purposes.

He was assistant to the Revd W. Uist Macdonald in an east-end parish in Dundee for two years before being ordained and inducted to Newark parish church in the shipbuilding town of Port Glasgow. He served there for seven years before spending four years as Church of Scotland minister in St Paul's, a church built by the Scottish Episcopal Church as part of the ecumenical experiment in Livingston New Town, West Lothian. Authorised by the Bishop of Edinburgh, Kenneth Carey, he shared eucharistic celebrations with his Episcopal colleague, Brian Hardy. A continuing interest in historical theology led to a later University of Glasgow PhD.

There followed 12 years from 1974 to 1986 as minister of the linked East Lothian parishes of Prestonkirk with Stenton with Whittingehame, during which time he participated in the Haddington Pilgrimage established by the late Lord Lauderdale (Patrick Maitland) and forged links with the neighbouring Cistercian monastery at Nunraw. Thereafter he was appointed to Crown Court Church, one of two Church of Scotland charges in London. He retired in 1997, his last years being spent in education.

He found the worship at Southwark Cathedral, and the preaching of the provost, David Edwards, with whom he had personal contact, helpful and stimulating. Similarly, St Mary's Scottish Episcopal Cathedral, in Edinburgh, has continued to provide a rich tradition of worship and witness, with opportunities for participating in congregational life through occasional guiding at the Song School (unique to Scotland), discussion and debate, and involvement in wider diocesan initiatives. Over the years, his interests have ranged from trees and bee-keeping to local history and Thomas Aquinas, an interest not entirely unrelated to the fact that his wife, Ann, is a medievalist.

David Jenkins

I had joined Roland Walls in Sheffield immediately after graduating from Cambridge; and, following my year in Sheffield, continued my preparation for ordination at Westcott House, Cambridge.

That year in Sheffield had unsettled us. This was due as much to our 'work experience' on the shop-floor as it had been to Roland's teaching and what we had learned together, although that had made a great impact on us. The genial, indeed rather self-indulgent, atmosphere of academia, combined with petty rules and regulations (i.e. no girls allowed to stay in after 11pm; husbands only allowed out for marital duties on a Friday night!) and a real lack at Westcott, at that time, of any rigorous or stimulating teaching provoked me, at any rate, to rebel! I had never been a rebel before; perhaps it was just a case of delayed adolescence! Ultimately, I was threatened with expulsion and was only allowed to stay at Westcott on the condition that I made no provocative remarks or asked visiting speakers awkward questions!

The most significant discovery I made at Westcott was Karl Barth. Reading his commentary on the Romans didn't change my life, but it certainly changed the way I thought about life. Cambridge at that time had not really woken up to the challenge of Karl Barth, though it has since. I had read theology for my degree; and 'Biblical theology', as it was called, seemed to be totally hung up on the authenticity and the authorship of the documents of the

Old and New Testaments, rather than on what they actually said or how they should be interpreted today.

Roland had a concern for the poor. Did that affect me? When I started my ministry, I was committed to working in industrial parishes – and the first three certainly would have qualified. However, the bishop directed my final move – and by then, married with children, I was happy to accept his direction! In a rather erratic way, my experience with Roland led me to be a little more understanding of the various vagrants who came my way. But somehow St Francis did not appeal to me in quite the same way as he did to Roland. Roland's ideals would be very hard to realise without celibacy. How difficult it would be to live out Roland's way in an ordinary career with a family and professional or even clerical commitments. Would one, for example, sacrifice one's wife or children to certain principles? The problem the C. of E. was clearly unable or unwilling to face up to was how Roland's inspiration could be channelled along more conventional routes; alternatively, it might have created a new movement, like the Franciscans or the Taizé brothers. Roland's revolutionary ideas actually require powerful structures to sustain them. Even so, those who had the privilege of knowing him and living with him can only be grateful for the light and hope and laughter he brought into their lives.

So, after Westcott, my career followed a very conventional pattern. I served three years as curate at the parish of Staveley in Derbyshire and had three further appointments at Billingham, Walsall and Whitchurch in Shropshire, where I spent my final 24 years as a stipendary priest.

Jeremy Tatham

(Derived from his poignant memoir, *A Book of Jeremiah – A Study in Hypocrisy*, Kit Publishing, 2003.)

Jeremy was born in 1934 on his parents' return from working in Malaya. An evacuee during the Second World War, he had an unsettled childhood. A public-school education, followed by National Service in the Royal Norfolk Regiment in what was then the Gold Coast, led to him going to read theology at Corpus Christi College, Cambridge. There he encountered Roland Walls, who was both chaplain and dean. Jeremy spent a year in Sheffield with Roland, as one of the Sheffield Twelve, and proceeded to Cuddesdon to train for the Anglican priesthood. Intellectually brilliant, he found himself overwhelmed by the gulf between the Church's words and its actions. He withdrew from Cuddesdon to become a teacher in local-authority schools. He and Hannah married, and Jeremy was appointed as lecturer in Divinity in a training college in Derby.

An original and exacting theologian, he made Nicene orthodoxy the foundation of his lectures. But his promotion of the fourth-century credal doctrines of Nicaea brought him into conflict with Church authorities and with the governors of the college. He resigned his post; he and his wife and three children had to find an alternative home, and Jeremy a new job. The purchase in Norfolk of a small guest house and a restaurant provided both home and work. But Jeremy's uncompromising conflict with the established Church, and his despair at the continuing gulf between the Church's words and its deeds, led to the break-up of the family. Hannah left with the children. Painful conflicts continued through turbulent years – and, through failing to make a maintenance payment for the children's education, Jeremy spent some days in prison. He continued to run the restaurant, and he loved sailing. He later had a share of caring for his two sons; but there was no reconciliation, and he and Hannah divorced.

Often in much distress, Jeremy would travel to visit friends, and he was in hospital several times. However, taking his stand on the words of Jesus in the Gospels, Jeremy used to write sermons on the contrast between what Jesus says and the day-to-day practice of the Church. Surreptitiously, and seditiously, he interleaved them with the official documents in cathedrals – Norwich, Westminster Abbey, St Paul's and Canterbury. He made his home in Sheringham on the north coast of Norfolk, where he lived with his father and earned a living as a successful watercolour painter. His father reached the age of 98, such good care did Jeremy take of him. Jeremy still lives in Sheringham, surrounded by good friends. His adherence to the strict meaning of the words of Jesus on marriage and divorce probably made impossible any hope of reconciliation and reunion with the family he loved.

1959/60

Patrick Casement

I was fortunate in being included as one of the second year of the Sheffield Twelve, as I was the only one not to have been an ordinand. It was, I believe, only because of my degree in theology that I had been included.

My time with Roland remained an inspiration, bridging across my subsequent breakdown and eventual breakthrough to a different kind of ministry. I found himself in psychotherapy out of need, and subsequently in psychoanalysis – again out of need. This became a great blessing to me, as there was never a sense of me having therapy or analysis merely as a training requirement *en route* to my eventual qualification as a psychotherapist, and later as a psychoanalyst. For me, it was never a matter of applying theory, either to my own life or eventually to my patients. Psychoanalytic theory only became meaningful for me through discovering it to be relevant, as and when it was. I needed there to be sufficient space for common sense and intuition, not always subjugated to theory.

This approach to theory, and to the practice of therapy and analysis, became a guiding light to me, which led eventually to my published writing: *On Learning from the Patient* (1985) and *Further Learning from the Patient* (1990), both in the Routledge series 'Classics in Mental Health'; *Learning from Our Mistakes* (which received an award in the USA for its contribution to psychoanalysis) and, most recently, *Learning from Life* – partly autobiographical – which I wrote after retiring from clinical practice.

For a long time, I turned my back on all Church practice, regarding so much of it as superficial and, often, as show. Dogma no longer appealed to me, as it seemed to threaten an imprisonment of the mind, whether that dogma be theological or psychoanalytic. Instead, I had come to value open-minded thinking, which I had learned from Harry Williams (my tutor at Cambridge) and which I felt Roland had also pointed to and represented in his own life.

It was only latterly that I was drawn back into being a communicant member of my local church, valuing again a sense of being confronted by transcendence, above and beyond all that we can conceive of or hope to define.

So, the circle has come to be almost completed, as I now treasure life still granted to me beyond the cancer that had severely threatened it. Roland was never far away from me on all of that journey.

Christopher Hall

Viviane and I were married the week after the Twelve dispersed from Iona in 1960. The next year, I started a curacy in a parish on the border of Sheffield diocese, in which one of my workmates from the Firth-Brown shop-floor lived. During my second curacy in Dronfield, I took a service in a vacant parish. I recognised one of the sidesmen as Mr Simpson, my department manager in Firth-Browns. He had not recognised me, and was visibly shocked to discover that the lad he had last seen in a dirty boiler-suit had just been preaching to him. In 1967, when we were about to move from Dronfield to an incumbency in Smethwick, I visited the shop for the last time. As I walked in, I was greeted with a yell: 'Eh yup! Ha'e ye cum for that crayne job, then?'

GKN's major production plant was in the parish in Smethwick. I never found the space to visit it. What I learnt from my time in Sheffield was that involvement with the shop-floor requires intensive long-term commitment; otherwise workers are left with the impression that the Church is not truly interested in them.

The parish was increasingly multi-racial. I was a founder member of a Birmingham-wide group, All Faiths For One Race. I became known as 'that wog-loving vicar'. When I arrived, a PCC member told me his three political heroes were Enoch Powell, Gerald Nabarro and Peter Griffiths. In time, that PCC member became a churchwarden. When I left, the next vicar appointed was an Indian. In protest at this new appointment, one of the members handed back her stewardship envelopes. She handed them to the churchwarden, who said to her, 'No, you don't need them. Evidently you haven't understood what Christianity is about.'

In 1972 I was elected to the Church of England General Synod; and, after being recruited to Manchester Cathedral in April 1975, I was surprised to be re-elected six months later. I then served for ten years on the C. of E. Standing Committee. I lost my seat in 1985, but was re-elected by Oxford in 1994 and served until 2000. From 1976 until 2000, I helped to publish *SYNEWS*, an informal A4 newssheet, every morning during the summer sessions in York.

For eight years in Manchester, as well as being a canon residentiary, I was Adult Education Officer, and continued as World Development Officer after I was shunted out to be vicar of Bolton in 1983. There I found myself chairman of the governors of two half-white, half-Asian Church primary schools and of the irredeemably whites-only Church Comprehensive School. Bolton Parish Church was one of those town-centre churches which attract the disaffected from other parishes avoiding commitment.

Ecumenism and world development have been priorities in my ministry. In 1982, I was short-listed for Director of Christian Aid, and in 1990 for General Secretary of Christians Together in England. Mercifully I was not appointed; but, for ten years from 1990 was co-ordinator of Christian Concern for One World, happily promoting justice, peace and environment awareness across Berks, Bucks and Oxon, and nationally. Jubilee 2000 was a major involvement, for which I imported and distributed 14,400 Fairtrade cotton rainbow scarves from India. Shareholder action with the Ecumenical Council for Corporate Responsibility found me proposing resolutions at the Shell AGMs in 1997 and 2006, and preaching at Ken Saro-Wiwa's memorial service in London.

Following the death in 1992 of Florence Li Tim-Oi, the first Anglican woman priest, her sister asked me to start the Li Tim-Oi

Foundation to empower Christian women to be agents of change in the Two-Thirds World – 350 in its first 18 years.

Christopher's primary concern through 50 years of ordained ministry has been to urge the Church of England at every level to respond to the demands of justice, peace and the global environment.

John Halsey

His history is contained in the book itself.

Peter Hipkin

Peter was one of the 1959/60 Sheffield Twelve. In November 1965, he made his way to the new Fraternity of the Transfiguration at Roslin, to test whether life in a religious community would be suitable for him. He had finished at Westcott House. While at Roslin, he was a care-worker in Rosslynlee, the nearby home for people with learning difficulties and psychiatric problems. He seemed likely to join the Fraternity, but in the end did not join. He left for South Africa, where he was ordained deacon. He was then ordained a priest in Johannesburg. He was caught up in the anti-apartheid movement. He returned to England but then changed his mind and went back to South Africa. In his new parish, at every meeting there were likely to be informers. He kept contact with the Fraternity of the Transfiguration, or the Community as it was called by that time. After some more years, Peter left South Africa again and worked in Birmingham.

By that time, he had become a Roman Catholic. He was a care-worker in Birmingham as he had been in Rosslynlee. It seemed that in some ways he was more comfortable with a role as a care-worker than as a priest. In Birmingham, he was in contact with Ted Longman, another of the 1959/60 Sheffield Twelve, and there were friendly contacts with the Community in Roslin.

After some years, Peter returned to South Africa; and there has been no further contact since then.

Ted Longman

Here is a summary of my ministry after my ordination, first at Michaelmas 1961 as deacon, and then in 1962 as priest.

I spent three years as curate at St Mark's, Broomhill, Sheffield, followed by nine years as vicar of St Thomas', Brightside, Sheffield. During this time, I also worked as a part-time chaplain with Sheffield Industrial Mission.

I enjoyed a one-year exchange (1972–3) with a parish in Brisbane, Australia, and then returned to England.

I spent ten years as vicar of St Edburgha's, Yardley, Birmingham and worked as a part-time hospital chaplain. During these years, I also served as rural dean.

Following my years in Yardley, I spent 12 years as rector of Holy Trinity, Sutton Coldfield, and once more served as a part-time hospital chaplain. I was also rural dean during this time.

Finally, I spent six years as priest-in-charge of Cerne Abbas with Minterne and Godmanstone, and continued with wider responsibilities as rural dean of Dorchester.

Although I came from a rural, agricultural background, my vocation was to urban ministry. In my working life, I gained experience in a wide range of urban settings. Broomhill was a middle-class parish area. Brightside was working-class terraced housing, and included a role as industrial chaplain in the local steelworks. Yardley was council estates and middle class, whereas Sutton Coldfield was a significant town-centre and residential parish.

With my last appointment, to Cerne Abbas, a rural benefice, I was leaving the urban setting for a rural setting such as I had known in my early years.

Ian Ross

Like Christopher Hall, John Halsey, Ted Longman and Peter Hipkin, I was a student at Westcott House. My year in Sheffield was marvellous – both for the experience of working in a steel mill and living in digs, and then having the extended reading time with Roland and the others. I was very disappointed that the C. of E. could not agree to continue with such a scheme. There were so many new experiences for me in the years 1958–62 that it is very difficult to say how each individual one of them influenced me. But there is no doubt that the year in Sheffield was an important ingredient. I returned to Westcott House after Sheffield for my final year.

I went to America on a World Council of Churches scholarship to spend a year (1961–2) at the Episcopal Theological School (ETS) in Cambridge, Massachusetts. I came back to England and was ordained in December 1962 to a curacy at Oldham Parish Church. In July 1963, I was married to Jean, whom I met at ETS.

In September 1965, I joined the staff of the Student Christian Movement as the Theological Colleges Secretary. In this post, I had the opportunity to visit the theological colleges and seminaries of the member churches of the British Council of Churches and the Roman Catholic Church. I also created ecumenical opportunities for students to visit the churches of the Netherlands, Paris, East Germany and Poland and to be present at the WCC Assembly in Uppsala, Sweden.

From July to September 1969, I was priest-in-charge of St Anne's Church, Brindle Heath, Salford. From September 1969 to May 1984, I was on the staff of Manchester Grammar School to teach religious studies and physics.

I returned to parish life in May 1984 as vicar of the parish of the Holy Cross (The Abbey), Shrewsbury. There I addressed the task of restoring the abbey church and opening it up for greater use. I retired in November 2002.

1960/61

Kenneth Boyd

Following a year in Sheffield, I returned to Edinburgh to complete a three-year BD at New College, and was licensed by the Presbytery of Tain in 1964.

From 1964 to 1969, I was Scottish secretary of the Student Christian Movement (SCM), and in 1965 Pat Barlow (the South of England SCM Secretary) and I were married by Roland in Rosslyn Chapel.

From 1969 to 1975, I was associate chaplain of Edinburgh University. (I was ordained in 1969 by Edinburgh Presbytery, with the Anglican and Roman Catholic university chaplains also laying on hands – so, arguably, not only ecumenically but also, on a Reformed view of bishops, episcopally ordained.) I completed my PhD in 1972 and was also secretary of the Edinburgh Medical Group, an offshoot of the SCM initially in London and then in most other UK medical schools. From 1975 to 1980, I was Research Fellow in Medical Ethics and Education at Edinburgh University, and for the last of those years also an acting hospital chaplain in North Lothian.

From 1980 to 1993, I was Edinburgh chaplain to international students, latterly part-time, being from 1989 to 1991 also Research Fellow in Medicine and Literature at Glasgow University, and from 1980 to 2005 honorary research director of the Institute of Medical Ethics, the national association of Medical Groups, of which I later became (until 2011) honorary General Secretary.

In 1990, I became Honorary Fellow, in 1996 Senior Lecturer, in 2002 Professor, and from 2011 Professor Emeritus of Medical Ethics in Edinburgh University College of Medicine and Veterinary Medicine, where I continue to teach as a Senior Honorary Professorial Fellow. In 1997, I was elected a Fellow of the Royal College of Physicians of Edinburgh and am honorary College Cleric.

I have chaired or been a member of several local and national committees and working parties concerned with different aspects of medical ethics, have written or edited a variety of books and papers on related issues, and was for ten years editor of *Contact*, the journal of pastoral care, and more recently an editor of the *Journal of Medical Ethics*. My current research interests – apart from medical ethics – include the history of eighteenth- and nineteenth-century science and medicine and in particular the philosophy and theology of S. T. Coleridge.

Until around 1980 Pat and I attended both Greyfriars Kirk (the University parish church) and St John's Episcopal Church on Princes Street. After leaving the University chaplaincy, I was invited to join (and continue to be a member of) the clergy team of St John's as a non-stipendiary associate minister, being given permission to officiate by the Bishop of Edinburgh in 1987, at that time also becoming an elder of St Cuthbert's Parish Church, which shares a local ecumenical project with St John's.

Although I met Roland on only a very few occasions after 1965, I realise, looking back, that our year in Sheffield had been like an underground stream, silently irrigating my life and conscience. Only the SCM, James Blackie who suggested I go to Sheffield, and Pat and other members of my own family have had a comparable influence.

Hugh Maddox

From 1961 to 1963, I was at Westcott House, with Sheffield in heart and mind. From 1963 to 1966, I was curate in Attercliffe, discovering how to say prayers and to minister to people in industrial housing. From 1966 to 1967, I was curate in Maidstone, where I met and married the vicar's daughter, which led to being curate from 1969–71 in Folkestone. Here I wrote a modern youth passion play, which led to 1971–4 as senior curate with Austen Williams at St Martin-in-the-Fields, where I founded Crypt Folk Club and created 'Alive', a street-theatre type of modern passion play, running for two years in the crypt, and taken around places including Wormwood Scrubs, Eton and Great St Mary's, Cambridge.

From 1974 to 1981, I was rector of Sandwich, a Kent Cinque Port, with a role in town life, encountering many distinguished people and working in schools, hospitals and industrial chaplaincy, and also with diocesan involvement.

From 1981 to 1983, I was vicar of St Peter-in-Thanet in Kent, a large, thriving, organised parish. Much went well, and much went wrong. It was not the role I was best suited for ... so in 1984

I took six months' sabbatical, three looking for work, three as Honorary Chaplain at Coates Hall, the Scottish Episcopal Theological College in Edinburgh. This was a relaxed, stimulating time in the city of my forebears.

From 1984 to 2003, I was vicar of Red Post, five small parishes in south Dorset. Here I fulfilled a country version of Roland's vision of 'a sacramental presence' among all sorts of people. It was possible to know every family in the five villages, weeping and rejoicing with them.

In 1985, my son suffered a serious schizophrenic breakdown. In 1998, my daughter got married and later rented a cottage deep in a wood in the parish. Our marriage broke up.

In 2002, I remarried and retired. Now I am occupied taking services and listening to people.

In each parish, I made trips to Iona, Taizé and other communities; I produced passion plays and undertook counselling and preaching in public schools. Roland's infectious humour, simplicity, devotion and free-thinking were a constant inspiration, along with his availability to the wretched of the earth.

[Hugh also wrote a book, *Tales of a Huggable Vicar*, available at www.fast-print.net/bookshop.]

John Oliver

Any young man preparing for ordained ministry in the Church of England in 1960 would have expected to start off with a curacy in a gritty northern industrial parish – or such was the impression formed at Westcott House in the time I was there. What better preparation, then, than a year in Sheffield, in a placement arranged by the Industrial Chaplaincy, and with the added incentive of a chance to sit at the feet of Canon Roland Walls?

What actually happened to me was that, after experiencing an amazing, stimulating, stretching year in Sheffield, I decided to get married and my beloved had just embarked on a Cambridge postgraduate course of research in theology. So I set out to make my own arrangements to do the same sort of thing, and was lucky enough to have Alec Vidler, the then dean of Kings, to supervise my work on social thought and action in the Church of England from 1919 to 1931 – a topic which grew naturally out of my Sheffield year.

When that was completed, a search for a first curacy led me, surprisingly and unusually, to the deeply rural south-west corner of Norfolk, mainly because of an outstanding training incumbent, from whom I learned a huge amount. These four years laid the foundation for what was in fact going to be a predominantly rural ministry, apart from a four-year stint as a chaplain at Eton. I subsequently spent nine years as team rector in overwhelmingly rural north Devon, and after three years in Exeter then became archdeacon of Sherborne, effectively a vast tract of rural west Dorset. From there, I moved to be Bishop of Hereford, the most rural diocese in the Church of England.

Does this mean that the year in Sheffield was wasted? Far from it, because I learned so much about the Christian faith and about people, and about the enormous benefits of friendly collegiality, all of which was of abiding value, and I remain immensely grateful for the time I spent with Roland Walls and my colleagues among the Sheffield Twelve. During my brief urban ministry in Exeter, I tried to develop a form of commercial chaplaincy to department stores and large offices, based to some extent on the Sheffield model, but adapted to a very different context.

I am seriously sorry that the Sheffield scheme was not perpetuated and made at least an optional part of ordination training. It had a good deal in common with experiments taking place elsewhere in Europe, not least in the specialised training and ministry developed by the Mission de France at the impressive seminary at Pontigny in Burgundy, from which teams of newly ordained and highly motivated priests went to work in some of the toughest urban and industrial settings in France.

Now, 50 years on, industrial mission has changed out of all recognition; jobs are hard to come by, and it is much more difficult to find temporary posts for ordinands. It is unlikely that anything like the Sheffield scheme could be replicated. It remains a short-lived but splendid episode, which will long be remembered with gratitude by those who were fortunate enough to take part in it.

John Ware

I was ordained in Sheffield Cathedral on Trinity Sunday 1962 to serve as curate in the large industrial parish of Attercliffe and Carbrook with many large steelworks and about 45,000 people mostly on shift work. There were four churches. There I fell in love with a local-authority childcare officer and married her in 1964. In 1966, we moved with our first child to the opposite end of Sheffield, where I was curate of St John's Ranmoor and the Church of St Columba in the parish of Crosspool. I was also chaplain to a small hospital for people with learning difficulties, and worked one day a week as an industrial chaplain with the Sheffield Industrial Mission.

In 1968, I was invited by the Bishop of Bristol, Oliver Tomkins, to be his social and industrial chaplain in Swindon, Wiltshire, and vicar of the small rural parish of All Saints Liddington on the edge of the town. I set up a small ecumenical team of part-time industrial chaplains in the railway works and in the car and tobacco factories of the town, and we worked with many other agencies in addressing the many needs in what was really a burgeoning new town.

In 1974, Bishop Oliver asked me to move to Bristol to lead the diocesan Social and Industrial Ministry in the diocese based on the ancient Church of St Thomas-in-the-City. The team of ecumenical chaplains worked in many of the major industries of the city, including the aircraft and engineering factories, the printing and packaging industry, the Avonmouth Docks and the tobacco industry as well as in relation to trade-union and employers' groups. We organised conferences on major social and industrial issues, and there was a sustained programme of conferences for young people leaving school and entering the world of work. We also worked with the Council for Social Services, the Council on Alcoholism and the Council for Racial Equality.

After five years, the bishop asked me to be vicar of the parish of Kingswood on the east side of Bristol. It had been a mining area noted for its lawlessness, and was famous as the first place where John Wesley had preached in the open air. The last of the mines closed just before the Second World War, but it had also been a significant area for the making of boots and shoes as well as for light engineering. It had two Anglican churches and several Methodist churches as well as Baptist, United Reformed, Roman Catholic and Congregational churches. While I was in this parish, I was appointed area dean, which involved overseeing about 19 parishes in east Bristol.

In 1987, it became necessary for me to move for health reasons, so the bishop suggested that I should move back to Swindon to take charge of two suburban rural parishes on the western side of the town. The job there was to prepare them for being swallowed up by Swindon. When I went there, the total population of the two parishes was about 2,500. The smaller of the two had about 300 people, but when I left in 2001 it had 5,000 and rising. While in these parishes, I was made area dean again, with oversight of 11 parishes. I stopped being area dean in 1994 and finally retired in 2001.

After retirement, I was a part-time chaplain at Bristol Prison for about four years, and a school governor until 2010; and I am still taking services most weekends, as there is a continuing shortage of clergy.

Notes

1 Chapter 1

1. *The Times*, Friday 22 April 2011.
2. T. S. Eliot, 'Little Gidding', *Four Quartets* (London: Faber & Faber, 1959), pp. 51–2.
3. Personal correspondence and discussion, 2009.

Chapter 2

1. From the papers of Kenneth Hughes, Sheffield Twelve, 1958–9.
'The Rule of the 12':
   1 Silent prayer: morning and evening.
   2 Mattins and Evensong: with silent pauses.
   3 The Eucharist.
   4 Weekly meeting for decisions and oversight on part of all.
   5 The special celebration of feasts of the Apostles.
   6 Economic interdependence.
   7 Minimum of possessions in the house: and simplicity of dress.
   8 Eight hours' work and prayers from everyone on 'weekdays'.
2. Ibid., personal correspondence of Kenneth Hughes, dated Ascension Day 1958.
3. See Appendix 1, which contains the complete list of the 17 members of the Sheffield Twelve, with brief notes of their subsequent lives.
4. Kenneth Hughes, *Memories of the Sheffield Twelve*, compiled and printed by Christopher Hall (The Knowle, Deddington, Banbury OX15 OTB), 2009.
5. Ibid., Hugh Maddox.
6. Ibid.
7. He was quoting from *The Bhagavad-Gita*, in stanza 12 of 'The Eleventh Teaching'; *The Bhagavad-Gita: Krishna's Counsel in Time of War*, trans. Barbara Stoler Miller (New York: Bantam Books, 1986), p. 99.
8. Matthew 17:2.
9. Hughes, *Memories of the Sheffield Twelve*, Kenneth Hughes.
10. Ibid., Patrick Casement.
11. Ibid., John Oliver.
12. Interview with Kenneth Boyd, August 2012.

13. Hughes, *Memories of the Sheffield Twelve*, Hugh Maddox.

14. Ibid., Kenneth Hughes.

15. Ibid., John Oliver.

16. The word for the 'Final Prayers of the Day' – the service that completes the day's prayer.

17. Interview with Kenneth Boyd, August 2012.

18. Hughes, *Memories of the Sheffield Twelve*, Patrick Casement.

19. John S. Peart-Binns, *Gordon Fallowes of Sheffield* (The Memoir Club, Weardale, County Durham), 2007, p. 139.

20. Ibid., p. 140.

21. E. R. Wickham, *Church and People in an Industrial City* (London: Lutterworth Press, 1957).

22. Interview with Kenneth Hughes, August 2012.

23. Hughes, *Memories of the Sheffield Twelve*, Rosemary Anderson (on behalf of her husband, the late Bruce Anderson).

24. Ibid., Ted Longman.

25. Ibid., Kenneth Hughes.

26. Ibid., John Oliver.

27. Interview with Kenneth Boyd, August 2012.

28. Minutes of Central Advisory Council for the Ministry, Ordination Candidates Committee, Meeting in Conference at Jesus College, Oxford, 25 and 26 September 1961. Minutes held in Church of England Records Office, London.

29. Ibid., Minutes of Meeting, 8/9 January 1962.

30. Personal letter, 8 October 1958, from Bishop Leslie Hunter to Kenneth Hughes, one of the first-year group of the Sheffield Twelve.

31. R. P. Reiss, *The Testing of Vocation: 100 Years of Ministry Selection in the Church of England* (London: Church House Publishing, 2013), pp. 201–5.

32. Hughes, *Memories of the Sheffield Twelve*, John Oliver.

Chapter 3

1. Ron Ferguson (with Mark Chater), *Mole Under the Fence: Conversations with Roland Walls* (Edinburgh: Saint Andrew Press, 2006).

2. Ibid., p. 42.

3. John Mantle, *Britain's First Worker-Priests: Radical Ministry in a Post-War Setting* (London: SCM Press, 2000).

4. Ibid., p. 42.

5. Ferguson, *Mole Under the Fence*, p. 41.

6. Ibid., p. 44.

7. Ibid.

8. Patty speaks with Rosemary Lee, July 2005.

9. Related by Roland to Jonathan more than 20 years later.

10. Matthew 19.16–22.

11. Little Gidding was the first Anglican Community to be developed after

Henry VIII's dissolution of the monasteries. Founded by Nicolas Ferrar in the village of Little Gidding in Huntingdonshire in 1626, it was a 'Lay' community; that is, its leading characteristic was that it was based round families as opposed to celibate monks or nuns. The Community dispersed in 1657.

12. Interview with Robert Haslam, July 2012.

13. Ibid.

14. Ibid.

15. Matthew 22.12.

Chapter 4

1. Joel 2.8 (Jerusalem Bible).

2. Interview with Kenneth Boyd, August 2012.

3. St Seraphim of Sarov (1759–1833), one of the most renowned Russian monks and mystics of the Orthodox Church. He is remembered for extending to lay-people the monastic teachings of contemplation and self-denial. He taught that the purpose of the Christian life was to acquire the Holy Spirit.

4. St Romuald (95–1027) from Ravenna in north-eastern Italy, was the founder of the Camaldolese Benedictines. Romuald brought together two strands of the Benedictine tradition, the hermit and the communal. Living in solitude, the monks met together for common prayer. His first foundation, which gave the movement its name, was in Calmadoli, a village in the mountains above Arezzo in Tuscany.

5. St Antony (250–356) was born in southern Egypt to wealthy landowning parents. Evangelised by the Gospels, he sold all he had, entrusted his young sister to a group of Christian women, and founded the tradition of desert monasticism. Famous in his lifetime, and even more so after his death, he was known as St Antony the Great.

6. Ferguson, *Mole Under the Fence*, p. 43.

7. From *The Manual of the Houses of the Transfiguration*, published privately, Roslin, 1984.

8. Père Loew, *Mission to the Poorest*, Catholic Book Club, 1951; quoted in Mantle, *Britain's First Worker-Priests*. Roland met Père Jacques Loew at Taizé in 1962. Loew remained very supportive of Roland and John through prayer and correspondence. He sent them a memento, now in the Community's chapel: a handwritten card from Pope Paul VI, given to Loew by the Pope when he was preaching at a papal retreat.

9. Mantle, *Britain's First Worker-Priests*.

10. Ibid.

11. Ibid.

12. Interview with John Halsey, March 2012.

13. Interview with Robert Haslam, July 2012.

14. Interview with John Halsey, April 2012.

15. Ibid., February 2012.

16. Luke 2.52.

Chapter 5

1. Richard Holloway, *Leaving Alexandria: A Memoir of Faith and Doubt* (Edinburgh: Canongate, 2012), p. 193.
2. The Revd Gavin White, friend and colleague of Neil in his Africa years, in correspondence, September 2012.
3. Recorded discussion between Patty Burgess and Rosemary Lee, July 2008.
4. Ibid.
5. Ibid.
6. Ibid.
7. Ibid.

Chapter 6

1. Kenneth Boyd, personal correspondence, October 2012.
2. Interview, November 2012.
3. Revd Dr Jamie Walker, retired Chaplain to St Andrews University, in private conversation, February 2013.
4. Ferguson, *Mole Under the Fence*, p. xvi.
5. Interview with D. W. D. Shaw, July 2012.
6. Ibid.
7. Interview with Elizabeth Templeton, June 2012.
8. Ibid.
9. Fr Brendan Pelphrey, *The Secret Seminary: Prayer and the Study of Theology* (Lexington, MA: Spring Deer Studio, 2012), p. 43.
10. Interview with Dr Monica Jackson, March 2012.
11. Monica Jackson and Elizabeth Stark, *Tents in the Clouds: The First Women's Himalayan Expedition* (The Travel Book Club, 1956).
12. Interview, June 2012.
13. Personal interview, September 2012.

Chapter 7

1. Pelphrey, *The Secret Seminary*.
2. Appendix 2 contains the 1973 version of the Rule of the Community of the Transfiguration.
3. Interviewed by Rosemary Lee.
4. John Halsey, 'Prayer, Politics and Transfiguration', in *Spiritual Journeys*, ed. Stanislaus Kennedy RSC (Dublin: Veritas Publications, 1999).
5. Ibid., p. 65.
6. Interview with the Revd Canon Alan Hughes, Vicar of Holy Trinity and St Mary, Berwick Parish Church, October 2012.
7. Personal correspondence from Bishop Neil, November 1981.
8. Ibid.

9. Personal correspondence with the Revd Canon Prof. Gavin White, September 2012.
10. Interview with Duncan Finlayson, March 2012.
11. Interview with Jean Vanier in Trosly-Breuil, November 2012.

Chapter 8

1. Personal correspondence, November 2012.
2. Lysergic acid diethylamide, abbreviated as LSD and known colloquially as acid. It is a psychedelic drug, well known for its psychological effects which can include altered thinking processes, closed- and open-eye visual experiences, an altered sense of time, and spiritual experiences. It played a key role in the 1960s counter-culture.
3. Edward FitzGerald, *The Rubaiyat of Omar Khayyam*, 1st edn (1858), stanza 39, in *The Oxford Book of English Verse*, ed. Arthur Quiller-Couch (Oxford: Oxford University Press, 1900).
4. Personal correspondence with Harold Palmer, January 2013.
5. Consecrated an auxiliary bishop in 1982, Bishop of Diokleia, he became metropolitan Bishop Ware of Diokleia in 2007.
6. A. M. Allchin (ed.), *Solitude and Communion: Papers on the Hermit Life* (Oxford: SLG Press, Fairacres, 1977).

Chapter 9

1. Julia Duin, *Days of Fire and Glory: The Rise and Fall of a Charismatic Community* (Baltimore, MD: Crossland Press, 2008), p. 87.
2. Maggie Durran, *The Wind at the Door: The Story of the Community of Celebration, Home of the Fisherfolk* (Eastbourne: Kingsway Publications, 1986), p. 14.
3. Duin, *Days of Fire and Glory*, p. 146.
4. Interview with John Halsey, January 2012.
5. Durran, *The Wind at the Door*, p. 83.
6. Ibid., p. 86.
7. Philip Bradshaw, *Following the Spirit: Seeing Christian Faith Through Community Eyes* (Alresford: John Hunt, 2010), p. 147.
8. A former member of the Community of Celebration has such a shell and a copy of the card, March 2013.
9. Duin, *Days of Fire and Glory*.

Chapter 10

1. *On Being Proud of Uniqueness*, lecture by Chaim Potok at Southern College of Seventh-Day Adventists, Collegedale, Tennessee, 20 March 1986, www.lasierra.edu/Potok.unique.html
2. Jeffrey Tigay, *In Memoriam Chaim Potok (1929–2002) (5689–5762)*

(La Sierra University, Riverside, California, www.lasierra.edu/Potok.unique. html).

3. Mishneh Torah, *Sefer Madda*, Laws of Repentance 3, 1.

4. Michael Dorris, in *Los Angeles Times*, 15 September 1991.

5. Elie Wiesel, *Night, Dawn, The Accident – Three Tales* (London: Robson Books, 1974).

6. Alan Ecclestone, *The Night Sky of the Lord* (London: Darton, Longman & Todd, 1980).

7. Ibid., p. 76.

8. Isaiah 53:5.

9. Ecclestone, *The Night Sky of the Lord*, p. 166.

10. Zvi Kolitz, *Yosl Rakover Talks to God* (London: Jonathan Cape, 1999).

11. Ibid., p. 24.

12. Interview with Jonathan Jamal, January 2013.

13. David Gilmour, *Dispossessed: The Ordeal of the Palestinians 1917–1980* (London: Sidgwick and Jackson, 1980).

14. Elias Chacour, *Blood Brothers* (Lincoln, VA: Chosen Books (Zondervan Corporation), 1984).

Chapter 11

1. From the transcription of a taped conversation with Roland Walls, recorded by Lesley Reid, Christmas 1999.

2. Jean Pierre de Caussade, *Abandonment to Divine Providence*. De Caussade (1675–1751) was a French Jesuit priest and writer known for this book (also known as *The Sacrament of the Present Moment*) and his work with Nuns of the Visitation in Nancy, France.

3. Interview with John Peet, October 2012.

Chapter 12

1. Kathryn Spink, *Jean Vanier and L'Arche: A Communion of Love* (London: Darton, Longman & Todd, 1990), p. 42.

2. Interview with Marguerite Kramers (née Millar), Edinburgh, January 2013. John's talk is recorded in full in Stanislaus Kennedy (ed.), *Spiritual Journeys: An Anthology of Writings by People Living and Working with Those on the Margins* (Dublin: Veritas, 1997).

3. Interview with Jean Vanier, November 2012.

4. Interview with Rosemary Lee, February 2013.

5. Interview with Marguerite and Anthony Kramers, January 2013.

6. Interview with Jean Vanier, November 2012.

7. Ibid.

Chapter 13

1. Ferguson, *Mole Under the Fence*, p. 38.
2. *The Rule*, Section I (Aim and Purpose), p. 4. Roland first produced the Rule in 1968. It underwent minor changes in the years that followed. The version in Appendix 2 of this book is the Rule as valid in 2001. The wordings of excerpts found in the text of this book are sometimes taken from earlier variants.
3. Recollections of Roland, in unpublished writings by Jonathan Jamal.
4. Ibid.
5. *The Rule*, Section I.
6. Interview, July 2012.
7. Ferguson, *Mole Under the Fence*, p. 108.
8. Ibid., p. 104.
9. Quoted, with permission, from the unpublished manuscript of the biography of Fr Jock Dalrymple written by his nephew (also called Father Jock Dalrymple), parish priest of the churches and parishes of St John Vianney's and St Gregory's Edinburgh, and Bernadette Campbell.
10. Annual Chapter Minutes, 31 July 1983.
11. Interview with Jonathan Jamal, January 2013.
12. Ibid.
13. In discussion at Nunraw, March 2013.

Chapter 14

1. Conversation at Nunraw, March 2013.
2. Ferguson, *Mole under the Fence*, p. 38.
3. Annual Chapter Minutes, 5 August 1977.
4. Annual Chapter Minutes, 1985, p. 67c.
5. Personal correspondence, January 2011.
6. Ibid.
7. Interview with Trevor Miller, one of the leaders of the Northumbria Commmunity, July 2012.
8. Ibid.
9. Annual Chapter Minutes, 1995.
10. Autobiographical sketch by Father Ya'akov Willebrands, 2002.
11. Ibid.

Chapter 15

1. Jonathan Jamal interview, January 2013.
2. Jodi Page Clark interview, July 2012.
3. Simon Hughes interview, November 2012.
4. Ferguson, *Mole Under the Fence*, p. 187.
5. Brother Johannes Küpper, 'Reminiscences', March 2013.

6. James B. Torrance and Roland C. Walls, *John Duns Scotus in a Nutshell* (Edinburgh: Handsel Press, 1992).

7. Annual Chapter Minutes, 1993.

8. The style of cross particularly associated with St Francis; see below.

9. Brother Johannes Küpper, *Reminiscences*.

10. Fr Maximilian Kolbe (1894–1941), a Franciscan friar who voluntarily took the place of a married man sentenced to die in a starvation cell following an escape by another prisoner. Canonised as a martyr in 1981.

Chapter 16

1. Douglas A. Templeton, *Re-Exploring Paul's Imagination: A Cynical Laywoman's Guide to Paul of Tarsus* (Germany: Eilsbrunn, 1988), p. v.

Chapter 18

1. Annual Chapter Minutes, 1990, p. 109.

2. Ibid., p. 88.

3. Ibid., p. 134.

4. Annual Chapter Minutes, 1991.

5. Chapter Minutes, July 1998.

6. The Rule of the Brothers and Sisters of the Third Order Regulars of St Francis.

7. Ibid.

8. Interview with Father Gero McLoughlin, February 2013.

9. Ibid.

10. Annual Chapter Minutes, 2007.

11. Chapter Minutes, 21 September 2007.

12. T. S. Eliot, 'The Dry Salvages', lines 210–12, *Four Quartets* (London: Faber & Faber, 1959), p. 44.

Appendix 1

1. Rule of Taizé.

2. Ibid.

3. Principles of the Society of the Sacred Mission.

4. Rule of Taizé.

5. Ibid.

6. Ibid.

7. Ibid.

Acknowledgements of Sources

The author and publisher are grateful for permission to quote from the following works.

Philip Bradshaw, *Following the Spirit* (ISBN 978 1 84694 294 5) (Alresford, UK: John Hunt, 2010).

Alan Ecclestone, *The Night Sky of the Lord* (ISBN 0 232 51397 X) (London: Darton, Longman and Todd, 1980).

T. S. Eliot, *Four Quartets* (London: Faber and Faber, 1959).

Ron Ferguson with Mark Chater, *Mole Under the Fence* (ISBN 0 7152 0832 2) (Edinburgh: Saint Andrew Press, 2006).

Stanislous Kennedy RSC, ed., *Spiritual Journeys* (Dublin: Veritas, 1997).

Zvi Kolitz, *Yosl Rakover Talks to God* (ISBN 0 09928423 5) (London: Jonathan Cape). Reprinted by permission of The Random House Group.

John Mantle, *Britain's First Worker Priests* (ISBN 0 334 027985) (London: SCM, 2000).

Brendan Pelphrey, *The Secret Seminary*, (Bastrop County, Texas: Spring Deer Studio, 2012).

Kathryn Spink, *Jean Vanier and L'Arche* (ISBN 0 232 51801 7) (London: Darton, Longman and Todd, 1990).